Praise for *Morbid Curiosit*

"It's a cliche that truth is stranger than fiction, but this compendium of real-life accounts of the bizarre, horrific, and just plain freaky proves it. Heartfelt, heartaching, and heart-attack fare all, these stories will haunt you long after the last twisted confession is told."

–John Everson, author of *Sacrifice* and *The 13th*

"A wild, exhilarating ride into the darker side of the human experience."

–Monica S. Kuebler, *Rue Morgue* magazine

"Nietzsche famously said that if you stare long enough into the abyss, the abyss stares back into you. Well here the abyss is poking back at you with a very sharp stick. *Morbid Curiosity Cures the Blues*–a testament to all that ever was great about the underground press–will crack through your armor, pry under your scales, and break through your numb envelope of reality to remind you what you're really made of. You'll shudder and cringe and laugh along the way, but the sheer gravity and humanity of every true story in this book will more than satisfy your morbid curiosity: it will change how you see the world for good. Well, until you die, anyway."

–Michael Arnzen, Bram Stoker Award–winning
author of *The Goreletter*

"I would be remiss if I did not point out that, at least according to St. Augustine, 'curiosity' is a grave sin. But I think in our age, a burning desire to acquire new knowledge and experiences is not our besetting sin; instead, we seem more prone to a kind of spiritual ennui, along with a flaccid and lazy intellect that does not inquire further and does not know real awe, joy, or anguish. And for that mental dis-ease, the always odd, often irreverent, frequently touching tales in this volume seem a delightful corrective. More than mere 'curiosity,' they are filled with a sense of wonder, of receptiveness and yearning for some hidden, better, higher meaning in our lives. This book makes you think as well as laugh, and that combination is as rare as it is enjoyable."

–Dr. Kim Paffenroth, Associate Professor of Religious Studies
at Iona College and author of *Gospel of the Living Dead,*
Dying to Live, and *Valley of the Dead*

Also Edited by Loren Rhoads

✧

Death's Garden: Relationships with Cemeteries

Lend the Eye a Terrible Aspect:
A Collection of Essays and Fiction (with Mason Jones)

Morbid Curiosity Cures the Blues

✦

True Stories of the Unsavory, Unwise, Unorthodox, and Unusual

EDITED BY

Loren Rhoads

SCRIBNER

New York   London   Toronto   Sydney

SCRIBNER

A Division of Simon & Schuster, Inc.
1230 Avenue of the Americas
New York, NY 10020

First Scribner trade paperback edition October 2009

SCRIBNER and design are registered trademarks of The Gale Group, Inc.,
used under license by Simon & Schuster, Inc., the publisher of this work.

For information about special discounts for bulk purchases,
please contact Simon & Schuster Special Sales at 1-866-506-1949
or business@simonandschuster.com.

The Simon & Schuster Speakers Bureau can bring authors to your live event.
For more information or to book an event, contact the Simon & Schuster Speakers
Bureau at 1-866-248-3049 or visit our website at www.simonspeakers.com.

Manufactured in the United States of America

1   3   5   7   9   10   8   6   4   2

Library of Congress Control Number: 2009024140

ISBN 978-1-4391-2466-6
ISBN 978-1-4391-3645-4 (eBook)

This book is dedicated to
Mason,
who has indulged my curiosity
for a delightfully long time.

Contents

CONTENTS

Gainful Employment:
The Morbid Things
People Do for Money

Curious Behavior:
The Morbid Catchall Category

Medical Adventures:
Morbid Medicine

Beyond Death:
Exploring Behind the Curtain

Epitaph:
The Final Word on Morbid Curiosity

Morbid Curiosity Cures the Blues

Illustration by Timothy Renner

Morbid Curiosity
Changed My Life

"In a time of universal deceit, telling the truth is a
revolutionary act."
                    —commonly attributed to George Orwell

I grew up on a farm. As a girl, I caught snakes bare-handed and
watched my dad dress slaughtered rabbits. I wasn't allowed to get
attached to the farm animals, because they were around only to
appear on the dinner table. When I graduated from my small-town
high school, I attended two years at the local branch of the University
of Michigan. In Flint. In 1981. Between the auto industry closing fac-
tories and the crack epidemic, there were vast stretches of the city
where a farm girl could be pulled over by the police, just for driving
while white. It took me a while to realize that I had to get out.

When I first moved to San Francisco in 1988, my husband Mason
Jones and I attended a slideshow about the early days of RE/Search
Publications. At the time, RE/Search was notorious for the books
Incredibly Strange Films, which introduced filmmakers Russ Meyer
and Herschell Gordon Lewis to the larger world, and the *Industrial
Culture Handbook,* which featured the noisy, challenging electronic
punk of musical terrorists Throbbing Gristle and Cabaret Voltaire.
RE/Search was the cutting edge. I hadn't yet realized they were San
Francisco–based.

The highlight of the evening was editor V. Vale's home photos fea-
turing William Burroughs, machine apocalypse artists Survival
Research Laboratories, and every punk band who'd ever played San
Francisco. Afterward, copublisher Andrea Juno (AJ to her friends)
announced that they were close to finishing their next book and could
use some help. I wouldn't have had the courage to step forward on
my own, but Mason volunteered us.

This was how we found ourselves going out for a vegetarian dinner
in Chinatown with Vale, AJ, and Catherine Reuther (RE/Search's

assistant editor). The three of them comprised the company's entire staff. We discussed publishing, starting with Vale's punk rock zine *Search and Destroy,* and dissected the small press world of the late eighties.

On our walk back through North Beach to their apartment, we stopped off at the RE/Search Typography office. Their books were not selling well enough to support anyone yet, which came as a shock. I had assumed that if we'd been able to find the books in Michigan, RE/Search must have been a huge organization.

On a small table, AJ laid out some page proofs that would become their next title, *Modern Primitives.*

She was struggling to lay out photos of a pierced labia. The plan was to have the books printed in Hong Kong, then shipped to the United States for distribution. AJ worried that if the Customs Office deemed the book pornographic, they might hold it up at the Port of Oakland. She wondered if she "split the split beaver" over facing pages, could it offend anyone? Could anyone find it prurient?

Here I was, a Michigan girl not long off the farm. It had never occurred to me that someone might wear jewelry in her genitals. I felt lightheaded as I stared down at the photographs.

Then AJ said, "If we have a split beaver, don't you think we ought to have a split penis, too?" She placed another page on the table. The photograph of a bisected penis dominated the text.

Morbid Curiosity magazine was born in that moment.

Of course, it took some time to work up to publishing my own magazine. Volunteering for RE/Search was a good education. It taught me how much of running a small publishing company involves carting around boxes of books, making trips to the post office, transcribing cassettes, maintaining a mailing list—basic clerical tasks, necessary to sell books.

In 1994, Mason and I founded Automatism Press and published our first book, *Lend the Eye a Terrible Aspect.* Grander in concept than execution, *Lend the Eye* was a collection of short stories, nonfiction essays, and artwork by underground artists from across North America. Mason's musical connections (he'd founded the Charnel Music record label in 1991) allowed us to solicit pieces from Dead Kennedys' former front man Jello Biafra, industrial musician Deborah Jaffe of Master/Slave Relationship, animator Stephen Holman (the *Phantom Investigators* cartoon on the WB), and Canadian prankster and performance artist blackhumour. RE/Search introduced us to spoken-word author Don Bajema (*Boy in the Air*) and Elizabeth

Borowski, who debuted her excruciating *Personal Tarot* in our book. Science fiction author Gregor Hartmann had been a coworker of mine at Pacific Bell. Writing for zines put us in touch with Mark Lo of the estimable *File 13*. *Lend the Eye* introduced me to contributors who later appeared in *Morbid Curiosity* up to its very last issue.

The *Lend the Eye* project came together more easily than we expected and left me eager to do a second book. When he was dying of AIDS, San Francisco photographer Blair Apperson gave me a shoebox of snapshots he'd taken in graveyards from the Caribbean to Yosemite. Originally, I planned to write the text for the book and simply showcase Blair's photos, but as I discussed the project with people, everyone had a cemetery story to tell. I found I wanted to explore the ways people related to graveyards: either places near where they grew up, destinations they'd sought out on vacation, or sites where their family members were interred.

When I finally finished the book, *Death's Garden: Relationships with Cemeteries* contained more than two dozen essays about graveyards from Argentina to Wall Street. The authors considered their own mortality, the loss of family and friends, the transience of fame, and the nature of death itself. Contributors included legendary spoken-word artist Lydia Lunch (*Paradoxia: A Predator's Diary*) and performance artist Pleasant Gehman (*The Underground Guide to Los Angeles*), and featured a gorgeous cover by artist Jane Handel (*Swimming on Dry Land: The Memories of an Ascetic Libertine*).

Death's Garden struck a chord. It sold out within nine months. Even though the book has been out of print since 1997, it was mentioned in a 2004 issue of *Artforum*. *Death's Garden* remains a sought-after collectible on eBay, going for many times its cover price.

Its completion left me casting around for a new project. The part I'd liked best about assembling both books for Automatism was reading submissions. I loved going to the post office to find entertaining, detailed, and emotionally wracking manuscripts from complete strangers.

So . . . how could I arrange to receive confessions from strangers? What kind of magazine would I have to publish? The title of the project was never in any doubt: *Morbid Curiosity* was the only one I ever considered. The title captured my motive in assembling the short memoirs and summed up the feeling I wanted to inspire in potential readers.

With a preacher's zeal, I feel that curiosity is the single most important attribute with which humans are born. More than a simple desire to discover or know things, curiosity is a powerful tool, like a scalpel or a searchlight. It allows us to look at something as abstract as behavioral patterns or as grand as history: to study it, dissect it, marvel over its component parts. Curiosity changes us. It is also a way to effect change, perhaps even on a global level.

While I've yet to turn up a definition of *morbid curiosity* per se, the *American Heritage Dictionary* has some interesting things to say about the concept *morbid*. From the Latin *morbus,* disease, which in turn comes from the root *mori,* to die, *morbid* is related to or caused by disease, a state that is psychologically unhealthy or unwholesome, characterized by preoccupation with unwholesome thoughts or feelings. *Unwholesome,* we are told, means injurious to physical, mental, or moral health, suggestive of disease or degeneracy, and offensive or loathsome.

The *OED* (my bible) says that *morbid* is chiefly applied to "unreasonable feelings of gloom, apprehension, or suspicion. Hence of persons: addicted to morbid feelings or fancies." Usage dates back to 1656.

To my surprise, I discovered that *morbid* does not imply an obsession with death. It doesn't necessarily have *anything* to do with death, only with sickness and "unwholesomeness." From the quotes collected in the *OED, morbid* suggests a condition from which one is likely to recover.

In 1750 Dr. Johnson, that feel-good rascal, wrote, "Every man comes into the world morbid." If that's true, how can a universal state possibly be unhealthy? To me, curiosity—even about "morbid" topics—is ultimately life affirming.

The goal of *Morbid Curiosity* was to explore the unsavory, unwise, unorthodox, and unusual—all the dark adventures that make life worth living. I made it my mission to convey that *all* curiosity is absolutely necessary.

When I began the magazine, my chief concern was how I would fill its pages. I contacted everyone who had submitted to the earlier books we'd published and asked them to pass the word. Then we set up a rudimentary Web page. Stories tumbled in.

I thought it would be best to start with a conservative print run for the first issue. Those thousand copies have been sold out for years. A year later, I bumped up the amount printed of issue #2. Those also sold out. The third and fourth issues followed suit. It's rare for a week to go by that I don't get another letter begging me to reprint the early issues so fans can complete their collections.

I appeared to be on to something.

• • •

So what was *Morbid Curiosity* magazine? I tried to create a forum where people could step forward and tell their own stories—not in the sense of a *Jerry Springer* freak show, but because "normal" people don't often have the opportunity to examine and discuss their lives. The magazine turned out to be cathartic both for authors and the audience, because readers definitely got a sense of "There, but for the grace of God . . ." I adored the confessional nature of the stories I read for the magazine.

The "reality" of TV reality shows is that they choose people because they aren't representative of you and me. They're prettier, or more messed up, or don't have any sense. Contributors to *Morbid Curiosity* were students and computer programmers, artists and file clerks, professional writers and people published for the first and only time. In other words, they're just like you and me, trying to make sense of events that changed their lives.

That said, there were many times I accepted a story for publication while privately wondering why the author would choose to share that particular aspect of himself. Of course, those were the people who astounded me by reading their confessions at a *Morbid Curiosity* event. I applaud and am inspired by that level of courage.

Over the course of its life, *Morbid Curiosity* developed several running themes. For a while, every issue had a dead pet story. Several issues visited concentration camps. Many contributors mourned their relatives. As the magazine (and its contributors) grew up, submissions shifted from doing drugs to surviving medical procedures—to such an extent that I dropped the *Illicit Substances* subject header for *Medical Adventures*. By their nature, good drug experiences are hard to record; they are fleeting. Most medical interventions unfold over hours, days, or months. There's plenty of time to think. Or . . . it could just be a factor of the encroaching middle age of *Morbid Curiosity*'s contributors.

One of my favorite sections of the magazine was called *Childhood's End*. Initially, I planned to limit that section only to stories about childhood, but the definition expanded to include any growing experience. Unless you're Ray Bradbury or Michael Hemmingson, the thrills and terrors of childhood can be tricky to recapture. And growing up, if done right, is a series of epiphanies and narrow escapes. The *Childhood's End* stories featured in this book include everything from sexual awakening to visiting mom in a mental hospital, from growing up in the bathtub of the dead to surviving having your face slashed at a bus stop. They're stories of the moments that created the people who contributed them.

Another section that was fun to put together was *Far from Home,* which originally contained travelers' stories, but swelled to include adventures outside one's comfort zone. I usually allowed each issue to sort itself by theme and mood, then gathered the stories loosely together, as one would a bouquet. Sometimes, I strained my metaphors. It couldn't be helped.

Curious Behavior was the catchall heading. In most issues, it was the biggest section of the magazine. Stories there might range from drinking blood to surviving a carjacking. Those stories tended to be the funniest, especially when read aloud.

For the purposes of organizing *Morbid Curiosity Cures the Blues,* I created the *Gainful Employment* section. Tales of bad jobs, crazy bosses, and unreasonable expectations for low pay recur throughout the magazine, but only after I started to sort things for this anthology did I realize how many I'd published. It's almost enough to convince you to become a stay-at-home mom.

The final section of each magazine was *Beyond Death.* Those stories explored what it's like to stare death in the face, but they were also about people who tried to peel back the curtain to see who was manipulating the machinery beyond. Hugues Leblanc wondered what lay inside the crumbling coffins in the local graveyard, so he looked. Leilah Wendell wondered what it would be like to make love to Death. Trilby Plants and Jill Tracy, among others, shared messages they received from beyond the grave.

Each issue of the magazine ended with an essay I called the *Epitaph.* Often these essays were entirely unlike anything else that appeared in the issue. Usually they conveyed something that I wanted to remain stuck in the readers' minds when they put down the magazine.

Three years after the magazine's final issue, the problem was not too few contributions, but so many it was hard to winnow them down to fit into this collection. I would have loved to include more of the earliest pieces here, but I've lost touch with their authors. That seems to be how things go. Some people appeared out of the ether with a story to tell, then vanished, never to be heard from again.

Which, I suppose, was the best aspect of *Morbid Curiosity,* the part that drew readers back issue after issue: the contributors' burning desire to share their experiences. The best stories were the ones where the author had some guilt or terror that could only be expiated by confessing it in a public forum. I love the stories that reveal the authors, that make me feel as if I know these strangers because I've seen their adventures reflected in myself.

This collection you hold in your hands represents some hard choices on my part. Each issue of *Morbid Curiosity* contained about 60,000 words' worth of essays. In the magazine's 10 years, that totaled more than 300 stories; over 250 authors, artists, and reviewers; and 600,000 words—all of which had to be pared down to a reasonable-sized book. (This isn't the phone book, after all.)

Some of the contributors complicated the selection process by submitting more than one strong essay. It was hard to choose Brian Thomas's piece about exploring Auschwitz over his touching burial of a very special feline or his work with the prop corpse who turned out to have a real human skeleton or his visit to Poland's Black Madonna or his night sleeping in the coffin or his excursion to buy a shrunken head in Venezuela. Claudius Reich's story "Why We OD" was a very strong contender, but in the end I had to pick his near escape from a pub bombing in London. And selecting that one meant I couldn't have his tale about hitchhiking with the "Crazy Mofo" through Oklahoma or what it's like to work with the San Francisco Needle Exchange or to grow up in a graveyard. In the pages of *Morbid Curiosity,* Dana Fredsti explored the origins of her fascination with darkness, hunted ghosts, learned to surf, starred in a B-movie, and petted a tiger. However, her experience in the Sunset Boulevard bikini bar remains my favorite meditation on the differences between the sexes that I've had the opportunity to publish.

Hardest of all was limiting myself to a single essay by Sacramento blood artist M. Parfitt. She was the only person to contribute to every single issue of the magazine. Her piece "Why," which ended the first issue of *Morbid Curiosity,* is such a perfect summation of what I tried to do with the magazine that I had to include it in this book. Still, I struggled with the decision. How could I pass up her eulogy to her muse and companion, Wilbur? Or the "Secret, Dirty Places" of her childhood? Or her discovery of the artistic possibilities of her monthly "curse"? Or dancing on the little girl's grave? Or her fascination with public toilets? Or shaving her legs for the very first time?

In the end, I wanted to incorporate as many contributors here as possible, to showcase the widest variety of the voices who've spoken in the pages of *Morbid Curiosity*. I wish I had the space to include everyone. That said, these are all stories that I would have loved to read anywhere. I'm thoroughly jazzed to have had the honor of publishing them again.

I find the world endlessly fascinating—from the ways people hide and reveal who they are to the elegant mechanisms of the human body to the mysterious workings of nature. I hope *Morbid Curiosity* will inspire you to look at the world with new wonder—despite discomfort or difficulties or the fear of what you might find.

Yours in search of satisfaction,
Loren Rhoads
San Francisco

◆

Childhood's End:
Growing Up Morbid

◆

Ephemera from the editor's collection

Why

by M. Parfitt

People ask me why I do what I do, why I use the materials I use to create my *stuff*. What could possibly inspire me to make art from hundreds of photos of dog crap, a quilt from used sanitary napkins, or a collage from bloody squares of gauze? The answer is simple. I blame my brother.

Back when we were kids, Joe and I delighted in offending each other. We mixed leftover food into concoctions that were deadly science projects. We tortured insects. We made spears tipped with dog droppings and flung them at each other in wild backyard battles.

I filled jars with water, grass, and bugs, then left them to ferment for months, only to uncork them—and release a mighty, noxious stench—when Joe least expected it. He chased me through the house with snot-covered fingers. We constantly tried to outdo each other with grossness.

Eventually, he won. He created something so disgusting, I had to admit defeat. And to this day, it makes its way through my subconscious and into my work.

The thing was so simple! A sheet of notebook paper, folded again and again, then opened to reveal a grid of individual squares. In each square, a carefully smeared booger or line of snot. Across the top, the neatly printed words: BOOGER SAMPLER. TAKE ONE.

In itself, the piece was shocking, sickening, a true masterpiece of warped imagination. But it led to a revelation which, for me, has justified all the pieces I've made since.

The revelation was a surprise to both of us. My brother, amazed and a little embarrassed by what he had created, put the Booger Sampler in his homeroom desk at school. During the day, class after class filed in and out of the room. Student after student sat at the desk. The next morning, back in his homeroom, Joe fully expected the vile thing to be gone, victim of a zealous janitor or horrified kid.

Reaching in his desk, he found the Sampler where he had left it.

He pulled it out. He looked at it. And there, along the right-hand side of the page, a square had been carefully torn out. Somebody actually TOOK ONE.

The lesson I learned from the Booger Sampler was this: there's an audience for everything. No matter what it is, someone will like it. Someone will appreciate it and understand it. That's the connection all artists hope for. So when I put my stuff out there for all to see, I know I'll probably offend some folks, but I also know that someone will see my work and connect with it.

Just like the lucky kid who, twenty years ago, reached into a school desk and discovered a treat.

Illustration by M. Parfitt

You Lock It Behind You

by Lee Smith

Things were going downhill fast. My dad had been a heavy drinker since he was seventeen. Recently my mom had joined him, probably out of self-defense. My first girlfriend, Peggy, and I were in the backyard one day when a truck pulled up and repossessed our furniture. After that, Peggy's mom thought that maybe Peggy was too young for a boyfriend. It didn't really matter, since a month or so later, we lost our house and I never saw Peggy again anyway.

We would never own another house. Instead, we shuffled through a succession of trailer parks, dingy apartments, relatives' basements: staying for a month or two, then moving on.

When we first moved into the little rented house, I wished, I pretended, I prayed that it meant the hard times were over. We were living in a house again, and surely that meant something. But house does not equal home, just as prayer does not equal a wish granted. My prayers hung in the air, unable to pierce the overcast sky as easily as the razor-edged

sleet that pelted us when we carried our boxes in on moving day.

My mom had a minimum-wage job loading *Magic Reveal-O Seek and Find* books into cartons. That frigid winter, the warehouse doors were constantly open so the cartons could be loaded onto waiting trucks. Mom packed and she stacked, over and over, all day long, until she got pneumonia. We weren't eligible for welfare or food stamps since my mom refused to toss my dad out. So she got pneumonia and kept right on working. Mom's checks covered the rent. Period. Not a penny more. Dad hung out at the Lazy W Bar, and I made water pancakes.

Day after day, I found myself making pancakes without butter, without oil, without eggs. We had no syrup, either. It was bitterly cold inside the gloomy—mostly empty—rented house. It was 1972. I was thirteen.

When the gasman came, I was home, sick. I knew who he was. I knew what he was there to do. I didn't answer the door when he knocked because it really wouldn't have made much difference. I hid against the dining room wall, listening as he turned the squeaky valve. The furnace coughed and banged and went out for good. I put my coat on over my pajamas and slipped my feet into my toeless, pink tennis shoes.

It'll be okay, I thought. *It'll be okay.*

The pink tennis shoes had gotten me beaten up at school. "Fag," somebody yelled. The next thing I saw was stars.

I was pretty used to getting beaten up. It happened a lot. I didn't fight back. I just let them hit me till they got tired of it or till some teacher came to break it up. "You didn't even hit them back," the gym coach said to me once. The sound in his voice wasn't surprise but disgust. I didn't tell him that when I fought back it was worse, that the beatings just lasted longer. I didn't tell him anything. I didn't say a word.

That was my MO: they could hit me, they could spit on me, they could chuck a hunk of that black ice that forms above the tires in the Midwest winter out the window of a moving car and knock me flat, busting my lip and blacking my eye, but I would never, *never* speak. Never tell them that my tennis shoes were pink because they got washed with a red shirt and we couldn't afford new ones. Never tell them, when I struck out on my turn at bat, that my dad was a drunk who never taught me to play baseball. Never tell them anything. I'd just stare at them. Hard. Right in the eyes. Stare like I was boring a hole right into their souls. A few times, that actually worked.

Once, a bunch of kids were getting ready to jump me. I turned and stared right at this one boy. He flinched. He tried to look away, but couldn't.

"Leave him alone," he shouted and pulled away the kid who was getting ready to hit me. "Let's get out of here. I can't stand the way he's staring at me." The boys backed off, incredulous that one of their own could be such a pussy. "I said let's go!" he shouted and they all ran, a couple of them calling over their shoulders that they'd get me later. There was always later.

Now the pink tennis shoes had holes where the toes used to be, but they were still warmer than nothing. The house was getting cold fast. When it got dark, I put on a pair of dirty pants and found a couple of dimes in the pocket. The nearest phone booth was about a mile away. If I walked there, if nobody from school spotted me, if my sister was at home . . . "If" is about all you've got when it's cold and dark.

As I walked, I thought about everything.

It was a couple of weeks before Christmas. In biology class, we'd made wreaths. I had gathered a bunch of dry oak leaves, ones that had been completely leached of their gaudy fall colors, and fastened them to a black coat hanger. In between, I stuck in some jet-black berries I'd found growing on a bush down the street. My teacher was aghast. "I can't hang this up anywhere. It looks like it was made for a funeral. Take it home!" I thought it was kind of beautiful in its own way. I stuck it in the trash on the way out.

I reached the phone. My sister was home. She came and picked me up—a lucky day, no doubt about it. Later, after we'd had some supper, my brother-in-law drove me home. I was a little surprised when he came in behind me.

"Sit down here." He pointed to the couch. I looked at that nasty old couch and couldn't remember where it had come from. My mom sat in the only chair in the house, on what I guessed was her fifth beer of the night. She was hacking something fierce.

"When'd you eat last?" the brother-in-law asked.

"An hour ago? At your house?" It wasn't really a question—just a kid's attempt to forestall what he saw coming.

"Before that."

"I ate before I came to your house."

"What'd you have?"

"Pancakes."

"What'd ya have yesterday?"

"Pancakes."

"The day before that?"

I didn't say anything.

"Go get your stuff," he said. "Schoolbooks, clothes, everything."

Between coughs, my mom got out, "Now wait just a goddamned minute!"

"I said go!" He shoved me toward my bedroom. My brother-in-law was a Cro-Magnon and very fond of sneering. He could sneer at you and make you feel like a bug.

I went into my room. I pulled out a couple of cardboard boxes. There were always cardboard boxes around. When you move a lot, you don't throw them away. I put in my schoolbooks and clothes. They only half-filled a lightbulb box. When I came into the living room, my mom was crying.

"It's okay, Honey. You'll be back soon. You'll see. Everything will be fine." She kissed me on the forehead.

When we were in the car, he said, "We're gonna go buy you some shoes. I don't wanna be seen with you wearing those fuckin' faggy pink shoes." A Cro-Magnon with a heart of gold.

7

Christmas came and went. I asked about Mom and Dad. My sister said, "They're fine."

Spring came, slow and rainy and gray. At Easter I got a new shirt and tie. I'd never tied a real tie before. My father had a thing for clip-on bow ties, god love him. The Cro-Magnon tied it around his neck, then pulled it off and shoved it roughly over my head. "Who the fuck doesn't know how to tie a goddamned tie?" he said. He called me "Clarabelle," which, I learned later, was the name of a clown on a television show.

I still asked, "How are Mom and Dad?" and still the answer was, "Fine." Nothing more. Just "fine." Like they were lost in some faraway wilderness and the messages that made it out could only be one word long: "Fine."

One day I came home from school and they weren't so fine. My sister was on the phone. "Whattaya mean, she's been asleep for three days? Nobody just sleeps for three days! Does she have a pulse?" Then she saw me and shooed me away. As I walked down the hall to my bedroom, I heard her say, "You gotta take her to the hospital."

She came into my room a while later. "Mom swallowed a bunch of pills about three days ago."

"Is she okay?"

"Destruction of Letterman Hospital, San Francisco," photographed by R. Samuel Klatchko

She looked away. "I don't think so."

"Is Dad gonna take her to the hospital?"

She didn't answer. She just got up, put on her coat, and left.

I didn't know what else to do, so I made dinner: grilled cheese and tomato soup. The Cro-Magnon would be home soon and I didn't want him to get mad because dinner wasn't waiting. When he came in, I had just put plates down in front of my nephews.

"Where's your sister?" he asked, that pissed-off sound creeping into his voice.

"Mom's . . ." I looked at my nephews, "Mom's . . . sick and I think she went over there."

"Goddammit!" he screamed. "I told her! I told her I'd let you come here only if she never saw them again!" He smashed the glass he was holding into the sink. Which was good in a way, 'cause at least it'd be easy to clean up. He got on the phone, calling one of my other sisters. I went to the sink to clean up the glass. He grabbed me by the arm and shoved me away.

"What the hell kinda boy are you?"

I didn't say anything. But I thought it. I thought: I'm the kind of boy who cleans up.

He hung up the phone and sat down at the table. He chewed his sandwich and laughed his lit-tle sadistic giggle that went everywhere the sneer was sure to go.

"They're taking her to the hospital. Locking her up."

I didn't say anything. I was confused. They "put you in" or "admitted you" to a hospital. They "locked you up" in jail. Were they taking her to the hospital or jail? The Cro-Magnon had his once-in-a-lifetime flash of insight: He got that I didn't get it.

"Locking her up in the nut-house," he said and giggled his little sadistic giggle. "When you try to kill yourself, they lock you up in the nuthouse and they can keep you there forever."

That night, once my sister got back, he took me over to my mom and dad's house. "Get the resta your shit," he said. "They'll be bootin' your dad's ass out in a coupla days."

Spring was all around outside, but inside it was still winter. I went into my old room. There really wasn't much to get. When you move three or four times a year, you lose things. Little pieces. A picture. A book. A transistor radio you won for being "Lucky Caller #3." You drop it. You leave it behind. It vanishes.

I looked over at my bed. There was a pile of paper. I picked it up to stuff it in the box. My mom's handwriting. Little notes, one written each night since I left. "Hi Honey! Just thinking about you. Things look bad right now but we'll be together again real soon." One from Christmas Eve: "I sure do miss you. This is the first Christmas you've ever been gone. We got a Christmas tree! They was throwing it out at the Lazy W Bar and your dad asked if he could have it. You would have laughed watching him and me trying to get that thing to stand up! See, it didn't have no stand and we tried to put it in that old pressure cooker and it kept falling over. Sure wish you'd been here to see it."

I sat with the notes on my lap, feeling empty. Feeling alone.

But I wasn't alone. The Cro-Magnon yelled from the other room: "Get a move on! I ain't got all night!"

When I started to stuff the notes into the box, one fell away. The last one, as it happened. "You've been gone so long. I guess maybe it's better for you this way. But I don't know what I keep going on for. Without you, it just doesn't seem to matter too much."

I felt a pain somewhere around my heart, like somebody was squeezing it in their hand. Squeezing it till it stopped. Squeezing it till there was nothing left but a handful of needles and sawdust.

"I told you to get a move on!" yelled the Cro-Magnon.

I folded up that last note and put it in the box with the rest and nobody—*nobody*—ever, ever saw them.

A few days later, the Cro-Magnon said, "Come on." He walked toward the door. We got in the car. We drove across town and out the other side. Out to where the woods were green and thick and the houses stopped, up a winding road in the most beautiful spring sunshine. We turned a corner and a group of buildings seemed to rise out of the hills. Old buildings. Slate gray. Gothic, like something out of a horror film. The sun seemed to grow dimmer the closer we got, until it was a faded, hazy, weak yellow. He stopped in front of the biggest building.

"Go on." He reached across me and pushed the car door open.

"What?" was all I could say.

"This is where your mom is. This is the nuthouse."

I got out of the car. He didn't. I held onto the door. This was not someplace I wanted to be.

"Go on in," he said. "Tell 'em who you are. They'll take you up to see her."

I waited for him to get out, but he didn't.

"Go on! You ain't scared, are ya?" He sneered and giggled and put the car in gear.

"Aren't you comin' in?" I asked.

"I got somethin' to do. I'll be back later." He stepped down on the gas. The door pulled out of my hand and slammed shut and he was gone.

I looked up at the doors, like a big mouth waiting to swallow me. I walked up the steps and into the lobby. A woman sat behind the desk, thumbing through a magazine. She said into the magazine, "Visitin' hours is over."

"I'm here to see my mom," I said.

Now she looked up, leaned across the desk. "I done tol' you, visitin' hours is over. So just go on home."

"He left," I said, not explaining who "he" was.

"Left?" she echoed. "Left?"

I nodded. She grumbled something unintelligible, sighed angrily, and stood up. "I ain't no babysitter!" she said. "Okay, fine. He left. So what am I suppos' do with you now?"

She looked at me like I was a soured mop left in rancid water. "Don't know why it's always me!" she said to no one in particular. "Always damned me has to do ever'thing!"

She came around the desk with a bunch of keys. "He left! Well, just fine and dandy! I cain't be watchin' after you!"

I told her my mom's name. She looked at a list.

"Ward C's what you want." She held up the keys one at a time. "This here one opens that door there. You lock it behind you. Go down the hall to the left. This here key opens the door at the end of the hall. You go through it. You lock it behind you. You go up the stairs. This here one opens the door at the top. You lock it behind you . . ." On and on she went: turn left, turn right, go up, go down, this key, this door, lock it behind you. I looked at the door.

"Go on!" she said. "You a big enough boy 'he' can just leave you here, you a big enough boy you can go in by yourself."

I opened the door and went through.

"Lock it! Lock it!" she screamed from the other side.

I locked it. My heart was beating so hard, I could see the red of my blood pounding in my eyes. I turned left. I went to the end of the hall. It was dim and quiet, not a soul in sight. It was all right. I was all right. Everybody was locked behind doors. I was safe as long as I opened the right doors.

I got to the top of the stairs, locked the door behind me. Where did she say to go next? Left? Right? I couldn't remember. I started to sweat, cold and burning like battery acid. I could go back. Give back the keys, go outside, wait. Then I imagined the Cro-Magnon sneering, "You fuckin' little chicken-shit pansy!"

"Just shut up!" I said out loud. "Just shut up and do it!"

I wandered down the hall to a door. I stood on tiptoe and looked through the wire-mesh window. Zombies moved around the room, going nowhere. One man reached into the diaper he wore under his open gown. He pulled out a turd and mashed it in his hand. He started to scream. I moved away. I wandered for a long time. Up and down. Left and right. I always locked the door behind me.

I found myself in the basement. The iron doors were old. Behind one, a man was screaming. There were no windows on these doors, no windows to see why the man screamed, which made it worse than the others. Then, right at my ear, from behind and very close, a man asked, "What the hell you doin' here?"

I turned around. He was big. He looked mean. Finally, I croaked out, "Ward C."

"Ward C? What about Ward C?"

I realized he was dressed all in white. He was an orderly. He worked there. He wasn't one of "them."

"You shouldn't be down here," he said, "and you ain't nowheres near Ward C." All in a rush, I told him everything: the Cro-Magnon, Christmas, the

gasman, my mom, my dad. Everything. He just looked at me standing there, shaking.

"Where'd you get them keys?" he asked, in the gentlest voice I'd ever heard. I told him and he nodded. "Come with me," he said and put his hand on my shoulder.

We walked up and up and he stopped me in front of a door.

"You really shouldn't go through this-a-way," he said. "But you be okay long as you stick right close to me. Don't pay no attention to what none of 'em says. Don't talk to none of 'em. Don't even look up. Just hold on to me and keep your eyes down on the floor. I get you through. Open the door." We stepped through. "Lock it behind you." I did.

I knew then what the word *madhouse* meant. The sound of hell: Screams. Crying. Cursing. Animal grunts. A man darted out of nowhere and grabbed my arm. I flattened myself against the big orderly.

"Get your hands off him now!" he yelled.

"I just want to touch him for a minute," the man said. "Just a minute."

I didn't look up—he told me not to and I didn't.

"I just want to touch him for a minute. He's so pretty."

The orderly shoved the man

aside. I heard him land, hard, several feet away. The screaming grew louder, deafening.

"We got to move fast now," said the orderly and we ran to the door at the other end of the room. He took the keys, opened the door, slammed it shut, and locked it.

"That scare you?" he asked.

I just looked up at him. I couldn't speak. My mouth moved like a fish, dying on a muddy bank.

"You okay now," he said. "This here Ward C. This where your mama is."

He took me down the ward to a little office, sat me down, told me to stay. In a minute or so, he came back with my mom.

She didn't really walk, just kind of shuffled and swayed, listing side to side like she was drunk. She burst into tears. "My baby. My baby," she said over and over, slurring the words. "My baby. My baby in this place." She cried and cried and hugged me close and petted my hair.

"He cain't stay but fi' minutes," the big orderly said.

She rocked me in her arms and cried. Rocked and rocked.

"You've gotta get better, Mama," I said. "You've gotta get better and come home."

She kissed me on the cheek. The orderly pulled me away gently. Our hands slid down each other's arms, lingering for a final second, touching fingers like Dumbo and his mom touched trunks in that final moment, when she's in the mad-elephant cage and they take him away.

The big orderly took me all the way back out. As I went out the front door, I could hear him screaming at the woman at the desk.

The Cro-Magnon was waiting. "So how's the nuts?"

I didn't say anything. I just stared at him, hard. Stared until he took his eyes off the road and looked at me. I stared right into his eyes with the most concentrated hate I had ever felt. He didn't say anything and looked away first.

She did get better. A month or so later, my sister and I went out to see her. We stopped and got Kentucky Fried Chicken. We took Mom outside and sat on the grass, eating, feeling the sun warm our backs. It was easy to pretend, there among the trees with the birds singing, that everything was all right.

Then a man jumped out from behind a bush, right into the middle of our picnic. No one breathed.

"Oh, boy!" he said, his voice full of childlike joy. "Chicken!"

Then he realized—it crossed his face like a storm—that it

wasn't his. He couldn't have any. He started to cry and tore at his T-shirt, ripping it, shredding it, while he cried and moved away.

My sister stared down at her food. I looked at my mom. She stared at the guy, still looking long after he'd disappeared over the hill. Then she looked at me and I saw it. In her eyes, I saw her realization that even if everything got better, even after they let her out, she would always be one of "them." Whatever she had thought of herself before was gone. From now on, she was one of "them." I wanted to tell her that I understood. But her eyes darted away, embarrassed, guilty, and the moment passed.

It was quiet in the car on the way home, the kind of quiet that pushes in on you. My sister switched on the radio. "Oooga Chaka! Oooga Oooga! Oooga Chaka!" sang Blue Swede.

My sister looked at me, puzzled. She pounded on the dashboard with her fist. "What the hell's wrong with this god-damned radio? It's been acting up all week!"

She pounded and pounded, pretending not to know that's how the song went. She was trying so hard, trying to make everything better for just a second. I knew that's how the song went and she knew I knew. But we laughed. We laughed so hard that she had to pull over. We laughed in that hysterical way that someone might if they'd just seen a headless body fly out of a car wreck. We laughed like one of "them" might laugh. And it was okay, because we were "them" or would be one day—me first, when I saw the devil taking a shower in Florida, and later her, when her son ran away from home. We were "them." And it was okay.

HOW THIS CAME TO BE WRITTEN

by Lee Smith

When I was a freshman in college, I was cast in a production of *One Flew Over the Cuckoo's Nest*. As part of the rehearsal process, the director arranged for us to tour Central State Hospital. It was one of the oldest "mental institutions" in Kentucky, dating from shortly after the Civil War. The place was a neo-Gothic horror and I shuddered as we were ushered in. Looking around at my compatriots, I realized that none of us looked too enthusiastic about being there, so I shrugged it off.

Our guide showed us some windowless cells in the basement, closed with huge iron doors. He opened a door and shined a flashlight in, revealing manacles on the wall. "But we've come a long way since those days," he said. "These rooms haven't been used in sixty or seventy years."

Without the sentence even forming in my mind, I blurted out, "That's a fucking lie."

No one was more surprised by the outburst than I. Why had I said that? And why was I suddenly pouring sweat, my heart racing? A glare from my professor made me apologize. I finished the tour with my eyes on the floor.

Twenty years later, I awoke in the middle of the night as if from a nightmare and wrote "You Lock It Behind You." My parents are both dead, so I sent a copy to my oldest sister.

"Oh, my God," she replied, "how could you remember so clearly? We all thought it was a blessing that you had forgotten all those years."

You lock the huge iron door behind you, but what's inside does not die. It simply waits.

The Barbie Wrecking Yard

by Michael Hemmingson

I was ten. I went to stay with an aunt and my cousin Veronique for a few weeks while my parents went somewhere. I took my G.I. Joe, my Evel Knievel, and my Six Million Dollar Man.

Veronique, who was eleven, laughed and said, "You have dolls."

"These aren't dolls," I said.

"They're dolls," she said, "like my dolls."

I asked what kind of dolls she had.

She took me to her room and showed me. She had Barbies, multiple Barbies. I'd never seen so many Barbies in my life. And accessories up the wazoo: dresses and shoes and gowns and cars and makeup kits and hats and bikinis.

"Where's Ken?" I asked.

"Barbie doesn't have a boy-friend." Veronique added, "But she *is* looking for one."

I never had any intention of allowing her Barbies to intermingle with my heroes. I had the action-size G.I. Joe of old, not those tiny things they sell now in conjunction with the cartoon. This G.I. Joe had a fuzzy beard and muscles, and came with an archaeological kit that would have made Indiana Jones proud. Evel Knievel had a white outfit and cape and his own motorcycle. The Six Million Dollar Man had a hole in the back of his head, which allowed you to look out of his magnified bionic eye. He also had a removable panel on his arm that revealed painted-in cybernetics.

"These are silly," Veronique said, inspecting my toys.

"They're not silly," I said.

"They are," she said. *"Boy* silly."

"And your Barbies *aren't?"*

"I wonder," she said, eyeing the three, "which one would Bar-bie fall for?"

"Fall?"

"Love," Veronique said.

I squirmed.

"Oh, come on," she said. "I bet they want a girlfriend."

"No," I said. "No, they *don't."*

"I think they do," my cousin said. "Now the Six Million Dol-lar Man—he has a girlfriend, right? He has the Bionic Woman. Evel Knievel—he's married, and he's just a fool who breaks his bones all the time. G.I. Joe, now—he's single, right? And he's a real man—he's macho, he's adventuresome, he's not always around to bug you. I think he would be perfect for Barbie."

"No," I said.

"Yes," she said.

Veronique had a playhouse in the large backyard of my aunt's house. This was where Barbie and G.I. Joe had their first date. Veronique lit candles and set up small plates on the table. Barbie wore an evening gown, cut low, with silver slippers. She smiled throughout the entire date. G.I. Joe didn't like her at first, then started to. At the end of the date, we made them kiss.

"Ooohhhhh," Veronique giggled, "those whiskers tickle, Joe!"

Over the next few days, Joe and Barbie saw more and more of each other.

"Ohhhh, Joe," cooed my cousin. "I think I'm falling in love and soon you may ship out to your next assignment. What will I ever do?"

The next morning, Veronique told me, "It's time."

"Time?"

"For Barbie and Joe to show their love for each other."

I didn't get it.

"They'll make love," she said. I still didn't get it.

She leaned close and whispered, "They're going to *fuck.*"

My jaw dropped.

Naked, Barbie was pink and shapely and had breasts. "She has no hair in the you-know-where," Veronique said, "but that doesn't bother me. Maybe she shaved it like this one high school girl I know does."

I struggled to undress Joe, feeling funny.

"He has no pee-pee!" Veronique exclaimed.

I blushed, feeling hot.

"Either does she." I nodded at Barbie.

"She does, too!"

"Does she *pee?*"

"*She does!*"

"This is stupid!" I said. "This isn't real!"

"*It is!*" Veronique sobbed.

I don't know what made us do it. We didn't discuss it. We undressed and compared ourselves to the dolls.

"I have a hole," Veronique said, "and she doesn't," touching Barbie between the legs. "Feel."

I felt Barbie. Smooth, cold plastic. I felt Veronique. Warm, a little sweaty.

"Put your finger in that hole," she said.

This wasn't the first time a female cousin suggested this to me: I was an expert by now.

Veronique tensed, let a breath out as my finger slid partly into her. "Barbie definitely needs one of these."

She grabbed my cock. "It's so

soft," she said. "Joe needs one of these."

My cock started to grow. I didn't like this at all. We got dressed and pondered what we should do.

Veronique went into the house and got a pair of scissors. Using one sharp end, she carved a whole between Barbie's legs. She was just full of ideas. She ran to her room, got a chunk of Silly Putty from its plastic egg, rolled a small phallus, and placed it between Joe's legs. "I hope it stays put," she said. Then we tried to make the dolls connect.

"We have to sound enraptured," she told me, "like on TV."

We made grunts and moans for Joe and Barbie.

"Does Joe want a cigarette?" my cousin asked when it was over.

"Joe doesn't smoke," I said.

"Barbie needs one badly," she said, "but I guess it isn't good for her health. '*Oh, Joe, I love you! Promise you'll come back alive and well from whatever top-secret mission you go on!*'"

They kissed.

My two weeks there were almost over. I couldn't wait to get back home. I hated my cousin. I didn't like what she made me feel. Lying in bed, I realized my hate was giant.

That night, I dreamt of gathering all her Barbies and Barbie accessories and taking them out to the huge yard where there was this special machine that tore them up. It was The Barbie Wrecking Yard. As I murdered her dolls, I laughed and danced. I heard a loud stomping sound. I looked up and saw a nine-hundred-foot Barbie, fully naked, with a hole between her legs, coming my way. She wasn't smiling. She looked angry. She was here to get vengeance for the dead Barbies. I started to run. The nine-hundred-foot Barbie was closing in. Strange fluids spewed from her breasts and the makeshift hole between her legs. I woke up screaming, my penis erect, sticky strange fluids on my thighs and pajamas.

"We Girls Can Do Anything"

1959 Barbie debuts at the American Toy Fair in New York City.

1961 Barbie has her first facelift, gives up her black eyeliner, stops plucking her eyebrows so sharply, and bleaches her hair, releasing it from its ponytail into a bubble cut. Ken is introduced as Barbie's "handsome steady."

1963 Barbie's best friend Midge arrives. She has a "fuller, freckled face," so she's less intimidating and sexual than the blonde bombshell.

1964 Skipper, Barbie's little sister, becomes the perfect babysitter.

1966 "Color Magic" Barbie comes with a solution to change the color of her clothes and hair. Francie, Barbie's mod cousin, appears in a polka-dot top and gingham bikini bottom. Who thought those would look good together? Apparently, *Gidget* inspired her personality.

1967 Mattel announces a Barbie trade-in: an old doll plus $1.50 got you a new doll. An African American version of Francie is introduced, but discontinued shortly afterward due to poor sales.

1968 Christie, another African American friend of Barbie's, finally integrates America's playrooms.

1969 Barbie's fan club reaches 600,000 members, second only to the Girl Scouts.

1971 Barbie goes under the knife again. Now, rather than glancing sidelong, she can look the world straight in the eye.

1974 Barbie has her Sweet Sixteen party, even though she's only fifteen.

1975 Barbie attends the Winter Olympics as a skier, skater, and swimmer(!) and takes gold medals in each sport.

1976 At the national bicentennial celebration, Barbie is entombed in America's Time Capsule. For the occasion, she wears a Betsy Ross dress trimmed with lace. Resurrected, Barbie changes her hairstyle for a feathered Farrah Fawcett 'do. Ken also has a makeover so that he looks more like Robert Redford.

1977 More plastic surgery makes Barbie's "golden smile" permanent.

1985 Yuppie "Day to Night" Barbie carries a calculator by day and wears designer gowns at night.

1986 Barbie becomes an astronaut.

1988 Barbie completes her MD.

1990   Mattel hosts a Barbie Summit in New York City, inviting thirty-nine children from around the world to discuss war, world hunger, and the environment. Black and Hispanic versions of Barbie appear, proving that "many girls may have the same name, but . . . can still be individuals."

1992   "Teen Talk" Barbie enrages feminists across the United States by informing girls, "Math class is tough." The Barbie Liberation Organization swaps voice boxes in some Barbies for G.I. Joe voice boxes, so that Barbie announces: "Vengeance is mine!" Editor's note: wish I had one of those.

1993   "Troll" Barbie commits a fashion faux pas. Despite this, Barbie sales reach one billion dollars.

1994   In the 1960s, the average household owned one Barbie. In 1994, according to Mattel's annual report, the average American girl between the ages of three and ten owns eight.

2009   Barbie celebrated her fiftieth birthday on March 9.

—Editor

"A Dark Playmate Is Made"
by Dorian Katz

A Real American Hero

1964 G.I. Joe is born as an eleven-and-a-half-inch doll with twenty-one moving parts and lifelike hair. He's named after a movie called *The Story of G.I. Joe.*

1968 Joe learns to talk.

1970 Joe's four friends form the G.I. Joe Adventure Team.

1974 Joe acquires a "Kung Fu" grip.

1975 Over a million "action figures" are sold in one year. A bionic warrior called Atomic Man is introduced.

1976 The first superhuman team member (named Bulletman) debuts. The Intruders—aliens with "Crusher Grip" arms—are created to give the Adventure Team someone to fight.

1978 The high price of petroleum ends the domestic marketing of G.I. Joe figures.

1982 Sixteen new three-and-three-quarter-inch toys debut. The new "G.I. Joe, A Real American Hero" figures are fully posable, but their uniforms are molded on.

1985 Drednoks are created to become Joe's latest enemies.

1986 According to *Toy & Hobby World,* G.I. Joe is the bestselling toy in America. Sgt. Slaughter becomes the first real person to join the G.I. Joe Team.

1987 To honor heroic children around the United States, Hasbro conducts a "G.I. Joe Search for Real American Heroes."

1991 G.I. Joe Eco-Warriors, bearing "Eco-facts" on their boxes, are introduced to combat C.O.B.R.A., evil toys who are destroying the environment. The good guys shoot water.

1992 G.I. Joe joins the "Drug Elimination Force." Hasbro funds in-school programs to teach kids about the dangers of drugs.

1993 Nearly thirty years after his inception, more than 250 million G.I. Joe action figures have been sold.

—Editor

The Fruit of All Evil

by John A. Domeier

In 1963 I was born missing a portion of three of my limbs. It was a difficult year for my parents. The ensuing years would be challenging for me, too, as I realized that, yes indeed, I certainly was shortchanged in the leg and arm department.

In 1964, a fake left arm and two wooden legs (yes, they were basically wood back then) allowed me to walk, ride a tricycle, ride a three-wheeled motorcycle, join the Cub Scouts, go to summer camp, pinch my neighborhood friends with my hook, and at least attempt to escape from the Frankenstein monster at Universal Studios. For a guy missing critical body parts, I did well in suburban California. Amazingly well, up until my encounter with the Catholic Church, a little girl, and an orange.

Before I entered first grade, my parents enrolled me, my younger brother, and older sister at St. Edward's Catholic School in Newark, California. They wanted to provide us with the best education possible. I'm sure it was a strain on the family finances, but parents make sacrifices for their children.

A child also makes sacrifices in schools like this. One should not stand out. We all know the drill, don't we? Conformity. The blue sweater and the white shirt. The black shoes. All the same. And then there was me. Part metal. Part wood. Good god.

My left arm prosthesis is technically called a *terminal device*. I and everyone else know it as a damn *hook*. When used correctly, hooks can manage many tasks. You can hold a pen or pencil and write. You can hold a cup and drink from it. You can hold papers and books. I never learned to use the clunky thing very well. I was much too busy hiding it under the desk or in a long-sleeve shirt. I was conscious of its look, of its connection to bad people and bad doings. This came mostly from movies and books. The hook's evil overtones were not lost on this six-year-old.

Because I never became adept at the evil hook device, my mom would help me here and there to make my life easier. Ever peel an orange with one hand? Oh, it's doable, all right. I've done it. But do it as a shy, god-fearing six-year-old with a Captain Hook arm in front of the two-armed freaks I knew as classmates?

I guess my mom knew my apprehension, so she peeled the oranges for my school lunch in the mornings. My mom is a great mom, but did she have to swathe the thing in Saran Wrap? Wasn't it embarrassing enough to have the tasty, juicy orb pre-peeled? Did she have to pile another embarrassment upon that one by encasing it in "the wrap"? Where was the edge to the plastic wrap? How, in front of gazing little boys and girls—and God, apparently—could I search for the edge and free my pre-skinned vessel of vitamin C? The plastic was more difficult to remove than the covering it was born in!

Part metal. Part wood. Did I really need to stick out any more? Hell, no.

So the orange, still entangled in space-age wrap with no edge, went straight into my flip-top desk in Ms. Collins's class. Where it stayed. And stayed. And, well . . . stayed. The wrap hastened the orange's ultimate demise into a fermented, decayed, mold-encrusted shadow of its former self. All conveniently wrapped in see-through plastic. I watched the atrophy like an experiment, safe (hope-fully) from harmful mold vapors. Every time I opened my flip-top desk, I'd note how the experiment had gone to the next level. Could I make penicillin from it? I didn't know.

I opened my desktop less frequently. I lifted it only halfway or less, until ultimately I learned to grab my school stuff through a slit, strictly by touch.

Even more amazing, the plastic became part of the horror. It morphed into the rot stew—becoming one with it. So there the nightmare sat, hidden inside its desk-tomb. Do you see my dilemma? How, in front of the class, was I to remove this madness from my desk? It not only looked bad, but it smelled, too.

What would Jesus do? Jesus would leave it in there, that's what. After all, we were always told that Jesus was everywhere. Maybe he was in my desk, decontaminating my orange. Maybe it would just go away. . . .

It was Valentine's Day, the end of the day—a Friday, I think. No more classes, but we did have homework. Catholic schools are good at that.

My comfy, if conformist, blue sweater had Valentine cards sticking out of various pockets. I think I made them stick out because I wanted my classmates to see the Catholic first-grade equivalent of bed notches. Oh, boy. What a metal-and-wood stud I felt like!

I knew I had homework. I knew my books and papers were in the desk-tomb. The experiment wasn't over! Didn't it need more time? Sure, it did. Everyone was around the sarcophagus anyway. I wouldn't dare open it. *The horror that lies within!*

So I did what any mortal would do. I left my books in there. They had company, after all. I walked proudly but with unfinished-homework anxiety out the classroom door and on down the outside walkway.

Until the oh-so-cute girl spoke to me. "Where are your books?" she asked sweetly as we made our way toward freedom.

"Oh, they are in my desk," I replied shyly.

"I'll get them for you!" she announced excitedly.

The little girl had given me one of my best Valentine cards. It was probably sticking out of my chest pocket next to my pounding heart. But it didn't matter. My feeble, "No, that's okay," went unnoticed. My internal screaming "Noooo!!" also went unheard to all but me. I shrank, just like my orange.

I tried to catch her before she flipped open the desk-tomb, but she was determined to help me. My wooden legs wouldn't carry me fast enough to stop her or beat her to it. Maybe she just wanted to make my life easier. Maybe she just plain liked me. No matter. The lid came up with a swift, hardy swing. Her face contorted in horror. The secret was out. The experiment was over.

The putrefied smelly orange stared at her through a fogged, wrinkled plastic window. What did the little girl think of me now? What kind of boy kept a heap of decomposed evil in his desk? I doubt if she even knew it was merely a neglected citrus. A dead mouse, perhaps? A turd? Something worse? Did the part-metal/part-wood terminal-device boy really harbor evil?

Illustration by Jim Wiz

What I do know is that I let two things go that, in their genesis, were innocent and sweet. I let the fruit decay instead of enjoying it in all its glory. And I lost the oh-so-cute little girl, who never spoke to me again.

Ostracism, conformity, and expulsion be damned. The fruit needed eating.

Gilding the Afterlife: My Pubescence in the Bathtub of the Dead

by Dean Estes

One of the hallmarks of the Church of Jesus Christ of Latter-day Saints—that is, the LDS church or Mormons—is the general lack of pageantry in their services. They don't have shiny embroidered robes or gilded chalices of sacramental wine. Instead, they have seven-year-old suits and Dixie cups of sacramental water. They never use the crucifix as a symbol ("We celebrate the life, not the death") and their austere churches are mostly bereft of décor, save the occasional framed print of a rather white Nazarene.

The various Mormon temples throughout the world, however, showcase a rich, if tasteless, decorative impulse and are home to eccentric neo-Masonic rituals of theological significance. The only temple I've been inside—the one in Oakland, California—is a special example of vernacular Mormon architecture. It sits perched in the Oakland hills, visible by both day and night throughout the northern Bay Area, a ziggurat intentionally quoting the pyramidal shrines of ancient Latin America. Why would this clean-cut, all-American cult-next-door wish to design God's house in the image of idolatrous pre-Columbian centers of abominable practices? The *Book of Mormon,* the notorious central scriptural tome of the church, is a "visionary" account of the spiritual heroes of the early Americas. The native "Nephites" and "Lamanites" of Mormonism's eponymous Good Book are generally understood, although without the blessing of official LDS theology, to have been the pre-Conquest inhabitants of the New World. Moreover, it *is* central to Mormon understanding that Christ walked the Americas, teaching his message of unconditional love and superior maize-harvesting techniques to the natives in much the same manner as he's more conventionally said to have done in the pre-Constantinian Roman Empire.

Much odder than the Aztec Moderne architecture is the "work" I participated in at the Oakland Temple in the mid-seventies: Baptisms for the Dead. In hindsight, I'm uncomfortable with the morality or appropriateness of inducting adolescents into mysterious rites of necrospiritual cleansing, but I and my young co-Mormons endured the event without evident damage. It helped that we were adolescent; we didn't really regard anything compulsory with seriousness.

In the Mormon universe, once a person ceases to exist on the mortal plane, the soul teleports immediately to literal Paradise, a sort of combination rest stop/Ellis Island in the sky. Paradise isn't Heaven. It certainly isn't the final destination. It also isn't the place where the Grand Truths are revealed; patience is required even in the Level Above Human. After dying, you won't know whether your religion or lack thereof had anything to do with What Really Is; you'll *still* have to decide for yourself. That's where the Mormons intend to rescue the dead, by performing surrogate baptisms on behalf of Paradise's populace, who will

The Oakland Temple photographed by Loren Rhoads

then have the choice of either accepting or rejecting the One True Gospel. Is this paradoxical, contradictory, unfair, and absurd? Of course. But then, the faithful aren't expected to fully comprehend God's mysteries.

The dead's choice upon baptism is crucial. Acceptance of one's newfound Mormon membership is a prerequisite for Higher Glory. Failure to accept will necessarily lead to Eternal Disappointment in knowing that, if only you'd played your cards Mormon, you'd have had a shot at your very own Godhood. Since the gospel in its Mormon aspect wasn't "restored" to humanity until the mid-nineteenth century, Baptism for the Dead represents a unique opportunity to the billions of souls who incarnated between True Gospels.

When Earth's sorry history is finally played out, the Big Judgment will come down and all souls will then be dispatched to their earned destinations in one of three levels of Heaven. That's right, three different Heavens. Gentiles—that is, non-Mormons—should be consoled by the generosity of the Plan of Salvation. Mormon lore has it that if only we could see the conditions of even the *lowest* of the three levels, the Terrestrial, we'd commit the sin of suicide just to get there. This bottom, third-world heaven is described like a superior, puri-

fied Earth. Souls are not exactly material, however, so you don't get to do satisfying things like eat or have sex. Eternal bummer, indeed. At least there's no sickness or further death.

Next flight up is the even-better Telestial Kingdom, nebulously described. You probably get unlimited chocolate rations there, but damn! still no sex.

Finally, the Celestial Kingdom awaits those who did all the right LDS things and are perfect by inhuman LDS standards. In this highest level, you and your spouse "for all time and eternity" get your very own universe where you'll be allowed to set the rules and spend your days making worlds. This is where you'll be allowed to have reproductive sex with your soul mate, for the purpose of populating all those planets you'll be busy baking.

This is all a pretty heavy burden for kids.

The first thing I can remember about my temple experience is the ride there. Seven noisy boys were crammed into Sister Alexander's Ford Family Squire station wagon, the one with the fading, peeling, simulated wood-grain stickers on the side. All the way to Oakland, I wondered if it was going to be a problem with the Lord that I'd been masturbating so much recently. I was thirteen and my bishop had specifically intimidated me on this point in preparation. You can't do temple work if you've been wiggling your willie or yearning with your yoni. I'm sure I'm not the only boy who lied when Bishop Garth leaned toward me over his big desk, looked me sternly in the eye, and asked, "Do you play with yourself?" This sort of obsessive denial of healthy human behavior is exactly the sort of thing that led to my eventual self-dismissal from the Mormon medicine show. That and the fact that I wanted to wiggle other boys' willies: a major crime against the prudish, heterosupremacist, sex-hating Mormon doctrine. My exploding sexuality *was* a bit of an issue later in the evening, although not for reasons of moral self-doubt. My body was simply at that hyper-hormonal stage when it had a mind of its own.

After arriving at the temple grounds, the boys met up with the girls in a waiting room annexed to the temple proper. We endured an embarrassingly racist little Mormon-made movie called *Johnny Lingo,* an inane fifties-style moral fable about the happy-happy inhabitants of an indeterminate Polynesian island who were concerned with the worth of young women. We giggled endlessly at the movie's unforgettable best line: "Mahona is a six-cow wife!" Adding fuel to

our group's embarrassment was the fact that half of us kids were either Tongan or Samoan. Even at that age, we were shocked at the tastelessness and insensitivity of being shown this movie. But then, the church at that time was just getting used to the idea that non-whites had any use in God's plan. What *Johnny Lingo* was supposed to teach us has remained beyond my grasp to this day. Another mystery, I suppose.

After a long wait, the girls were ushered into the temple by a tall, thin alien of a man for their turn at saving dead people from a cut-rate afterlife. We boys became more restless and fidgeted in our seats while telling unkind jokes about the girls and how many cows they were worth. I wondered if Jesus was going to walk by and hear us.

Finally, Brother Alien returned and smilingly showed us to our changing room, after handing us our one-size-fits-all temple garments. These clothes were thin, loose-fitting cotton, entirely white. We were instructed to leave our shoes outside the changing area and switch into these purified costumes, which resembled karate outfits.

For some reason I can't fathom now—but must have had something to do with boys being boys—we handled the situation of changing together with a lot of randy talk and peeking at one another's developing bodies. This was sheer hell for me, as I had the additional burden of having to pretend that I wasn't aroused by the horseplay and needing to control my body accordingly.

The baptismal room of the Oakland Temple was something else, a minimalist Moctezuma's inner sanctum as visualized by Busby Berkeley: white marble floors, white ziggurat patterns on the walls, cubist brass sconces, Delphic tripods bearing ferns. The most spectacular feature was the baptismal font itself. It was a very large golden bowl mounted on twelve life-size gold-plated oxen. The sculpted oxen represented the Twelve Tribes of Israel by some arcane semiotics. Each one was unique. Much was made of how each bull's face bore a different expression. At the rim of the font was a platform with a desk and public address system from which the details of the baptisms were observed and recorded. We waited on a long bench, more fidgety than ever, across from the font assembly.

One by one, we were called into the water by the presiding Elder on the platform. I was terrified to realize that the man doing the boy-dunking was a particularly handsome youngish Elder from my own "ward," on whom I had a fierce puppyish crush. He always wore these box-contour-ing Brittania jeans to weekday church functions. My first crotch. I had to redouble my efforts not to get an erection in front of Jesus and the dead and all.

My name was eventually called. Time froze. Gathering all my mental energy to focus only on things holy, I climbed the steps between the fore bulls and then down into the surprisingly warm water. The water felt good. Too good. Between this visceral stimulus and the nice paternal way that Brother Stud held firmly onto my arms and shoulders, I lost control and got an underwater boner in a big way. I became dizzy, as if I were in some alternate reality, drugged by the stress of hoping my condition wouldn't be noticed while I was giving someone's great-granddad the chance of an eternity. I knew then that I was either going to go to Mormon Hell or going to escape this bizarre belief system and have a good life. I chose life. Thanks, Brother Stud. Thanks, boner.

Routine prayers were read with the name of the dead person inserted. At the "amen" of each prayer, the big Elder dude would forcefully push me backward, fully submerging me in the purifying waters, fully making my dick stick out. I silently prayed that no one would notice. By the time I'd been dunked for about ten souls or so, what physical thrill there had been at first became waterlogged. I was just flaccid enough to climb out of the water without embarrassment. As I ascended the steps, heavy with my wet garment, I looked down to realize that the water had rendered the clothing totally transparent. If any spirits had dropped in to witness their promotion, they would have seen how excited I was to have been of help. I furtively looked around and was relieved not to see any holy ghosts.

I was then debriefed by another Elder, who told me how proud I should be to have participated in this very sacred work. I felt humiliated. He gave me a list of the names of the dead I'd saved. For the first time, I considered the presumption of what I'd just done. What if those nice Victorian-sounding names had belonged to Muslims, Buddhists, or Navajo? Indeed, in later years, major Jewish groups asked the LDS church to cool it with their ancestors. For the first time, my religious guilt came not from considering, "What if it's all true?" but rather from, "What if it's not?"

I didn't stop questioning the religion I'd been raised in and,

when I finally accepted my non-Christian spirituality and homosexuality, neither the church nor I had much interest in each other.

Although it had been a few years since I'd stopped attending any Mormon services, Bishop Richards asked to meet with me when I came out at eighteen. I agreed, hoping for a wonderful excommunication. Instead, I was intensely berated by some quack psychotherapist whom Richards had invited, and whom I'd never met before. This fraud asserted that I'd *chosen* to be gay to hurt my mother. Where he got this conspiracy theory, I'll never know, but it was gratifying that my mother thought it was disgusting. I declined to dignify Richards and his psychoquack's anti-family hate-mongering with an argument, and chose instead the dignity of proper self-acceptance over the mediocre charade of Mormonism.

I'm glad I got to see those golden bulls, though. They were cool. I'm happy I saw a bit of the temple, too; the experience afforded me the glory of Eternal Dish.

Still, I'm sorry if I offended any ungrateful dead.

LET'S LEARN ABOUT MORMONISM

The prophet Joseph Smith Jr. was fourteen when two divine personages approached him on his family's farm near Palmyra, New York. They told him to refrain from joining any existing Christian sect.

In 1823, the angel of the Prophet Moroni told Smith that records written in "Reformed Egyptian" on gold plates, along with two stones to help in the translation, were buried in a nearby hill. Smith uncovered them four years later. The English translation was published in 1830 as *The Book of Mormon.*

This book tells the story of a tribe of ancient Israelites who sailed to the Americas about 600 B.C.E. They "maintained a civilization in the Americas for centuries." Christ even visited them, after his resurrection. Their civilization ended in the time of Mormon and his son Moroni (about 400 C.E.) when the Lamanites, ancestors of the Native Americans, overcame the Nephites, the descendents of the righteous Israelites. Moroni buried the history recorded by his father. It was hidden in the hill for more than fourteen centuries.

The "latter day" in Latter-day Saints refers to the 1820s, when Smith's revelation restored the true church to the world. Christ, the Bible, and America are central tenets in Mormon thought. Also important is the symbolism of Israel, the chosen people who wander, are mistreated, and finally settle.

According to *The Perennial Dictionary of World Religions,* rites in Mormon temples resemble Masonic rituals.

Ten million members strong throughout the world (as of 1998), the LDS church boasts more than eighty thousand converts yearly. This may be due to the missionary work all men are expected to perform in their twenties. Unless specifically excused, they are required to devote two years, at their own expense, to service to the church.

African Americans were among the early converts, but were relegated to second-class status by proscriptions in the Books of Abraham and Moses. In the middle of the twentieth century, African Americans were banned from the priesthood. This was repealed by a new ordinance in 1978. The revelation came from a living prophet named Spencer W. Kimbal. It was hailed as the "most momentous decision for the Mormon faith this century." Kimbal died in 1985 at the age of ninety.

Women derive their religious status from their husbands. Marriage comes in two flavors: for time (the customary Christian marriage till death do you part) and for eternity. A marriage for eternity makes the couple eligible for the "highest opportunity of salvation."

Marriages may be performed vicariously by the living for those who died before they could accept Mormon teachings.

God is a self-made, finite deity with a material body, according to Joseph Smith, who also set forth degrees of progression through eternity. In the final state, humans can become like God himself. Human beings are "gods in embryo," reports *The HarperCollins Dictionary of Religion*.

Anyone can gain entrance to Christ's earthly kingdom through repentance and baptism by immersion. *The Perennial Dictionary of World Religions* confirms that even the dead can receive baptism and "thus share in the millennial age." Until the kingdom comes, the baptized who die wait in heaven with material bodies identical to those they had on earth.

According to the Los Angeles stake (a stake is about three thousand to five thousand members in five to ten congregations), "baptism by proxy for deceased ancestors is still being performed." Justification for the practice comes from no less a source than the Bible itself. In his first letter to the Corinthians, Paul says, "What do people hope to gain by being baptized for the dead? If the dead are not ever going to be raised, why be baptized on their behalf?" (1 Corinthians 15:29)

The church maintains that the soul on the eternal journey has the right to refuse or decline its baptism. The Latter-day Saints protest that any allegations of mass baptisms of Holocaust victims are "hooey."

—Editor

This Is a Very Old Scar

by Dorian Katz

> No foreign sky protected me,
> No stranger's wing shielded my face.
> —Anna Akhmatova, "Requiem"

Before waking to the alarm clock, I dreamed I was asking my father and sister to drive me someplace important. Each had promised to take me, but they weren't budging. Finally, I just left their house alone; I was running late.

In my desperation for work, I had scheduled a second interview with UPS. Walking down the block to catch the bus at Fillmore and Oak, I glanced up at the sky. It was an unusually warm and clear night. San Francisco seemed peaceful. I told myself, *Nothing bad can happen to me on a night like this*. It was three A.M.

Sitting at the bus stop, I brushed my thick dark hair and waited. Few cars passed. The neighborhood was silent. From across the street, a handsome man came toward me with an unlit cigarette dangling between his fingers. "Do you have a light? Are you on your way to work?" he asked. I replied no to both questions. He then moved away from me to stand outside the bus shelter. I resumed brushing my hair and assumed he was waiting on the bus, just like me.

Within minutes, the assault must have occurred. I do not remember and doubt I ever will. I assume that I was hit in the head with something hard and jagged. I was knocked out cold and left alone.

I remember opening my eyes to see I was lying on the sidewalk. I knew I had been assaulted. I touched my forehead. It was warm and damp, so I knew I was bleeding. Looking around, I noticed that my backpack was gone. My coat lay a few feet in front of my head. A surge of adrenaline boosted me up off the pavement. I grabbed my coat, then rushed back to my flat, one block away. I don't remember any thoughts beyond my desire to get home.

My house key was in my stolen bag. I rang the buzzer and pounded on the door simultaneously. My friend Amy opened the door. The horrified look on her face reminded me of Edvard Munch's painting "The Scream." I had not seen my reflection and felt unsettled by her alarm.

I commanded her, "Call the police! Call me an ambulance! Bring me water," while trotting up the staircase, then down our long hallway to the bathroom. I heard our other roommates, Hank and Marc, rousing from their beds and getting dressed before emerging from their rooms.

Amy brought a bowl of water into the bathroom. I stood before the mirror. I could not tell how deep the wound on my forehead went. Tattered flesh hung down. There was a lot of blood and something the color of egg yolk. Instead of placing the washcloth against the injury to stop the bleeding, I wiped at it aggressively. When Hank joined me in the bathroom, he delicately put his hand on the washcloth and began to press. Looking at my reflection, I asked, "Is that my brain?"

Hank said, "That can't be your brain. If that were your brain, your skull would be cracked and you wouldn't be conscious." He was always so practical.

Unfortunately, the cops came far sooner than the ambulance. One of the beefy officers joined Hank and me in our long, skinny bathroom to bombard me with questions. "What's your name? What happened? What were you doing out there? What did he look like? Was he black? Are you drunk or on drugs? Do you know what day it is?"

I was terrified of this cop. I didn't feel he had my best interests in mind or even a morsel of compassion for me. I sat down on the cold tiles, squeezing myself into the corner between the toilet and the sink. Looking up at Hank, I said, "Don't leave me alone with him. He's scaring me." As the questions were repeated, I grew tired of answering, so I asked Hank to respond for me, but the cop would not allow it.

The other officer peeked into the bathroom. Mostly he spoke with Amy and Marc in the hall. He told them that I might have brain damage.

Eventually my ambulance came. In the beginning, the paramedics weren't any kinder than the cops. I overheard an EMT advise Amy to remove the bloodstains from my wool coat with a meat tenderizer. (As if she gave a damn about the condition of a coat at that moment.) I decided that the paramedics were hardened by life on the job. My survival instinct was keen, so I decided to be charming in hopes that would get me the best care possible. An EMT radioed in, "This is a code three." I later learned that code three meant lights and sirens on, get there as fast as possible.

At the top of the stairs, I requested a gurney. After all, in the movies, doesn't every patient about to be whisked off in an ambulance get carried away on a gurney? Well, since I could walk, there was no gurney for me. I settled for an arm to link with mine. I clutched the banister with my other hand.

Amy rode in the front of the ambulance. Marc and Hank followed in Hank's van.

When we arrived at San Francisco General's emergency room, I was wheeled inside on a gurney. As we passed a cluster of hospital workers, I overheard someone say, "Oh, my god! What happened to her?" SFGH is known for its excellence in dealing with trauma victims. I figured they'd seen it all and much worse, so I must have been in pretty bad shape.

At first, I had to wait alone on my gurney in the hallway. I was given heated blankets that lost their warmth too quickly. I realized I was in shock, because I was severely cold.

Every so often, someone came by to ask whether I knew my name, the date, who was presi-

dent, and where I was. (I could have asked them the same questions, but refrained.) Basically, the nurses were checking to see whether I had a concussion. The possibility of a concussion was also their excuse for not supplying me with the morphine I requested. Actually, I wasn't in pain. I just asked for morphine, because my friend had it when she lost three toes in a bicycle accident.

Alone in the corridor, I sang myself lullabies. I also prayed to God: "Just let me be able to think when this is all over. I don't care what I look like." I feared brain damage, yet I comforted myself with assurances that I was going to survive.

Within half an hour after arriving at the emergency room, it seemed as though my spirit moved outside of my body. My spirit fit into a space tiny enough to accommodate a hovering insect. That space was located underneath the fluorescent light fixtures on the hospital ceiling. Alone in those corridors, I was my own guardian angel. I kept watch over myself.

A paramedic, Dwayne, saw the hairbrush tangled in my hair and apologized for not noticing sooner. Dwayne visited me several times, just to keep me company. When he came to say good-bye at the end of his shift, he showed me three small scars on the top of his bald head and told me he healed well because he was Native American. I thought, *I'll heal well, too, because I'm a woman.*

Eventually I got to choose a friend to keep me company through the rest of my wait. Amy held my hand and wiped away the blood that dripped toward my eyes from beneath my bandage. I made jokes that weren't especially funny to try to keep us entertained.

In the ER, people are treated according to their priority of need. There was a man screaming in Spanish, who had been stabbed in the stomach. He was wheeled into a room immediately. From near that door, I had the impression that I didn't need to scream, because somehow we were linked and he was screaming for us both.

The wait went on for hours, so I had Amy trade places with Marc. Marc can be downright obnoxious and I wanted him to recklessly complain on my behalf until a doctor would see me. Within twenty minutes, Marc and I were in a small room waiting on a plastic surgeon who had been woken up to do the sutures. Someone figured he'd do a neater job, which I appreciated, since this injury was on my face. When the bandages came off, Marc turned green, so I sent him back to the waiting room. After

all, he had done his job well and I felt fine about being alone in the doctor's care.

The light of the surgeon's magnifying lamp warmed me. That felt great. He injected Novocain into my forehead and got to work. The surgeon and I chatted away. I asked questions about him and he told me stories to pass the time. Sometimes I watched him sewing through the layers of my skin by looking at my reflection in the glass of the magnifying lamp.

Oddly enough, I never felt much physical pain with this injury. During the surgery, I moaned at times. Then the doctor would ask if he was hurting me. I told him, "No, it just feels good to moan." He gave me more Novocain after these moments and told me to let him know if I felt even the slightest bit of pressure. It took him several hours to finish. He lost track of how many stitches he put in, but estimated around a hundred in the three layers on my forehead and a mere six at the bridge of my nose.

The plastic surgeon, who did a terrific job sewing me up, told me I would probably need plastic surgery and to come back in a year. I dismissed this comment without having any idea how well my scar would heal. I figured I'd wait and see. If I was severely disfigured, I would go back to see this nice surgeon later.

Psychologists believe trauma survivors try to make sense out of their experiences. I did this for the first few months by compulsively drawing and writing every detail I could remember. The writing was linked to my hope that someday I might remember the actual assault itself. Did I yell or scream or fight back in any way? Since I had suffered a blow to my head that knocked me out, I may never know how it happened or what I was hit with.

The attack colored and dominated my worldview. I felt powerless against the depression that came in response. I call the two years that followed my personal Dark Ages; I had little hope for my future. I told myself that if in ten years I was still so miserable, I could kill myself, but not now, not yet.

Borrowing from the ritual of clean and sober friends who celebrate their yearly anniversaries, I made May 11, the date of my assault, my personal holiday. I tried to take the day off from work and make time alone for contemplation. I ate chocolate cake with mint tea and bought myself flowers. It was a holiday I did not share with friends.

On my tenth anniversary, I

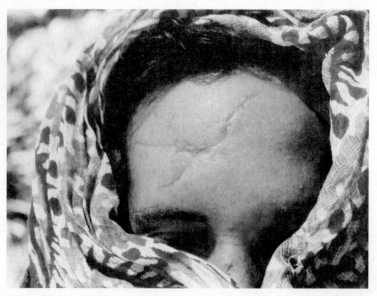

Photograph of the author

made an exception. I threw my scar a party and invited a small group of close friends over for desserts. At ten, my scar was much too young to go out for cocktails and dancing.

Before sending off the invitations to my scar's birthday party, I had misgivings about hosting a partially self-indulgent affair. Ultimately, I decided I would regret not following through on the wacky idea and rejoicing over how much I had grown in these ten years. I'd had to relearn to be comfortable enough to leave my house at night. I had to foster the pleasure of adorning myself with joy and creativity.

It was wonderful to honor myself this way. We even played "Pin the Tail on the Scar." I painted the form of my scar—which has always resembled branches to me—in crimson on a silver background and cut out various shapes of things I like, such as a high-heeled boot, a bird, and a cat, to stick on the branches. Everyone received a prize I'd gotten from the dollar store.

Within the first year after the attack, I had a memorable dream. I dreamed I met an elderly African American man working in a bar paneled with fine wood. This man had a scar on his forehead. Its shape resembled my scar's. When I remarked on it, he said, "This is a very old scar."

I'm glad I promised myself ten more years before taking drastic action. I never wish to revisit my personal Dark Ages or anything remotely similar, but I am grateful to have more faith in my inner resilience.

The Road of Life

by Simon Wood

A few years back, before I left England, I was doing my usual thing—burning the candle at both ends, trying to compress a thirty-six-hour day into twenty-four. My lifestyle consisted of working full-time while studying for a post-graduate diploma. I would finish my workday, race through fifty miles of rush-hour traffic for a quick meal, then off to college. If my timing was crackerjack, everything would go like a breeze and I'd be home before midnight. Living like this changed me. I was impatient, never suffering fools gladly. Everybody was an obstacle. On that particular night, my obstacle was some moron on a bicycle.

I peeled off the roundabout doing thirty-five. The ineffective speed bumps did little to slow me. The more effective traffic-calming device was the BMX rider.

A hundred feet ahead of me, he launched his bike off the curb without a moment's thought for oncoming traffic. Legs a blur, he weaved back and forth like a drunk in the lane in front of me.

"Prick," I mumbled to myself. "I'll fucking teach you."

It was something I said but didn't mean. He was fucking with my schedule, and I wanted to vent. But someone somewhere granted my wish.

The street ahead was clear. I jinked onto the wrong side of the road, giving the kid the widest berth possible, and floored the gas pedal. Inches from being passed, the BMX rider veered hard right and directly into my path as my speedometer needle touched fifty. The kid was broadsided. He didn't stand a chance. Neither did I. We were both passengers on a nightmare ride. I never had a chance to hit my brakes.

Books always describe a body hitting a car with a hollow thud. That's bollocks! A body striking a car hood and an unprotected skull smacking a windshield sound nothing like anyone can possibly describe. The sounds are twisted and contorted. I tried to comprehend these noises as the teenager's body rolled up my car's hood.

The kid tumbled like an acrobat until he blotted out my windshield. I stiffened like I had rigor mortis. My legs spasmed. I found the brake pedal. The car's hood dived. The kid, still conscious, was flung to the unforgiving asphalt. I was treated to the sight of the boy hitting the ground on his back, his head exploding on the tarmac. My car stopped a few feet from his twisted body.

I'm not a bad person, but my first thought was to run. I glanced at my mirrors and around me. More than a dozen people stared at the disaster. I weighed it up—if I fled, would anyone be able to describe the car, my license plate number, me? My mind bounced the idea back and forth in a nanosecond, changing the answer from yes to no and back again. But my conscience got the better of me. I had to stay. I guided the car around the kid to the correct side of the street, parking half on the sidewalk and half in the road.

I clambered from my car on unsteady legs. I got as far as the rear of my car and crumpled, collapsing into a heap on the curb. I stared at the kid. Blood bloomed at a phenomenal rate to form a slick around his head. The blood's color was like no other I'd ever seen, dark and rich, like a royal seal on a death warrant—my death warrant. The boy was still.

A balding man exhibiting some first-aid knowledge approached the boy. A woman with a cell phone called 999. People stared at me, forming opinions and prejudices.

The woman with the cell came over to me. She was full of concern. "Are you okay?"

I mumbled something to say that I was, but I wasn't.

She sat beside me. She was kind and motherly. It wasn't what I was expecting. I'd expected a lynch mob.

"What happened?"

I explained. My voice was monotone with a manic streak fighting to get out. I never looked at her. I stared at the balding man who was at a loss about what to do with the boy.

"It's my fault," I murmured.

"It's an accident," the woman said.

"I should have stopped."

"You couldn't have. No one could."

She didn't understand. She wasn't in the car with me. She didn't know my foot was on the gas and not the brake. She didn't know I'd wished bad things on the kid.

"Do you want to call someone?" She offered me her cell.

Who was I going to call? I was too ashamed. Besides, this was something I needed to face alone. The condemned prisoner never has a friend's head in the noose with him when the hangman pulls the lever. I wanted to be held at the moment, but I was embarrassed to ask.

The boy sprang into a sitting position. My heart stopped as his started. The balding man leaped back. The woman and I jumped to our feet.

"Are you okay?" the balding man asked, resting a gentle hand on the boy's shoulder.

"Oh, yes." The boy nodded, flicking blood everywhere. He had a South African accent. "I need to get home." He bent to pick up his buckled bike.

"You're not going anywhere," the balding man said.

The boy spotted me. "I'm really sorry. It's all my fault. I wasn't looking."

"I think you should sit down." The balding man relieved the boy of his bike. "Where do you live?"

"I just need to get home." The boy sounded drunk, but lucid.

I couldn't speak.

He turned his back to me. The back off his skull was a mess. How he was standing, let alone speaking, I never understood. The boy tottered around to face me and started to say something else, but never made it. His eyes rolled back and he went down like a sack of rocks. He hit the sidewalk unconscious. The balding man dropped to the boy's side, but recoiled when the

boy went into violent spasms. We all watched helplessly. It was a blessing when he stopped.

"Where's that damn ambulance?" the balding man whimpered.

The *damn* ambulance arrived a few minutes later. The paramedic demanded details. "Has he been like this the whole time?" she snapped.

"No, he was unconscious at first, then conscious," I said, trying not to let the hysteria show. "Then he collapsed and had a fit."

The paramedic tried to revive him, but the boy was unresponsive. They were loading him into the ambulance when the police arrived. The first officer ordered me to stand by his vehicle while he took statements. A panda car arrived minutes later; the two officers conferred with the lead officer and examined my car and the crash site.

I listened as the witnesses condemned me. An elderly Sikh man claimed I was speeding and that I was a menace to society, but when pressed, admitted that he'd seen nothing, only heard events. Others told similar stories. A mantra chimed in my head, "You're fucked. You're fucked. You're fucked."

Two pre-teens who'd been closest to the accident came to my rescue. They explained that the boy had been riding recklessly and turned right across me as I was going past.

"Was the driver speeding?" the officer asked.

"Don't know. I just know he was trying his best to avoid him."

The officer dismissed everyone and told me to get in his car. The two support officers moved everyone on. The officer interviewed me and took my statement. He asked me to read it before signing. I stared at the words on the page, unable to take any of it in. It might as well have been written in Greek. I signed.

"Okay, you can go."

"What happens now?"

"Come into the station with your license and proof of insurance and that should be that."

"Will I be charged?"

The policeman wrinkled his nose. "I shouldn't think so. You'll get a final decision from the chief constable within three months. As far as I am concerned, it's been a tragic accident."

He led me back to my car and the other policemen. "Not too much damage," one of them said. "The dents in the bonnet should come out easily enough."

He was right. There were only two dents, one from the impact of the boy's head, the other from the bike's saddle. How could the police be so callous? Was it the job? Had they seen this atrocity so many times that it meant noth-

ing to them anymore? Were they just humoring me?

"Mind how you go, son," the lead policeman said, signaling for us to draw a line under events. He might, but I knew I couldn't.

I wanted to confess. Tell them that I was guilty. Malice had been on my mind before I hit the kid. But I didn't. I didn't want my life to end, too. They halted traffic and waved me on.

The nightmares came, of course, but not the sort you might expect. Definitely not the sort I expected. My nightmares never surrounded my guilt. The phantoms that skulked in my dreams hurled horrors of my loss. I was being made to realize that I came within a fraction of losing everything important to me: my freedom, my dreams, my future. Everything I held so dear could have been snatched away. That scared the shit out of me. The boy I had chopped down never entered into the scheme of things.

That bothered me and still does, on occasion. How could I not feel anything for another human? Was I that dead inside? I had no answers; neither did anyone else I spoke to.

My doctor signed me off work for two weeks. Psychiatric help was available if I wanted it. I declined. I wanted to solve my own problems.

My dreams were telling me something. The answer to my sanity was here: *What is important to you, Simon?* It was a simple enough question, but damn hard to answer. I looked at the world I'd created for myself and didn't like what I saw. It's so easy to lose sight of what is important. I'd lost it.

Like the cops, I drew a line under the experience. I didn't blot out what I had done, but I saw no point in torturing myself. I'd been given a second chance. Every day had to be lived like it was my last. The world could come to an end in an instant and I didn't want to be saying, "If only . . ."

Within a month, I'd quit my job, much to my boss's disgust, and taken a new one, working freelance. I booked my dream vacation. Another trip was lined up a few months after that. I bought a race car, returning to a sport I had loved so much. I learned to fly light aircraft. I climbed a volcano. I got out more, played more, enjoyed myself. I rediscovered what life was all about.

I never did find out about the boy, not even his name. In England, police and hospital policy protects the identities of the parties involved, unless a case is made. I used to wonder about him. It's history now—something to be remembered and respected, but not to be dwelled upon.

So much has happened in the six years since the accident. I've come so far. My world has changed many times, always for the better. Don't ask my ambitions for the next five years; I couldn't tell you. Life is too difficult to predict, so why try? Just live it. For me, it took a tragic accident to learn that.

Far from Home: Morbid Curiosity on the Road

Ticket to Auschwitz from the author's collection

Souvenir of Hell

by Brian Thomas

I've always found something compelling about following history's path. I've even sampled military reenacting, shouldering a musket, drenched in sweat and inundated with gunpowder smoke, reliving battles centuries past. I happened to be working in Northern Europe during the fiftieth anniversary of the end of the Second World War. A lifelong history buff, I loved having the chance to be amidst it all. Mostly, thought, I followed the headlines on CNN International from my hotel room. Watching it on European TV was no different from watching it on TV at home. It was all so abstract.

I'd spent four months working nonstop on a film job that had—with the exception of the month shooting snowbound and isolated in the mountains—allowed little free time outside the city limits. During my free weekends, I'd seen pretty much all there was of Oslo. National capital or no, thousand-year history aside, I'd done a pretty thorough job of doing the town.

So when the entire country of Norway shut down for Easter Week, I found a bargain excursion to Poland, a country I'd long been fascinated with.

One thing I love more than history, it's the odd underdog. Hence my fascination with Poland, butt of innumerable Polack jokes. Home to Europe's oldest working democracy. Country voted most likely to be invaded. A people that not once, not twice, but three times saved the Western world from being overrun: twice by Islam in the sixteenth and seventeenth centuries, once by Bolshevism in the twentieth. No kidding. Look it up.

Poland has literally been wiped off the map. The place wryly calls itself *God's Playground,* but prefers not to advertise that it was also Hitler's slaughterhouse, home to the most efficient network of institutionalized human destruction outside of Germany itself.

During the train ride to Kraków, the young architect I shared the compartment with advised that I not attempt the late afternoon tour, but spend the night getting myself ready for it. At suppertime, I made my way through the rain-slicked streets of the medieval city, getting psyched for the day to come.

For a major Polish city, Kraków is an anomaly. Deemed by the Nazis too beautiful to bomb into rubble, it served instead as base of operations for the occupying High Command—once they threw out all the Jews.

I spent the evening church-hopping. You can't go more than a block without coming across a Catholic church, let alone a full-blown cathedral. Good Friday penance services seemed to be going on around the clock.

As I knelt in church after church, hearing services in Latin or Polish, I looked around. Invariably, more than half the people around me were in their seventies: old enough to have been through the War, the Occupation, the scouring of the ghettos.

Poland had been one of the few countries in Europe to open itself to the Jews back in the Middle Ages. With only a few brief occasions, the country had been something of a haven for them. During the War, of course, all that changed. When the Nazis struck out at the Jews, more than a few Poles helped. Actively.

Since the country is and has been more than ninety percent Catholic, it was a good bet that a significant number of these older folks had taken part. As I lost myself in clouds of incense and the steady murmur of prayer around me, I wondered how many in each church reflected on the souls of the murdered Jews—and who among them were begging forgiveness for betraying them.

At midnight, I sat in the town square, listening to the mournful tones of the *Hemnjal,* a bugle call that repeats four times, every hour on the hour. The call always ends abruptly to mark the moment, centuries ago, when a city trumpeter was felled by an invader's arrow.

Every place has its sad stories. Poland always seems to have one more waiting.

The tour left just after sunrise. The trip through the Polish countryside took the better part of two hours. The tour bus was clean and new, packed with folks from a half dozen countries. The whole thing had a festive atmosphere. These folks were, like me, on an excursion package. I was one of four Americans. The other three were Italian Jews from New Jersey, going because their parents thought it would be a "character experience." They talked about picking up souvenirs from the camp bookstore, then getting the hell out. They couldn't imagine why I was going alone.

The bus paralleled train tracks that led into town. Local children played alongside, putting things on the tracks like kids probably always will. One watched as our bus passed. I had déjà vu to a particularly chilling scene in *Schindler's List*. Instead of drawing a finger across his throat, the boy just gave us a bored look: "Oh, great. More tourists."

Suddenly, we passed through the town of Oświęcim, and just as quickly out of it, approaching arguably the most infamous place on earth.

A common misconception is that Auschwitz was one big camp. Actually, it was four, the smaller one being Auschwitz or Camp 1, laid out in orderly blocks of squat two-story brick buildings, like some very spartan private university, except for the guard towers and the barbwire-topped wall at its perimeter. The front gate was adorned with *Arbeit Macht Frei*. Work will make you free: the carrot on a stick that made up the Nazi work ethic.

The larger complex is a few kilometers down the road. The Germans called it Camp 2 or Birkenau. It's the one that comes to mind when people hear *Auschwitz*—images of low barn-like barracks, endless ugly barbwire fences strung on hooked concrete pylons, squat guard towers, and towering crematorium smokestacks.

There was a third camp called Monwitz, where the more political prisoners—Poles and the like—were held.

Last of all was Buna where, with a steady supply of free labor, the German industrialist I. G. Farben set up shop, manufacturing synthetic oil and rubber for the Nazi war effort.

Four camps in all, each with a different purpose, ultimately to be known under a single name.

The parking lot, an enormous gravel and cracked concrete expanse, hinted at the numbers who make the pilgrimage. As we parked, a half dozen other buses arrived.

When we stepped off the bus, the chatter died off as we crossed some unseen meridian separating the realm of package tours and the not-so-distant atrocity. When the tour groups converged on the entrance, they did so in silence.

Some things were almost reassuring in their normalcy, like the modern tan brick-and-concrete visitor center. It could just as easily have stood outside Dinosaur National Monument. Right next to it, a kiosk sold souvenir booklets, slides, Holocaust memoirs, and, oddly enough, ice cream. Although the camp had opened at eight, the kiosk was closed. I bypassed the Jerseyites, who were making plans to buy slides and already consulting their guidebooks for the afternoon salt mine tour.

I fell in at the tail of a random group as they entered the visitor center. One of the first things I saw was a large glass urn shaped like a child's top, balanced on a black marble stand. Layers of ashes, made up of many small measures gathered from several dumps around the area, filled the urn. Finer powdery ash drifted to the bottom, then different levels with different shades and degrees of coarseness piled toward the crown, culminating in bits of charred white bone.

In heavily accented English, an elderly man told a teenager how tons of the powdered remains were dumped into the river Vistula, buried in pits, or pulverized and used for agriculture. Think of that: human ash as fertilizer.

Standing in the entrance hall, while people edged past as I tried to frame a photograph, it occurred to me that I was taking a group portrait rather than a still life. This urn held all that remained of untold hundreds—perhaps thousands—of people.

This first phase of the museum held fairly typical exhibits, what you'd expect in a Holocaust museum. There were multiple-language placards next to photo-graphs and framed documents, but most of the items required minimal explanation. Beyond the ashes in the entrance hall, the initial presentation wasn't dramatic.

Then I went upstairs. It was a simple one-story walk-up, but the indication of how many people had passed this way was inescapable. The concrete and stone-chip steps were glass-smooth in places, with deep, visibly curving depressions worn into them. How many pairs of shoes does it take to do that?

I came across a scale model of the crematorium workings, encased in glass. Cutaways of the structure showed small white plaster figures in poses approximating the day-to-day ritual of extermination. For the mechanically and organizationally inclined, there were labels and charts in the languages of both guilty and victim.

Across from this display stood a series of exhibits that needed no words whatsoever. Floor-to-ceiling glass-enclosed stalls had been filled with different masses of objects. One was full of suitcases, the next with toiletries and every kind of brush imaginable. Then eyeglasses . . . clothing . . . shoes . . . an entire stall filled six feet deep with human hair. Faded and brittle with time, the hair was now mostly yellowed gray with waves of dusty brown and veins of black.

Stare into the bins too long and you see things: a name and address chalked onto the side of a cracked leather satchel. Initials on a toothbrush. A spiral of dark hair that might have been a *peyot*. A clump of curls with what could be a faded chunk of ribbon in it, hinting at a hasty and brutal clipping.

There were two types of people in this room. Some walked in, took one look, and retreated hastily. Others stared into the bins, seemingly mesmerized, as if looking for some answer, some hidden definition within the mute proof housed here. Perhaps they sought some trace of a lost relative.

Even the fascinated, myself included, could only stare so long before an urgent need to breathe fresh air overtook the will to face—to absorb—the sadness of these jumbled traces.

The morning was chill and clear as we milled through the passage into the main compound. People broke into small bunches or split off on their own. No one spoke except the tour guides, all saying pretty much the same thing in their various languages. Our guide suggested we start inside the nearest barrack, then head for the far side of the camp and work back to the exit.

I lasted about two minutes with this group. Not intention-

ally, but it was hard to keep pace. The guides had their schedules and I had mine. Keeping up with them meant an informative tour through one of mankind's best arguments for the existence of Hell. Owing to group size and time constraints, however, it also meant an abbreviated tour. While not a bad thing in itself—to spend as little time as possible in this place—I'd come a long way to be here, even if for the most roundabout reason.

The lower floor of the first barrack was full of rooms that the guide kept disappearing in and out of, leaving more people behind each time. Taking a cursory stroll down the hallway, I glanced in to see what was so captivating. Each room bore a different display with corresponding photos and text boards. Lots of information. Chapters of it, in no fewer than half a dozen languages. This, apparently, was the starter exhibit, a way to show what would be waiting the deeper one delved into the camp. I was surprised by how many people could just stand there, rapt, when the real thing lay just beyond the front door.

Looking back, it was very much like a civilized form of the skull and crossbones signs that used to adorn dangerous places in the old days. People were hesitating at the threshold of an evil known only through books, fading movie film, and the stories told by survivors.

"Abandon all remaining innocence, ye who enter here," the bones were saying.

I decided to strike out on my own, finding a pace suited to my own attention span.

Inside the camp stood block upon block of redbrick barracks. Each one had contained a liberal mix of what the burgeoning Greater Reich deemed to be the undesirables of their self-bequeathed continent.

Now each one stood as a memorial to a different persecuted group. There were barracks set aside for Hungarians, Czechs, Dutch, French, Danes, Gypsies, and homosexuals. The lower floors of each building were kept in a semi-preserved state, complete with latrines, bunks with rough straw pallets, and rude implements such as brooms and scrub brushes stacked neatly in the corners. Tattered striped prison smocks hung on wall pegs. Worn bowls and broken spoons gathered dust atop rough cupboards. An institutional gray-green paint scheme gave it all a sickly cast that the thin April sun did little to dispel as it pushed in through the dusty yellowed windowpanes.

The upper floors of each barrack had been turned into a memorial gallery with artifacts and original works of art, many by survivors or their descendants. Often the hallways were adorned with black-and-white 5 x 7 blowups of the incarcerated, enlarged from their original camp ID photos.

In one barrack, gaunt, defiant women gazed outward, their pink triangles evident even through the yellowed monochrome. I saw faces with expressions no different from ones I'd seen on the street in San Francisco or West Hollywood. The level, unbending stare of tough dykes masked the certain hurt acceptance of one more indignity, mixed with the kind of hard defiance that must become second nature in a world that doesn't accept you. I wondered how many, if any, of those women were still alive.

To this day, it hurts me to see a woman with extremely short-cropped hair or a shaven scalp. No matter how beautiful she is, no matter how healthy, whether gay or straight: for me, color fades to black-and-white and, briefly, I'm back in that dim hallway with the defiant, murdered dead.

For hours I wandered the camp, no form to my explorations, no reason other than a need to see it all. In many of the barracks, I was arrested by the artwork. Some of it was compelling. More than a little of it was nauseating.

In one blockhouse-turned-gallery, I found a quartet of mannequins, German uniforms painted onto their smooth bodies. Their mouths were smashed in and the jagged holes rimmed with broken glass. In different poses, each one depicted the systematic dismantling of a line of gray mannequins who'd had their chests hollowed out, or the tops of their heads cracked open. Rotting black rubber hoses swarmed from the German figures, probing the brutally opened voids of the prisoner figures.

A blank book sat on a stand in front of the installation, inviting comments from passersby. I looked over lines in several languages. The one line in English, scrawled with fading blue ballpoint, read: *Everything stolen is less valuable than the ashes which remain.*

The medical experimentation block, with its dingy examining rooms and stained white porcelain operating theater, stood nearby. Here Dr. Mengele committed one unspeakable act after another, because he could.

Next door to the medical block sat the interrogation block, complete with its portable gallows. The guardrooms held racks of truncheons and canes. An occasional chair waited with heavy leather restraints. In some rooms, the wooden floors were webbed with gouges. The patterns of curved scratches hinted at the unending volleys of kicks from hobnailed boots.

A small group of tourists headed downstairs after a guide. The few words I caught were in English, so I followed them into a dark little hall that bisected a concrete cellblock.

The guide was an elderly man in a long black coat. One room at a time, he took the group through the various cells that had been left open. They were pretty much the epitome of a nightmare jail cell: narrow, cold, concrete, maybe five feet wide by seven feet deep, with a tiny ventilation grate at the top of the rear wall, angled up toward the outside. The guide told us that the very first trial Zyklon B gassings were conducted on a hundred Russian POWs in these very cells—using those same vents.

Pointing unsteadily to the small grate, he intoned quietly, "History begins in very small places."

He stepped away from the cell, leaning heavily on a narrow stand-up radiator on the wall. It struck me as unusual, having a heater in a jail cell. Then I considered its true function, beyond the comfort of the SS men who might be conducting an interrogation down here. A metal loop welded to the top of it hinted at its use as a restraining point, implying a truly sadistic application of steam heat. The old man nodded.

"One more stop," he told us in his heavily accented English.

At the far end of this lower level was a room—larger than the rest. A tiny barred window and a single bulb in a caged fixture illuminated it. On one side of the room stood a series of four tall brick-walled booths, in various stages of assembly. The one at the far right was completely built up, filling the space from floor to ceiling. The one next to it had the bricks removed to shoulder height. The next reached only knee-high. The final one was simply a single layer of bricks forming a square outline on the floor.

I'd heard about these cells in parochial school. My seventh-grade homeroom teacher's father had been a death camp liberator. It was unusual, in 1975, for a junior high history class to have a section on the Holocaust, but Mr. Vanderbildt had been very determined that we get an early look at the reality of the world outside our safe, suburban, Catholic existence. He told us about the gas chambers, about the endless ditches that were bulldozed full of bodies, about the tortures (the arm hooks, the pillories). He told us about these cells, which were about the size of a phone booth. The Nazis would shove you in

through an 18 x 24-inch door at the bottom, and you'd have to stand up inside, with as many as four other people, breathing each other's air, smelling each other's smells . . . until they let you out or, more likely, removed your corpse.

The guide explained all of this, in a couple of languages, for everyone's benefit. Then, with a gesture more suited to showing off a game-show prize, he wordlessly extended an invitation to enter the booth of our choice.

One or two people stepped into the knee-high space. Two couples faced one another from opposite corners of the brick outline, laughing nervously before stepping gingerly out. A middle-aged woman shook her head in disgust and left the room.

No one seemed inclined to try out the pair of more complete cells. The guide paused, hand extended to the slightly ajar hatchway of the complete cell, then to the door that led to the hallway and the stairs out of this place.

I hung back until the group shuffled out.

I've never been afraid of small places. A little over a month previous, I'd wandered off from a mountain location set, slipped, and gotten myself wedged a good dozen feet deep in a mountain crevasse. Not a lot of fun, but not a big enough influence to keep me from trying one of these booths for size.

The basement level of Block 11 was silent now. Only muted footsteps upstairs and the occasional drone of a guide's commentary filtered through to me.

This might be the only time in my life I'd be at Auschwitz. It was my intention to absorb every impression I could. The only thing that prevented me from doing it when the group was there had been the thought of the guide rushing me along. Once I broke the ice, others might want to try it.

Yeah, right.

On hands and knees, I headed through the hatch. The door was a two-part affair. Half was a solid wooden hatch, a good inch and a half thick, drilled with air holes. The other half was a steel grating with a sliding latch. Taking a breath, I slipped inside. It was a little awkward, but not overly so. Still on my knees, I pulled the grating closed after me and stood.

My eyes tried to adjust to the darkness. An elongated square of dim light played across my feet. Kneeling again, I decided to pull the outer door nearly shut, to cut off as much light as I could. I wanted to get the "full experience."

Looking back, I suppose I could have simply closed my eyes.

Hooking a fingertip through one of the air holes, I eased the hatch ninety-five percent closed. Standing again, I felt for the wall behind me. I leaned back, breathing shallowly almost by reflex. I tried to imagine being in there with four other people.

It had been fifty years since the last body had been pulled from the tiny space I now occupied.

A scraping sound drew my attention to the hatch. At first, I thought someone was opening it. Quite the opposite. With a dull thump and metallic clatter, the door latched shut from the outside.

I couldn't hear any tour group out there. Someone had obviously seen me enter the cell and decided to be a comedian. This was, to say the least, an unexpected taste of living history.

Dilemma. The easiest thing to do would be to drop to my knees and start banging on the door. While in no mood to play along with the joke, neither was I in any hurry to be embarrassed in front of the next tour group. I opted to wait things out, see what happened.

With the hatch closed, the silence and darkness thickened around me. I couldn't make out any sounds of other people. I wondered if the door leading to the main hallway had been closed as well. Leaning back into the corner of the cell, I waited, listening to the sound of my own breathing. It echoed from the walls I knew were within arm's reach.

I wondered what time it was, wishing I'd paid better attention to my watch, which had no light on it. The darkness was so complete, so uninterrupted, there was nothing for my eyes to grow accustomed to.

Being the Saturday before Easter, it was always possible that they might close the camp early. A voice in the back of my head reminded me that this was deeply Catholic Poland; most of the country had already been shut down since Holy Thursday. Would they perform idiot checks at closing time for foolhardy American tourists? No way would this place be open tomorrow . . . it might not even be open on Easter Monday.

Suddenly, it seemed very possible that I was looking at forty-eight, maybe sixty hours in this cell—an interesting notion, in a *Twilight Zone* way. I imagined them unlocking the door come Tuesday, pulling me out dehydrated, shell-shocked. A born-again claustrophobe, all because I wanted the "full Auschwitz experience."

As more time passed, it became increasingly difficult to think of myself as being alone. Despite my eyes' failure to adjust

to the darkness, it was too easy to see the emaciated features of prisoners past. No matter how I shifted or moved, I was standing in the footsteps of someone who had died in that precise spot.

The air came alive with the odor of uncounted unwashed bodies. It wasn't me. A quick check verified that English Leather was still working overtime inside my jacket.

My thoughts raced. I wondered how many coats of paint had attempted to cover this funk. I wondered if there was any graffiti on it. I wondered who these people were . . . are . . . who even now stood nose to nose with me.

I talked aloud, if not exactly apologizing, then at least attempting to explain that I meant no disrespect. Suddenly, I was trying for all I was worth to assure the dead that they hadn't been forgotten at all, that their ordeal had been and would continue to be told.

Taking out my camera, I clumsily shot a picture toward the floor. The hard light of the flash took forever to fade, impressing into memory a view of the surroundings that so many had endured at the end of their lives, sight unseen.

The return of the darkness brought something else to me: not merely a renewed sense of how small the surroundings were, but of genuinely not being alone.

Kneeling again, I knocked tentatively at the hatch. This time it swung out easily. No sound of unlatching. No evidence that anyone was outside the door.

I don't even recall getting out, but literally the next thing I knew, I was standing in the empty hallway looking for any sign of the person who had released me. The wooden stairs were noisy enough to set straight any notion of someone letting me out, then slipping away unheard. Thinking a quick good-bye to the ghosts and whoever let me out, I made my way outside.

At the end of the alley between the two barracks stood a chipped and broken wall, its bricks blackened. Flowers and small stones were piled before it. This was the "black wall," site of uncounted executions. It is one of the few reconstructions in the camp. Former inmates pulled down the original in a rage, after the camp's liberation. I had no desire to put my back against this one.

I headed back toward the camp entrance. Somehow I found myself at a narrow gateway that felt like it might be an exit. It was, in a manner of speaking. I'd found an earth-mounded structure with a squat chimney: the camp's original full-time gas chamber and crematorium.

You could walk on top of the structure. Once there, wood and tin vent covers could be easily lifted to observe your fellow tourists in the concrete rooms below.

This place was a model of terrible, straightforward efficiency. The ovens, with their shuttles and ramps, were located in a room directly adjoining the gas chamber. It was a wide, featureless room where, depending on the volume of people coming through, they would close the doors behind you if you asked.

Maybe I was numbed by my

Photograph by Brian Thomas

experience in the standing cells or I'd simply chosen a different place to cross that line. Discreetly ignoring his very German accent, I took a fellow tourist up on his offer to close the door behind me. The others around me hastened toward the ovenside exit.

Not as deadly quiet as the cell, the whole atmosphere of this chamber was still pretty . . . stagnant. I broke the silence by snapping a couple of photos, all the while trying not to think too much. Then a scraping sound from above made me jump. A narrow shaft of sunlight, bright as any desperate hope of Heaven, dropped into the gloom around me, broken by the indistinct shadow of whoever looked in at me. Just as I had been looking in minutes earlier. No amount of not thinking could mask that I was seeing the world via the same perspective as unknown thousands who died precisely where I was standing.

Unlike them, I'm here to tell you sunlight and fresh air are never again commonplace, not once you've sampled them through vents meant for Zyklon B.

Out in the parking lot, I discovered I had missed my bus. My ticket, according to half a dozen different tour drivers, did not entitle me to catch a lift with them. Fortunately, a young couple from the States (who lived in Germany) had also missed their bus. Since we had the same sad predicament, we hired a local driver for twenty bucks American to not only take us to Birkenau but also wait for us outside the gates until closing, then get us to a decent restaurant and the railway station by nightfall.

The couple, it turned out, were photographing Holocaust monuments all over Europe. To hear them talk, Birkenau's collection was the equivalent of Nelson's Column, the Lincoln Memorial, and the Hiroshima Atomic Dome, all rolled into one.

After going up to the gate tower observation deck together, we set a rendezvous for five P.M. and split up.

From that vantage point, the camp filled one's entire field of vision, horizon to horizon: an entire landscape of rotting barracks, worn concrete foundations, and crumbling chimneys, bounded by hard angular rows of barbwire. In some places, the wire was still militarily straight; in others it jangled loosely from cracked cement pylons. The whole unappealing tableau was divided by a railroad siding that led nowhere. Two kinds of paths, muddy or sharp stone, crossed it.

One of my fellow crewmembers back in Norway worked here filming *Schindler's List*.

According to him, most of the barracks near the gate were down-to-the-nail accurate reconstructions, done for the production. Once downstairs again, I decided to check them out. The barracks in question were part of the men's quarantine camp. Their construction suggested a function something closer to stables.

It was hard to think of them as rebuilt. They had an all-too-convincing smell and feel, like any barn or attic that's stood too long without cleaning.

The bunks were hard and every bit as uncomfortable as one might imagine, built in tiers of three. The stained wood was full of splinters in some spots, worn smooth in others. Not quite six feet tall, I still felt jammed in, head to toe. As with the cell, it was impossible to get a feel for the full reality of this position without at least three other men wedged in there with me, let alone that I was well-fed, fully clothed, and not suffering from dysentery.

Barn swallows or their Polish equivalent flitted from rafter to rafter. I wondered if they lived here during the nightmare. Were they caught and eaten—or were they more valuable as a reminder of life and freedom?

Something occurred to me as I got out of the bunk. Faded graffiti was scratched into the wood. It didn't seem like teen vandal stuff. I wondered if it was prison graffiti, but a lot of it seemed incomprehensible, not the dates I would've expected.

The main litter I found was flowers, flattened on some bunks. A bouquet tied with string settled inside the barrack's heating stove.

I walked the wire perimeter facing into the camp. A nasty surprise: the barbwire had been replaced with authentic, brand-new, sharp steel-tined stuff. Since I'd already done a few foolish things that day and had had tetanus shots recently, I experimentally wrapped a hand around one section. A barb penetrated my palm easily. Minus the electric charge the fence should have been carrying, it was every bit as daunting as it would have been back in 1944.

No way they'd have something like this back in the States. I thought back to Manzanar, the American concentration camp I'd visited in the California desert. In some ways, that was very similar to this place, a vista of old wire and empty foundations. Only we dismantled our camps, let the desert reclaim them. Except for a roadside plaque, nothing remains to tell the tale, to cop to our own guilt. And why not? We only imprisoned a single race, only tried to murder their self-esteem, personal honor, and reputation.

In the end, we wrote the survivors checks sufficient to buy a nice Buick.

Apples and oranges. I was here for German guilt, right? But the thought wouldn't go away entirely. Not then, not now, writing this from the comfort of my home. Auschwitz, it seems, has served its purpose the way those who argued for its preservation meant it to.

Point to you, Mr. Wiesenthal.

I spent the next hour crisscrossing the front half of Birkenau. The women's camp had brick-and-cinder block buildings with broad open windows that must have exposed the prisoners to both the elements and the ever-prying eyes of their captors.

I found more flowers, more notes. I hardly saw another person. I always felt watched. The camp was a crowded void: dead, but not so. Grass grew among the gravel between the huts. Birds sang. Spiders made webs in a window that glistened in the late afternoon light.

Who'd looked out that window? Was she still there, admiring the spider's work and thinking how she once crocheted lace in Murmansk, Lódz, Prague, or Le Havre? I spared a smile for the woman who might not be there.

My own grandmother was Slovak, but she had the fortune of being part of the pre-War generation that made it to America. But for that accident of location, I could have been searching for some trace of her. She would have been a only a face from a photograph whose loving voice I might never have known, whose cookies, soups, and pierogi I never would have enjoyed at Christmas. If this sounds maudlin, I have a number of friends who would have to to go to Auschwitz or the dozen places like it to trace families they never got to know.

The sheer scale of what I'd seen still hadn't fully sunk in. Distances gauged from the single-page map I picked up at the front gate turned out to be meaningless. I still hadn't seen the cemetery at the far side of the camp. It was nearly four o'clock. The camp closed at 5:30. I needed to find the young couple I'd planned to head back to town with and tell them to go on without me.

I trekked back to the woods—and the burial pits within them—via the railroad track that bisected the camp.

When I paused to reload my camera, I discovered two things. First, I hadn't taken nearly as many exposures on this roll as I thought. Second, I was standing at a railway siding directly adjacent to ruins of one of the crematoriums.

I imagined the endless lines of ragged prisoners, freshly arrived to the camp, hauled out of the boxcars, propelled along by shouts and blows into twin lines facing the selections officer. Sometimes that man would be Dr. Mengele himself. By all accounts, he cut an impeccable figure, handsome, suave, polite to a fault. A single word from him, or the slight motion of his hand, translated to life or death— or worse, if you were a twin or a dwarf, or in some other way caught his fancy. Then you were damned to the living hell of his experimentation blocks. Vague nausea moved into my chest, and a strange, fluttering chill. I could almost see the ghosts still shuffling past.

The nausea gave way to something else. I wanted to yell my fury, my frustration, to the blameless dead around me. "There were tens of thousands of you! Only hundreds of them, guns or not!" The unspoken words piled up behind my teeth. The rush of anger shocked me. I wanted to shout at the phantoms, "Why were so many of you sheep?"

My mind immediately countered with hard logic, pure math. Assume four hundred guards, armed with bolt-action rifles at five rounds each or perhaps machine pistols, each loaded with thirty-two rounds of 9mm ammo. Even at the economical rate of two rounds per prisoner, that was more than 1,200 dead before the first reload. That pause might take eight seconds. The first minute of my idealized revolt meant nearly four thousand casualties. Add the machine guns in the tower at seventy-five rounds per drum, with a cyclic rate of nine hundred rounds per minute, and another two thousand went down.

I was including missed shots, but there wouldn't be that many, given most of the targets would have been starving and half of them would have been women and children. All would have been easily distinguishable, thanks to their dingy striped prison smocks, with a colored triangle or star-shaped target sewn over every breast.

The wounded wouldn't have fared any better, since the officers would have carried sidearms with eight shots in the clip and at least one extra clip. So, assuming sixty officers, each delivering sixteen separate coups de grâce . . . Well, there was close to another thousand that I'd just coldly estimated the logistics of eliminating. Which was, in all probability, exactly the sort of possibility some SS supply officer would have calculated, down to the last projected bullet, with margin contingencies for gun oil and barrel replacement afterward.

That I could, in these surroundings, coldly play guesswork games regarding the lives of people already long dead was disturbing enough. The realization that I achieved even a fleeting mental equivalence with the people who murdered them was chilling. True enough, I was only approaching it via my background as a movie weapons handler. But it was easy to see how simple math could translate to unthinkable equations. There was a clue there, like the memory of our American camps, that wouldn't go away. The germ of it is there, it seems, in each of us. But to recognize it, to be repulsed by its hinted implication, is important. Auschwitz has all kinds of lessons it sneaks in when you're not paying attention.

The whole thing leaves me to wonder: What good, if any, occurred in this place? There were no doubt countless instances of compassion, quiet courage, love, honor, sacrifice, maybe even humor—a great many of these instances held dear, no doubt, in the memories and souls of the survivors. For the life of me, standing amid the bones of misery, I couldn't think of a single one I might have read or heard of.

Why wouldn't there be? There were human beings here, after all, despite being thrown in a collective pen, bereft of past, present, and future, shorn of outward identity beyond the numbers on their arms and the patches on their breasts. They must have become all the more human in many ways, more vital in spirit. The simplest emotions must have been magnified tenfold. The fear, agony, and desolation all certainly were.

I thought again of the Nazis, both old and new, and the Polish thugs who collaborated with them. Once they realized that their crimes couldn't be conveniently swept from the memory and judgment of the world, the unrepentant bastards who built this artificial universe of torment would no doubt prefer fear, agony, and desolation to be the sole legacy of this place: *Never forget, Juden, what has gone before can come to pass again.*

Then, in the back of my head, the underdog-lover chimed in, shouldering aside the statistician. An incident—such glory as might be possible in a place like this— pushed past the cluttered scrapbook of a lifetime's worth of devoured history.

Something *had* happened here, late in the War—something

heroic: the revolt of 1944. An obscure fact to much of the world, to be sure, but I couldn't believe I had forgotten it. Now, when I needed it, the memory grew stronger. My mind flooded with details. I remembered a name: Robota.

The slaughterworks had been going for the better part of four years when, in 1944, a handful of *Sonderkommando* working with the camp underground staged an uprising. Yes, there was an underground in Auschwitz. For those of the TV generation, think *Hogan's Heroes* without a slick tunnel system, day-trips to Paris, wisecracking well-fed heroes, and *no* cuddly, gullible Germans. Even that pared-down vision doesn't come close to the truth, but things did go on that the Nazis were never able to fully control, things like hope, nerve, and defiance. Sometimes that's all you need for a revolt.

Anyway, these *Sonderkommando* were prisoners responsible for the actual hands-on work of operating the crematoriums, herding prisoners to the gas chambers, maintaining and even operating the ovens, disposing of the ashes. . . . It was as hopeless a job as anyone could ever be condemned to do. Especially considering that, sooner or later, the Nazis would eliminate entire squads of *Sonderkommando* to make room for a fresh batch.

These prisoners had decided that enough was enough. Working with the camp underground, they established contact with a young woman named Roza Robota. Roza, working with a bare handful of women from the camp's slave labor munitions factory, spent the next few months smuggling out a steady trickle of chemical compounds. Eventually, they had enough to create several explosive charges, powerful enough to destroy at least the camp's busiest crematorium, #4.

According to the map, it was still quite a walk to #4 from where I was standing, so I attempted to head off "as the crow flies." No luck. While most structures had been pulled down or allowed to decay, the barbwire fencing was taking its sweet time. In some places, the wire was pulled back in broad tangles to leave gaps for off-path navigation of the grounds. Problem was, once you entered one of these gaps, you could easily find yourself moving down lanes that led nowhere until you found another narrow, makeshift passage that led you even further off course.

I felt a sting of empathy for the *Sonderkommando* who tried to make a break for it the day they blew up #4. The revolt was a bloody, confused affair, short-lived and tragic. Some forty of them lived long enough to make it through the wire perimeter in a fierce rush. Unfortunately, in the confusion, most got turned around and forced back via the electrified wire alleys into the camp. Those who did breach the walls wound up lost in the woods bordering the camp. Most were hunted down with the help of local farmers. Once back in the camp, they were spared the farce of Birkenau's usual "repatriation" ceremony: being whipped through the camp wearing a clown suit, forced to beat a drum and chant, "I'm so glad I'm home." All the *Sonderkommando* were dead by sundown.

Speaking of which, the sun was definitely on its downward course. I'd led myself into a rusted steel maze. I was lost, even without identical buildings to confuse every twist and turn. No one was chasing me with dogs. No Klaxons were blaring or bullets streaming toward me from the deserted watchtowers. Why was I doing this to myself?

According to the map, the ancient-looking, mossy, shattered brick ruin ahead of me was Crematoria #4.

Finding an area of sagging wire by one of the curved pylons, I pried the rusted strands aside and slipped through. Half a century ago, going through the wire the way I did meant instant death. I reflexively spared the

corroded insulators a glance, calling once more on that portion of my brain that so coldly put down the prison revolt. It assured me that this wire no longer posed any threat, just as the unoccupied guard towers had no guns, probably not even ghosts. All had gone to Hell.

I slipped almost entirely through the fence. Then the very thing I'd been trying to avoid happened. I felt an insistent tug at my jacket and knew I'd become snared in the wire. Twisting to free myself, I stepped into a pair of broken coils looped close to the pylon, making things worse. Wire loops attached to the old insulators twanged, sending forth a spray of ceramic chips and clouded rust. They kept hold of me.

I'd straddled a hydrogen bomb once, in the United States Air Force Museum, waved my hat and made like Slim Pickens in *Dr. Strangelove.* I wish I could say that, in Birkenau, I emulated Steve McQueen in *The Great Escape,* coolly understanding that I'd been tangled in the German wire and ready to accept my capture. Mostly I felt stupid, like at the bomb when a retired Air Force vet saw me. I got a good talking to and almost got booted from the Air Force Museum, mostly for being a stupid kid. Accidentally ripping out the wires of a shrine to six million martyrs because I couldn't stick to the path . . . that was something else. But no tourists or grounds maintenance personnel came to my rescue or accusation.

As gently as I could, I extracted myself, except for the original strand that caught me. Wriggling out of my jacket, I freed it with an angry snap. I felt some measure of satisfaction as the wire sprang back to tangle against itself.

First the cell, now this: Auschwitz 0, Brian 2.

I finished my trek to the rubble of #4. It had no plaque, no flowers, no bullet scars on the bricks, no defiant commemorative graffiti. The rubble, like the dead and decaying camp around me, was its own testimony, I suppose. Time and history were finishing the job the rebellious *Sonderkommando* began. This legacy, measured in hopeless courage, outshone any numbers on paper.

In the end, only three guards were killed, a few more wounded. Nearly five hundred *Sonderkommando,* whether they took part or not, were executed. The Nazis counted themselves lucky. Had the revolt had more time to get organized, it might have gone worse for them. They were afraid a signal had been sent: that they could be, even briefly, repulsed.

Without much trouble, they traced the explosives to the women from the munitions works. Roza and three others were captured and sent to the basement of Block 11 in the main camp. They tortured her in the same rooms I'd walked through hours before. She never gave up her secrets, her contacts, or the names of the underground.

The Nazis made sure she and her three sisters in resistance—Ester Wajcblum, Ala Gertner, and Regina Safirsztain—were the last ones hanged before they began to shut down the camp.

Before that, though—not long after the revolt, when it was clear the war was too far gone against them—the Nazis dismantled the rest of the ovens and the smokestacks clogged with human fat.

The honor of demolishing Crematoria #4 went to the women and men who chose to risk all and, ultimately, die on their own terms, rather than end their lives in its mechanism.

I felt uncomfortably superfluous. I'd wanted to find this spot, to be here to gain some reassurance—something, anything, to balance against all I'd seen that day. There was nothing more I could add. My mind was suddenly too full.

Off in the distance, I saw white markers, denoting various sections of the mass graves. Heading in their direction, I discovered a break in the wire just off the main path. Really, I would've liked to go on, but something inside was telling me *no more*. I'd hit some hidden limit as far as this place was concerned.

The route to the graves was open and clearly marked. I could've been there in five minutes, tops. If my earlier explorations had been any indication, I probably wouldn't be satisfied until I'd stretched out in some convenient patch of earth and pulled the sod over myself.

The shame that hit me came as a complete surprise. In all the years I've known of this place's existence, not once had I doubted the truth of any of it. Yet, like the Apostle Thomas probing his fingers into the wounds of Christ, I had to know this place with my own senses, as best I could.

To what purpose? To be a better, more informed witness to the Holocaust? It feels almost meaningless to try. Visiting Auschwitz is really a trade-off. You go and you learn, you see proof, but there's a catch: you find that no matter how well you pay attention to the things you see, smell, feel, and walk among, it's impossible to do the place justice in words.

The light was definitely going. The wind had picked up. I decided to find the main gate.

A few buses remained, but no cars for hire. Trusting luck, I fell

in at the back of a line boarding one of the larger buses. As I stepped up to entrance, the driver looked at me oddly, but said nothing.

Finding an empty bench near the back, I settled in and tried to look inconspicuous. Then it hit me. Hardly anyone was talking. Most looked out the windows away from the camp. I noticed a patch on one tourist's windbreaker: the Deutsche tricolor. Listening carefully, I discerned the language being spoken so quietly. I'd picked the one busload of German tourists in the entire parking lot. No wonder it was so quiet here.

Given my earlier reminder about Manzanar, I couldn't feel particularly smug.

Predictably, the silence lasted until we hit the main road out of Oświęcim. As we crossed the river, the final psychic breaker was tripped and I found myself riding on just another holiday excursion bus. I was totally baffled as to whether I should be depressed or encouraged by this.

Back in Kraków, I walked the streets, trying to sort it all out. Finally I took refuge in the cabaret below the clock tower in the town square. Ordering hot mead, I just sat, taking up a stool, warming my hands on the cup, and wondering why I was still so cold in this crowded place.

The bartender asked me something in Polish. I had no idea what he said, but figured he wanted me to pay up and move along. Digging into my pocket, I dropped the contents on the bar, trying to make sense of the baffling *zlotys* so I could leave a decent tip. He slid back most of it, along with my tour ticket stub.

Leaning close, he raised his voice over the din. "Oświęcim?"

I nodded. After regarding me for a long moment, he took my cup. With a sideways glance to see if the boss was watching, he ladled in another portion of the strong, sweet drink, sliding it toward me. He never said another word, but as long as I allowed him to, he refilled my mug, never charging me.

THE MECHANICS OF GENOCIDE

Once genocide had been decided upon, there was a lag before the Nazi killing facilities were prepared. In the interval, German soldiers were ordered to assassinate large numbers of Jews. Many of those men snapped, choosing to commit suicide rather than continue to execute women and children. Himmler reportedly became ill while watching a mass execution. Afterward, he ordered "more humane" killing.

Auschwitz was chosen to be an extermination camp because, according to *The Nazi Doctors: Medical Killing and the Psychology of Genocide*, "its location was favorable for communications and transportation, as well as isolation and camouflage." Commandant Rudolf Hoess took his charge seriously and searched for an alternative to shooting, which "placed too heavy a burden on the SS men who had to carry it out."

Hitler himself suggested the use of carbon monoxide. This was tested at Brandenburg, a prison converted into a killing center. Twenty prisoners at a time were led naked into a specially constructed "shower room." Carbon monoxide gas was fed through fake water pipes. The SS reported that victims "toppled over . . . without scenes or commotion."

After visiting the death camp Treblinka, Hoess rejected carbon monoxide. The truck engines did not always produce sufficient gas to do the job; victims sometimes had to be shot. In his absence, his deputy SS Captain Karl Fritzch experimented with Zyklon B on Russian prisoners in Block 11, Auschwitz's punishment block. Zyklon B killed within four minutes. Wearing a gas mask, Hoess observed a repetition of the initial executions firsthand.

The Nazis had plenty of the insecticide gas on hand to kill lice. Zyklon B was the trade name for a combination of Prussic acid (another name for hydrocyanic acid) and an irritant. Cyanide gas is colorless, so the irritant was added to prevent accidental inhalation. The Nazis negotiated with the German manufacturer of the gas and had the irritant removed so that the victims' deaths would be "more humane."

Poisoning: Toxicology, Symptoms, Treatments reports that hydrocyanic acid is "among the most potent and rapidly acting poisons known." A concentration of 0.2 to 0.3 milligrams per liter of air is almost immediately fatal. Collapse is instantaneous, accompanied by a loud cry, convulsions, and unconsciousness, followed almost immediately by death. Women and children are more susceptible to the poison than men.

Mass killing of Jews began in late 1941 or early 1942. Approximately four million people were murdered at Auschwitz. According to the *Oxford Family Encyclopedia,* the world's largest burial ground is at Birkenau.

—Editor

Happy Trails in Southeast Asia

by Jessica Eisner

Machismo. As an educated, well-traveled woman, I didn't think I could fall prey to the enigmatic lure of having to prove myself to someone for no good reason. I was wrong. Unfounded machismo led to my first experience with hallucinogens while traveling in Southeast Asia. In retrospect, I think my pride at being so familiar with Asian customs was what got me into trouble in the first place. That, and being American.

It was my first full day in Singapore and, still a bit jet-lagged, I opted to walk around the neighborhoods surrounding my rather plush, but isolated, hotel. After walking only a few blocks, I realized I was hungry and thirsty, so I began peering closely at the goods offered by fruit vendors I passed. I was about to settle for a breakfast of bananas and the omnipresent Coca-Cola when I happened upon a strange fruit. Pale green and about the size of a football, it was covered with tough pyramidal spikes: sort of a large, biological grenade. I thought it was a mean, stunted

variety of jackfruit—a giant, citrusy melon I'd eaten quite a bit of in the Philippines. The elderly Chinese man who ran the stand laughed.

"It durian," he said in a thick Singaporean accent. "American no like durian."

I was immediately insulted. I was not your average American who only ate hot dogs and cheeseburgers. I'd lived in Asia for a year now. I'd eaten rambutan, mangoes, jackfruit, and all sorts of intensely salted fish with vigor! How could he assume that I wouldn't like durian?

"How do you know?" I countered.

"American no like durian," he repeated. "Maybe you like banana."

As far as I was concerned, the gauntlet had been thrown. I wasn't just representing myself now; I was representing all of America. I couldn't let this man pigeonhole our entire country! Machismo took over from there.

"I'll try one," I said. Astonishment crept over his placid features. "A big one," I added.

"But you no like it," he assured me.

I couldn't be swayed. "We'll see."

The man helped me pick out an appropriately ripe durian and cut it open for me. I should have had the sense to stop right there, but I thought the smell was coming from one of the few open sewers in the shabby precinct. Clearing a spot on a gingham-covered "eat-in" table, he prepared a similar-sized durian for himself and proceeded to show me how to eat the new food. Avoid the seeds. Simple enough, but what was that smell?

I took a bite. The fleshy fruit melted into my mouth; the flavor was reminiscent of almond egg custard. Then I took a breath and the second sensory wave hit me like a cannonball blast. The sewer smell was coming from the fruit. I felt as though I had just inadvertently licked the inside of a Dumpster. The stinging, rotten odor of putrefied cheese, crusty old socks, and fetid unwashed genitalia bombarded my olfactory cortex! The old man stared at me for signs of rejection. His eyes twinkled with the anticipation of being right about Americans. Emotionless—but in sensory agony—I pressed on.

Two and a half pounds later, I stumbled out of his stand, nearly fatally engorged on durian but with my—and my country's—

pride intact. Never again. On my previously empty stomach, the durian somehow had the effect of giving me a potent buzz. I wandered the streets of Singapore in a daze for several hours until the high wore off. Luckily I had cab fare to get back to my hotel when I returned to my senses. The worst part was getting the stink out of my system. The stench of durian leaked from my pores for almost four days, despite numerous showers and cologne.

Durian is a fruit indigenous to Southeast Asia. I later found out that the experience of eating it has been likened to "eating custard . . . over a public urinal." I've not come across a more apt description. Durians grow from tall trees in the Asian forest. When ripe, they fall to the earth below—often a trip of more than thirty meters. People have been killed by falling durians. There are five popular varieties, most of which grow in Thailand. Each has its subtle distinctions. I've heard aficionados describe the flavors as ranging anywhere from butterscotch custard to onion-and-sherry-flavored cream cheese. Durian lovers speak less of the smell, but I'd say they all stink. Otherwise, why would there be a law against bringing the fruit on Singapore's subways?

For several years I tried unsuccessfully to find the chemical entity responsible for durian's intoxicating qualities. Aphrodisiac rumors abound (as do anecdotal tales of renewed potency). Durian is said to be particularly intoxicating (even lethal) when mixed with alcohol. However, none of these claims has been scientifically investigated. Durian eaters prefer it that way. From my experience, however, I'd say the combo of drinking a carbonated beverage and eating a very large durian first thing in the morning on an empty stomach might give any Westerner a psychologically

THE KING OF FRUITS

I wasn't able to turn up any information on the hallucinogenic properties of durian, so Jessica might have discovered something new. My favorite description of the flavor comes from *Travelers' Tales: Thailand,* in which the editors compare the flavor with eating your favorite ice cream while sitting on the toilet. The Philippine ice cream shop in my neighborhood illustrates durian in its menu with a gasoline nozzle.

Bao Sheng Durian Farm in West Malaysia (www.durian.com.my) grows ten species of durians, with names such as Hor Lor, Red Prawn, D-600, and Green Skin Ang Bak. Trees on this plantation produce fruits with a wrinkled texture and smooth, thick, creamy flesh that tastes sweeter and has a stronger fragrance than your average durian. "Durian lovers know," they say, "there's no kick consuming the fruit without its scent."

Durian season down on the farm can last from the beginning of May to the end of July, dependent on the weather. Durian is best when eaten within twenty-four hours after it falls from the tree. According to Bao Sheng, Thai durians are inferior because they are picked rather than being allowed to fall on their own. Hence, they aren't completely ripe.

Bao Sheng Farm strongly advises against washing down your durian feast with alcohol. "The flesh of the durian is rich in protein. When high protein mixes with alcohol, it becomes yeast. You will feel uncomfortable and you may need to visit a doctor then." Consider yourself warned.

—Editor

pricey (but unique and legal) high. I'm glad I tried it, but I'll never (intentionally) eat it again.

If you're interested, you'll probably have to go to Asia to try this fruit. It starts fermenting the moment it falls from the tree. Attempts to export it have proven largely unsuccessful. Canning doesn't stop the fermentation process, so the fruit can cause the containers to explode. In addition, there are nightmarish tales of travelers becoming ill when durian smugglers have tried to use the overhead bins of passenger planes for their nefarious purposes. You can buy the fruit frozen at some well-stocked Asian food stores, but I hear it definitely loses some pizzazz in the cold transpacific journey. That probably means no buzz.

My next stop was Thailand. Having had my "natural high" in Singapore, I was in search mode. I'd heard of a substance called *betel nut* that was supposed to get you where you were going. Reportedly it was legal and sold everywhere, but it took me a few days to locate a vendor. I didn't know exactly what I was looking for and, coming from American society where only alcohol was legal, I was afraid to ask. In a chaotic street market that specialized in bootleg copies of American music and computer software, I came across a stooped old lady selling red paste rolled into leaves.

"What is this?" I asked in phrasebook Thai.

"Betel," she replied impassively. The lit end of a cigarillo rested inside her mouth on a shelf of gum where molars should have been. Many old Thai women smoke with the lit ends of cigars inside their mouths.

I was ecstatic to have found betel nut, but fearful of reacting. She might sense my eagerness and raise the price. Or she might not sell it to me at all. There is a certain thrill to having been raised in a puritanical society and then being unleashed into the rest of the world. Composing myself, I asked for one.

The woman mixed up a new batch of powders and herbs into a thick red paste and spread it on a crisp new leaf. Sensing that I'd not had it before, she showed me how to place the plug in the side of my cheek. She then hawked up a bright red gob of her own betel nut juice and spit it on the pavement to illustrate that I was not to swallow the concoction. Smoke poured out of her nose and mouth as the cigarillo never left its place on her gums. I thanked her and walked off to indulge myself.

The taste was disappointing, chalky and bitter. I didn't chew it. I stuffed the leaf-wrapped packet between my cheek and gum like the woman showed me and let it sit there and ooze. They just call it chewing, like "chewing" tobacco.

After twenty minutes of wondering if I'd gotten the right kind of betel, it finally kicked in. It wasn't the cloudy, distorted high of durian. Betel was a true buzz, like having had way too many cigarettes and beers in one sitting.

In all, I probably had it in my mouth for thirty to forty minutes. Once the buzz kicked in, I got a bit frightened and spit it out so I wouldn't spiral into an uncontrollable high. Spitting in public was quite uncomfortable for me, so I probably swallowed more juice than I should have.

Alert but slightly disoriented, I weaved through the colorful, fragrant spectacle of the open street market for another forty minutes before the high wore off. I felt like myself again almost immediately. Unlike my experience with durian, I smelled like myself, too. The only undesirable side effect was a toothpaste-resistant red stain on the inside of my mouth where the packet had rested. It went away after a few days.

Betel nut (*Areca catechu*) is a large seed of the Asian palm tree family *Palmacea*. It is ubiquitous in Southeast Asia but not limited to that region. It is also popular and grown in India, Malaysia,

and Polynesia. The current practice of mixing the ground nut with burned lime (hydrated calcium oxide) and wrapping it in a leaf from the unrelated betel vine (*Piper chavica betel*) has a long history that varies from culture to culture.

The Vietnamese have a folktale that explains the mixture. The king of ancient Vietnam had two identical twin sons. Far from being competitive, the boys were very close. One was ultimately chosen to marry the neighboring king's only daughter and the brothers were separated. The single brother died from grief and loneliness for his brother and grew into an Areca tree. Walking by the riverbank one day, the married brother happened across the majestic tree and sensed it was the incarnation of his brother. Overwhelming sentiment killed him and he became a large limestone at the base of the tree. Then the widow suffered a similar realization and, after perishing, became the betel vine intertwined between the two brothers. Years later, the boys' father, King Hung-vuoung, passed by the riverbed and was told the story of his sons and the wife. He chewed some betel nut with betel vine and liked the taste. Then he spit on the limestone and saw it turn red. He took the crimson stain as a sign of the deep love between the trio and asked that his people build an altar there. The modern-day incarnation of that altar is the practice of chewing betel nut. Poignant, eh?

Whatever its origins, chewing betel nut is an active practice in many parts of the world. Unlike durian, the chemistry of the betel nut's active ingredient has been well described. Arecoline, a volatile oil, is released from the nut by saliva and lime. Arecoline is a "mood elevator" or, technically, a mild central nervous system stimulant. In small amounts, it causes a "buzz"–increased alertness and faster breathing and pulse. In larger amounts, however, it can cause vomiting, diarrhea, and convulsions. Due to these side effects, the fact that it has no nutritive qualities, and arecoline's link to esophageal cancer, it cannot be imported to or sold in the United States or Canada. If you want to try it, you're looking at a trip across the globe.

My remaining attempts to legally "trip" in Southeast Asia were largely unsuccessful. A friend sent me a page from *The Anarchist Cookbook,* which described how to extract a hallucinogen from the insides of banana peels.

I tried the shake 'n' bake method on about fourteen of the fifty varieties of bananas grown in the Philippines before quitting. Apparently there is no hallucinogen in bananas that can affect my physiology. Maybe you've had better luck?

Back in the United States, I settle for mild, legal highs. I don't smoke but I do drink coffee daily and occasionally have a drink. I am no longer obsessed with seeking out altered states. I suspect that any I find will, ultimately, be illegal, embarrassing (e.g., licking frogs), or worse, fatal (mushrooms, fugu fish). In any event, I would be penalized for my natural curiosity.

It is my belief, however, that the drive to experience altered states of mind is a trait not unique

"Thunder in the Butterflyshroud"
by Timothy Renner

to humans. There have been studies that show that a rat will forgo food for a diet of cocaine or an electrical intra-cerebral blast in the hypothalamic pleasure center. There are the Siberian reindeer that have the uncanny ability to specifically sniff out the most hallucinogenic of mushrooms. After nibbling their fill of the fungi, they are found dazed–staggering about and falling in the snow. If reindeer can fly, then why, oh, why can't I?

MELLOW YELLOW

"Believe it or not," *The Anarchist Cookbook* begins, "bananas do contain a small amount of *Musa Sapientum bananadine,* which is a mild, short-lasting psychedelic. There are much easier ways of getting high, but the great advantage to this method is that bananas are legal."

After peeling and *eating* fifteen pounds of ripe yellow bananas, the *Cookbook* instructs you to scrape the insides of the peels with a sharp knife. Boil the scraped material with water for three to four hours until it becomes a solid paste. Dry this paste in the oven until it becomes a fine black powder. Only then may you smoke three or four cigarettes rolled from this powder.

Drugs from A to Z: A Dictionary reports that users claimed that a high from four bananas' worth of skin was comparable with half a marijuana cigarette of 1966 window-box weed; "However, the inhalation of large amounts of corn-silk smoke would probably produce a similar state of mind." In my household, we call that an oxy-dep buzz. "Inhaled in sufficient amounts," the *Dictionary* continues, "banana smoke probably does produce a mild, drowsy, fuzzy mental state, which users equate with a high. No hallucinations have been reported."

Federal authorities claim the resultant high is a hoax.

—Editor

THE MOST POPULAR HIGH IN THE WORLD

More popular worldwide than tobacco or alcohol, betel nuts are "chewed" by approximately one-tenth of the world's population. Regardless of age, Christians, Buddhist monks, and observers of indigenous faiths throughout Southeast Asia use them.

Classified as a stimulant in *The Alchemy of Culture,* betel nut increases mental and physical stimulation without impairing the user's performance of daily tasks. Ethnographer Alfred Gell, studying the drug in Papua New Guinea, describes betel's effects as "a sensation of mild dissociation, an unwonted feeling of reduced gravity, a dulling of hunger and fatigue, and a sharpening of visual acuity. In short . . . a 'marginal' state of consciousness, putting the user slightly 'outside' himself." The book reports, "hallucinations have been reported by some consumers."

Chewing betel nut increases the flow of tears, sweat, intestinal juices, and produces copious amounts of red saliva. The buildup of lime caused by frequent use will blacken the teeth. Betel nut use increases respiration while decreasing the workload of the heart. According to *Reader's Digest*'s *Magic and Medicine of Plants,* the stimulant imparts a feeling of general well-being, aids digestion, sweetens the breath, and strengthens the gums. The betel nut contains tannins, which give it an astringent effect, and several powerful alkaloids—especially one called arecoline—which kill tapeworms. Arecoline was once used to treat urinary tract disorders, but "in large doses, it can have severe toxic effects in humans." It is still sometimes used in veterinary medicine.

Travelers should note that betel has been used to treat cholera, dysentery, fever, gonorrhea, hysteria, malaria, scabies, smallpox (hopefully not recently!), and stomachache.

Offering betel to friends and strangers is a common form of extending hospitality and goodwill. Just be warned: betel nuts are widely believed to be aphrodisiac. In fact, they are a traditional bride price in some Southeast Asian cultures.

Use originated in prehistoric Southeast Asia. The betel palm grows everywhere from Tanzania and Madagascar in the west, across the Indian subcontinent and Southeast Asia, and in the western Pacific Islands.

Partakers wrap a leaf of the spicy betel pepper vine (*Piper betle*) around a small piece of freshly roasted betel nut, add a pinch of powdered lime, and place the mixture between their cheek and gum. A variety of flavor enhancers can be added, according to taste: rosewater, saffron, ground cloves, cardamom, turmeric, melon seeds, tamarind, musk, or ambergris.

Like anything else, the marks of a user's status are apparent by the tools with which he accessorizes his vice. Some spatulas for scooping lime into the mouth can be considered high art. My favorite accessories mentioned in *The Alchemy of Culture* are made by the Trobriand Islanders. They make lime pots out of the skulls of their dead relatives and spatulas out of their bones. Cool old Aunt Millie can still hang out with you, even after she's dead and gone.

—Editor

Museum Pieces

by Julia Solis

"Tombs are now by common consent invested with a certain sanctity, but when they have been long tenanted, it is considered no sin to break them open and rifle them, the famous Egyptologist Dr. Huggyns explaining that a tomb may be innocently 'glened' as soon as its occupant is done 'smellynge,' the soul being all exhaled."
—Ambrose Bierce, *The Devil's Dictionary*

When delving into the history of museums, one has to concede that these tastefully arranged institutions have often served the admittedly mundane purpose of providing new ideas on home décor. Frequently, visitors admiring a Cézanne or an elegantly shaped Greek vase at the local art museum find themselves compelled to locate a copy to grace their living rooms. There is a whole industry of museum shops selling reproductions for this very purpose.

Yet there are few museums designed to provide fun, interactive settings, where visitors may not only admire what is on display but also are given the opportunity to pocket an authentic museum piece as a souvenir. One of the more generous muse-ums in this respect is the Museo de las Momias in Guanajuato, Mexico.

The museum came into existence when the city began recycling graves due to limited space (exhuming those deceased whose surviving relatives stopped paying taxes on the burial sites). The townspeople came to realize that the soil in the Pantheon of Guanajuato has a special mineral combination that naturally preserves corpses. When the workers dug up the bodies, they found many of them intact, wearing shreds of their clothing: boxer shorts here, a formal suit there. Most of the bodies still had hair and teeth, their still-recognizable faces twisted into grotesque expressions, their eyes having dried up in such a manner as to preserve the natural color of the iris.

A natural tourist attraction, in other words. The townspeople swiftly constructed a fine museum on a hillside, first displaying the mummies leaning against the walls in two facing rows, then splurging on an elegant glass case for each specimen. Throughout the years, news of the museum spread. Now an occasional tourist can be found gawking at the interesting patterns of exit holes left by various sarcophagidae and conicera tibialis.

Following the tradition of museum visitors throughout history, Alan and I stopped in front of one of the glass cases and admired the old woman's discolored front teeth.

The author gleaning, photographed by Al Ridenour

Those were pretty decorative, we decided. Teeth such as these would look lovely in our living room. In perfect agreement, we left the museum halls and set off along the winding road toward the Pantheon.

The walls enclosing the cemetery had that peculiar brightness that comes from being the only white surface in a sun-drenched black space. The upper level of the graveyard was entirely deserted for the hour or two we spent there. This was fortunate, as we had just discovered a crumbling coffin and the grave from which it had been disinterred.

Beside the grave, the freshly excavated mound of dirt awaited the next burial. Alan and I quickly sifted through the soil, keeping a close watch on the gate through which a caretaker could enter at any moment. I admit to some squeamishness: the interior of the heap was moist, speckled with fragments of teeth and bone. Alan exclaimed in delight when he found a "finger joint," a knucklebone. I was less lucky: bone splinters and coffin fragments. Porous ivory slivers wedged beneath my fingernails.

Next to me loomed the open grave, its interior multilayered like a crumbling chocolate cake.

I descended into the pit to have better access to the remains. When I lay down on the moist, leveled ground and looked up at the sky, I was very startled by what I saw. It is not such an anomaly to find bones in the soil; even teeth seem somewhat natural in the ground. Something about the texture, the color, blends into the earth. But what seems abnormal nearly to the point of obscenity is to look at the soil and find protruding hairs. Long, gray hairs were sticking out of the grave walls above me. That, and nothing else, gave me the sense that I was lying in a place previously inhabited by a corpse.

I pulled a few tangles from the chocolate-colored strata of soil. As I did so, I apologized to persons unknown. Even if the bodies were deemed suitable for public exhibition and sort of "free-for-all," an apology seemed to be required for pulling hairs.

The city workers who exhume these corpses surely ask for forgiveness beneath their breaths.

How to display our museum pieces? The choice of containers was tough. My personal finds were placed into a mustard jar with an understated black lid, resting on a living room shelf until someone saw it for the treasure it was and swiped it. It didn't exactly catch the eye; but whenever someone noticed the coil of gray hairs, my heartbeat—a true collector's—did quicken just a bit.

MUSEO DE LAS MOMIAS

Compiled by Julia Solis and Loren Rhoads

Number of mummies: 118

Cemetery constructed: 1853

First cadaver exhumed: 1865

Most recently added mummy exhumed: 1984

Corpses exhumed from the graveyard that are judged fit for display: about two percent.

Admission price in 1998: about $2, plus an additional $1 for a photo permit. You know you want to.

In the tradition of sugar skulls for the Day of the Dead, this is an all-ages attraction.

Tours were conducted in Spanish. Groups of thirty were hustled through.

The Museo is air-conditioned.

Fifty-eight miles west of San Miguel de Allende lies Guanajuato. During the 1500s, vast amounts of silver—still being removed—were found beneath its streets. It became one of Mexico's wealthiest cities and still boasts lots of Spanish Colonial architecture and several stunning churches.

Even before Diego Rivera was born there in 1886, the town had run out of room in its cemetery. In the 1860s, the city fathers developed an inventive way to recycle the land. When someone died, the survivors were given five years to pay under seventy U.S. dollars for the burial. Five years turns out to be about the length of time it takes the mineral-rich soil to completely leach the liquid from an interred corpse. If the fee went unpaid, the unlucky decedent was unearthed. Most were cremated, but especially beautiful or horrifying mummies were put on display.

The word mummy came from the Arabic word *mummiya*, meaning bitumen or pitch. According to the book *Egyptian Mummies* by Carol Andrews, the blackened and brittle appearance of the badly embalmed bodies of the Late Egyptian Period suggested that they had been dipped in bitumen, seemingly confirmed by their ability to burn easily. Wallis Budge, once the keeper of the British Museum's Egyptian collection, described how "the arms, legs, hands, and feet of such mummies break with a sound like the cracking of chemical glass tubing. They burn very freely and give out great heat." Who started setting mummies on fire? That's the unanswered question.

Amsterdam

by Christine Sulewski

I walked the streets of Amsterdam for days, in the rain mostly, with no idea how I'd gotten there. Not yet having figured out how to travel, I spent most of my time in museums or poring over guidebooks, trying to plan an itinerary. I was lonely, bored, and frustrated. My body felt thrashed from standing on marble floors. My eyes ached. Already I'd forgotten why this trip seemed so necessary. I'd had a great life in San Francisco. I worked in a record store, had tons of friends, a motorcycle. Now I had nothing. I'd even sold my bed. Had my lifelong masochism caught up with me, driven me away from comfort, love, and happiness?

I was tempted to return my Eurail pass and go someplace where experience was not kept in a museum. Americans were everywhere in Amsterdam. Where could I go, how could I get away from what was familiar to me?

As I wandered the streets, I came across a poster of a wooden chair, with straps and iron spikes on it. *What's this?* I was standing in front of the Torture Museum. My fatigue dropped away. I bought my ticket from a bored man in a glass booth and entered the dimly lit wooden building as if I were entering a church.

Rickety steps led up and up four stories. There was a guy on the second floor and a couple on the third, so I went up to the fourth and wandered around in a daze. I didn't know how authentic the implements were, but in the low light it didn't matter. The chairs, pincers, racks, and iron maidens were only there for atmosphere anyway. The real attractions were the woodcuts, blown up on transparencies and displayed on light boxes, accompanied by explanatory text in six languages. The text was well-written and printed clearly: all the usual stuff about when and where the implements were used, by and on whom, and when the practices were made illegal.

The woodcuts were almost pornographic. I loved one of nuns whipping a young novice, her habit around her waist, her long dark hair loose as she threw her head back in ecstasy. Another one I especially liked was of a naked prisoner surrounded by three men, two of them holding iron tongs to his nipples. One squeezed; the other prepared to squeeze. The third man watched his face, which was distorted in pain. Good thing there was a bathroom on every floor. I locked myself in and barely touched myself before I came.

I spent two hours in that museum, reading everything, examining every woodcut and every implement of torture on display. Delicious. I remembered what kind of person I was and what I liked. I felt revitalized and ready to explore other cities and other torture museums. On my way out, the guy in the glass booth gave me a look, I thought, of disgust. I returned a wicked smile.

Torture collage by Mike Hunter

CHRISTINE'S ASIDE:

I just found my ticket stub. It simply says, "TORTURE MUSEUM/AMSTER-DAM." And, in Dutch, "BEWIJS VAN TOEGANG." It also says, "BEWAREN EN OP VERLANGEN TE TONEN," which sounds delicious.

Christine's friend Justin translated the Dutch for *Morbid Curiosity*:

BEWIJS VAN TOEGANG = proof of entry
BEWAREN EN OP VERLANGEN TE TONEN = to be shown on
demand, literally "keep and on demand to show."

CHRISTINE ADDS:

Did I mention that the Torture Museum is no longer there? Everyone I know who's been to Amsterdam in the past couple of years has looked for it in vain. Perhaps you'll be lucky, though.

The 1996 *Time Out Guide to Amsterdam* listed the Torture Museum at Damrak 20–22, open 10 A.M. to 11 P.M.

CHRISTINE'S FINAL COMMENT:

The world has changed since this story was written. I do not condone non-consensual torture of any kind, at any time.

Dragon's Teeth

by Claudius Reich

Cloudless sky, lambent sunlight, silken breezes—it's a gorgeous afternoon, luxuriant as a long soak in a clawfoot tub. I'd needed to get out of town for a few days; my life was *not* working. Since I hadn't seen my friends Nik and Greg in way too long, I flew to London for a long weekend. (Which already helped—there's something about jaunting a third of the way around the planet, for less than a week, for mere pleasure, that's as deliciously self-indulgent as peeled grapes on a silver platter.) Greg had to work that day, and Nik needed to run a few errands, so I went into central London by myself, with plans to meet up with Nik at Comptons, this one bar on Old Compton Street in Soho (heart of the gay section, London's analog of the Castro or Christopher Street). We met there, had a pint, and went out wandering around Soho, late on a beautiful spring afternoon.

Can't recall specifically where we sauntered—we weren't being terribly goal-directed—other than this place that sold (I guess you'd call it) ravewear. Nik was flirting shamelessly with the *very* appealing twentysomething at the counter, while I grinned and industriously browsed the silver and safety-orange vinyl frocks.

It was getting toward sunset when we headed back to Old Compton Street for another pint. It was Friday, April 30, 1999, May Eve, the start of a three-day weekend (Bank Holiday, as the Brits call it). The area was packed: gorgeous men spilling off the sidewalks, chatting one another up in front of a café or hanging out with friends just inside an open-fronted pub.

We went back to the same place, managed to wedge ourselves into a bit of defensible space in front of the horseshoe-shaped bar, got our drinks. Think I may have had one or two small sips of my cider, when the pub down the street blew up.

Along with the tremendous *boom!* came a short sharp gust, a pop, like some drunk over-pronouncing a word with lots of plosive consonants right in your face. Nik and I were in this

LONE NUT

In 1999, three nail-bomb attacks in London killed three people and left more than one hundred injured, some critically.

The first bombing occurred on April 17, 1999. A bomb packed with nails exploded on Brixton High Road, in the heart of the large Afro-Caribbean community. A twenty-three-month-old boy was permanently crippled when a nail punctured his skull. Two men were blinded and another seriously injured.

A week later, another nail bomb exploded near Brick Lane in East London, the center of the largest expatriate Bangladeshi community in the world. Six people received minor injuries.

In several phone calls, a neo-Nazi group called Combat 18 claimed responsibility for the bombings. A splinter of Combat 18 called the White Wolves sent hand-written letters to minority leaders and newspapers, warning that Blacks, Muslims, Jews, gays, and Catholics were being targeted in a new race war.

On April 30, the Admiral Duncan public house—called a "gay rendezvous" by the *London Times*—was bombed. Among the dead was twenty-seven-year-old Andrea Dykes, who was four months pregnant. She had been visiting the pub with her husband, twenty-six-year-old Julian Dykes, who was seriously injured, and their best man, John Light, thirty-two, who was killed instantly. Many of the bomb's victims were lacerated by flying nails or severely burned by the explosion. Some lost limbs.

David Copeland, a twenty-two-year-old engineer from Sunnybank Road, Farnborough, Hampshire, was arrested on May 2, 1999, following the release of a closed-circuit television tape that recorded him in Brixton on the afternoon before the first explosion. In the film he wore a baseball cap and a "zipper jacket."

Copeland was not affiliated with any neo-Nazi group. Police did not believe he was responsible for any of the hate mail sent to the media after the bombings.

Police said the crude bombs were primed in an apartment Copeland rented in Central London. All the bombs were hidden in sports bags.

Copeland was found guilty of murder and three counts of causing explosions. He was sentenced to six consecutive life sentences.

—Editor

two- or three-meter-deep nook between the bar and the tall open windows. Some people were leaning out or running out the door to see what was up. I think I was a little stunned. My pint was sitting on the bar. I picked it up but there was too much to chug down. I wanted to run out and see, but what about wasting the rest of the pint, what about our jackets, what about . . .

I'd read the news stories about the bombings the previous two Saturdays in Brixton and in Brick Lane. A couple of neo-Nazi groups were claiming responsibility but no one had been caught, so it didn't take long to click. I remember saying, more to myself than to anyone nearby, "The bastards did it." The syllables seemed to echo, the way words do when you've got a head cold, or talk aloud in an empty room. I was starting to come out of my paralysis: Wasted Booze vs. Terrorist Bombing was not a real complicated equation, even for an old alky like me.

Then Nik said matter-of-factly that we'd better get going. The police'd be sure to cordon off the area and he wanted to get his bicycle out first. (Of course, this was the guy who observed, in a phone chat shortly after Oklahoma, "You people aren't used to bombs yet, are you?" with the earned aplomb of a man whose morning commute took an extra twenty minutes because of the IRA bomb check.) So I swigged a bit more cider, we set down our near-full drinks, grabbed our jackets, and headed out.

We walked down Old Compton Street, in the direction of what used to be the Admiral Duncan. The air and sky were grayed out, or sepia, like the moments before a summer thunderstorm hits. This was probably about a minute after the explosion, though I wouldn't swear to it. Shock had messed up my time sense. Each stride seemed to take ages to complete. The door and windows of the Admiral had all been open before, so spatially it wasn't much different, though I think I remember seeing the ledge and door frame before the blast. Those framing elements were absent now. A stream of smoke was still billowing out of the top meter of the pub—maybe the smoke rose, inside, before escaping into the ambient air. Bits of rubble were lying about: charred wood and seared cement, nothing large enough to identify as a barstool or pillar.

All the windows in the vicinity had shattered. Broken glass lay all over the street and sidewalk like the jagged shards left after hurling a framed photo across the room.

Think I recall one or two people (shapes, really) ducking into or out of the pub, maybe checking for survivors. For the most part, the arc in front of the Admiral, the path of the explosion, was only thinly populated. Everybody was at its edges, even at this point. A bunch of people were coated in blood, or soot, but it didn't stand out in the dimness. It was like the homeless, or gutterpunks, where it's not until the second glance that you realize, *Hey, this guy's really fucked up.* There weren't any police or paramedics on the scene yet.

Street was chaos, a broken anthill—some people sitting or lying on the sidewalk directly across from the pub, others crouching next to them, some staggering toward or away from the blast site, others moving with lots of purpose but no visible aim.

Nik and I walked through, quickly. I didn't want to rubberneck and didn't see how to help. We sidestepped briskly around the broken glass or the wounded, and then past. I've read a lot of sci-fi where movies and news have evolved into *sensies,* where the tech is such that the medium engages all your senses, envelops you. I'm not quite so much a fan of the idea as I was. One thing I've thought about since all this is that *Yeah, it was just like a bombing on TV, except that in real life the smoke makes you wheeze, your eyes tear, and you can smell sulfur in the air, with just a hint of barbecue.*

Nik's bicycle was a block or

two away, in a cul-de-sac. While he was unchaining it, some guy leaned out of a ground-floor window to ask what had happened. I told him, "They've bombed the Admiral," saw his face go as shocked and frozen as mine felt.

We left the alley, started walking away. Nik very casually mentioned that, after our earlier wanderings, he'd considered suggesting we drop by the Admiral, instead of going back to Comptons. If he'd spoken up, I'd've said, "Yeah, it's my vacation, I want *more* bars" . . . and we'd probably have planted ourselves by the windows, good spot to check out the talent strolling down the block . . . which would've put us . . . oh, I guess, a meter or two from the bomb itself. Oh fuck. *Oh fuck.* **Oh fuck.** My freak-out jumped a few more points on the Richter. Nik then finished with, "But I thought to myself, nah, the trade's better at Comptons." (As he observed later, "Every now and again, your dick can lead you *out* of trouble.")

We walked a bit further, Nik hopped onto his bike and rode off, and I walked down into the tube station.

When I stopped by an off-license on the way home to pick up some cider (I had no intention of dealing with this sober, not just yet), I told the guy at the counter that I'd just been near a bomb going off. I suppose I could rationalize it as my way of explaining, *Why is this man buying nothing but liquor, and that with shaking hands?* Actually, I *needed* to tell someone about it. It was as though the fact of the bomb and my nearness to it and accidental escape were too much to handle, too large to hold in something that was only six foot high and a foot or so wide. I *had* to spread it about.

Got back to the flat, and Nik got back, then Greg got home from work and we told him all about our day. I made some calls Stateside: my folks, since I knew they watched the BBC news on cable sometimes, and this one friend, a thorough heterophobe, whose usual response to the unspeakable is to exclaim, "Straights!" (For once, I wasn't planning to quarrel with him about it.) Their answering machines picked up.

We stayed glued to the news for the rest of the evening, on any and every channel showing it. The bomb had been worse than it seemed, even. It was packed with nails, dirt, broken glass—one nurse they interviewed on the telly said that she hadn't seen wounds that bad since working in Belfast in the seventies.

I proceeded to get sodden drunk on thoroughly mediocre canned cider. Helluva shock? Sure. The utter atrocity of it? No question. But mostly, that it had been such a glorious afternoon, a feast for the senses, perfect weather and the company of a dear friend and gorgeous men and other revelers all about—one of those excruciatingly rare moments when life is *not* all about shoving your goddamn rock uphill—and then getting sucker-punched, a visceral reminder that someone so loathes you as to *exult* in taking it all away.

Around 10ish, we crashed. No one suggested going out. I turned off the lights in the living room, crawled into my sleeping bag, and cried myself to sleep.

•   •   •

"Ghost" by Timothy Renner

After the first bombing in Brixton two weeks before, the British police had publicized a picture of a man, taken by videocam outside some store, who they thought might be the bomber. Eighty minutes before the Soho bomb went off, someone who thought he recognized the guy called the police. Late that Friday night, the bomber was under arrest. Turned out it was just this lone hater, building bombs and setting them off. It didn't come out until the trial that the Olympic bombing in Atlanta had been his inspiration. Appalling, but unsurprising. Shortly following his arrest, it had occurred to me that, were I such a thug, all this would've been *very* encouraging. Three separate bomb sites, three deaths, 139 injuries (many maimed for life), front-page headlines, a major metropolis on high alert for a fortnight . . . and all it took was one guy. Sure, he got caught—the trial occurred during the writing of this piece, he's in prison for six consecutive life sentences—but *kamikaze*'s not an impossible slot to fill. There's always room for one more inside.

Y'know, I keep on forgetting how many people want me dead. While homophobia has had a horrendous impact on the lives of me and mine, it's rarely this damn visceral. So much of the worst of it was during childhood and adolescence—while you don't get over that, not unscarred, nonetheless that was still half my lifetime ago. While I remain braced against fools acting hateful—when you're on the Better Dead list, though any given minute will likely be uneventful, you *don't* drop your guard—most days, the problem's absent or at worst negotiable. I don't cry easily. That some scumbag out there, who hates me for something that's properly none of his business, can make me sob, pisses the hell out of me. That my anger is merely the shield arm, protecting older wounds, makes me seethe. That there's nothing I can do—no cure, no defense in or from this fallen world—enrages me most.

I'd love to be left alone in a room with this bomber, or Pat Buchanan, or the guys from Laramie—just me and my steel-toed Docs and more righteous fury than I know *how* to live with day to day. There are those who've harmed me and mine in ways I can neither fathom nor condone walking freely upon the earth. I have seen the face of mine enemy and I'm more than ready to rise up and smite him. I yearn to see him put down like a rabid dog. I hope I get to watch.

Unfortunately, I imagine that's how the bomber felt.

Holiday in Genoa

by Dan McQuillan

On July 17, 2001, I traveled with my friend Norman Blair to Genoa to join protests against the exclusion of ordinary people from the decisions of the G8. I believe their decisions are based on profit and exploitation rather than on cooperation and human need.

On Saturday the twenty-first, I witnessed large and peaceful sections of a legal march being gassed and attacked by police. These events contributed to the atmosphere of fear in the city that evening.

Norman and I were staying at the Scolastica A. Diaz, a large empty school building opposite the Genoa Social Forum Media Centre. The school was covered in scaffolding; I assume it was being renovated during the school holidays. We'd been told it was a safe place to sleep. On Saturday night, a lot of mostly young people were staying at the school. The ground floor was a colorful patchwork of sleeping bags. A quiet stream of people came in to check their e-mail on the free computer terminals.

Norman and I shared a first-floor room with Sam Buchanan. Belongings of at least two other people were in the room, but they didn't return that evening.

About one A.M., an explosion of noise woke me. Norman looked out the window to see police charging into the building. We heard glass smashing downstairs and people screaming.

In fear, we tried to hide our belongings so the police wouldn't realize our room was occupied. As the rampage grew closer, we hid under one of the tables at the back of the room. The police pounded on the door of our room, then kicked it open. They advanced into the room, waving a flashlight and their truncheons.

We stood up with raised hands. I said, "Take it easy, take it easy." With the corridor lights behind them, I saw them only in silhouette. The police advanced on us. The leading one struck a hard blow on the left side of my head with his truncheon. Things went white. I fell to the floor and blows rained down on me. It was a frenzied attack. I rolled onto my right side and curled into a ball. I raised my left arm to protect my temple just in time to deflect a truncheon. I yelled in pain and fear.

Eventually they stopped and backed out of the room. The last two paused by a stack of wooden door frames beside the door. In a last vindictive gesture, they threw these onto us.

Other police came in to drag us to our feet. We were herded downstairs past officers clad in body armor. I received at least one more blow to the head on the way. I was already bleeding heavily from the initial head wound.

We were taken into the main room and made to kneel facedown on the floor with our hands stretched out. My blood pooled in front of me.

After some time, we were told to sit back against the walls. It looked like the aftermath of a bomb blast. Thirty or forty people sat around the walls, many of them bleeding or obviously injured.

The police pulled a frightened

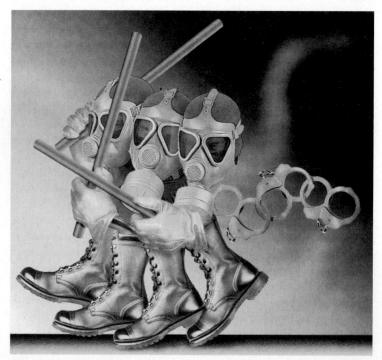

Illustration by Mike Hunter

young woman into the room. She was dark-haired and slim. Two police shouted at her in Italian, which she didn't seem to understand. One struck her upheld wrist with a forceful blow, then she was shoved, crying, into a corner.

Many of the police wore plainclothes under their body armor. They could have easily passed for demonstrators. This made them even more frightening. Some wore handkerchiefs across their faces to mask their identities. I particularly remember a tanned police officer with a long black ponytail.

I tried to stem the flow of blood from my head. The shorts and short-sleeved shirt I wore were both soaked in my blood. I started to shake.

Norman whispered, "Oh shit, Dan. You look bad. Are you okay?" He held my free hand and told me not to worry, that whatever happened, he would make sure we stayed together. He wouldn't leave me.

Beside us, a woman tended her completely unconscious boyfriend while another woman held his legs up in some sort of recovery position. His body twitched spasmodically. I feared he was dying.

At the other end of the room, police searched a great jumbled pile of people's belongings. They ripped open bags and scattered their contents, leaving clothes and documents to be trampled.

During this time, I saw at least one older man in a suit survey the operation. He conversed with two of the truncheon-wielding officers before leaving.

A couple of paramedics came into the room. They poured a fizzy liquid on wounds and applied basic dressings. They tore the cardboard backing off pads of A4 paper to use as splints.

Ambulance staff in orange jumpsuits began to load people onto stretchers. Both the ambulance staff and paramedics seemed very agitated.

I was loaded onto a trolley stretcher and wheeled out of the room, accompanied by Norman. Near the door of the building, we were physically blocked by a helmeted officer who had a shouting argument with the ambulance woman pushing the stretcher. She said to me, "Sorry. I must give him this," and removed my money pouch, which contained my passport, credit cards, and about £500 cash in sterling and Italian lire, as well as my contact lenses. No one since has admitted any knowledge of this pouch or its contents.

Out in the street, I remember lines of police, camera flashes, and furious shouts of *"Assassino!"* One woman shouted in English, "We will not forget this!"

•   •   •

The ambulance took us to the Galliera Hospital in Genoa. I waited in a queue with many others from the school. The hospital staff was noticeably kinder when there were no police officers present. While I was in the lift going to X-ray, a nurse said in broken English, "This is not Genoa. We are not doing this."

Medical staff said I had a fractured left wrist, but no skull fracture. My foot had also been badly beaten, so I was limping. My arm was put in a cast and my head wound stitched. The medical staff gave me my X-rays in an envelope, along with a photocopy of my diagnosis. Because I was shivering badly, they also gave me an old sleeping bag to take with me.

After the X-rays, a plainclothes officer–who said he worked at the hospital–took my name and date of birth.

Ten of us were put under guard in a Carabinieri van. The police convoy swept through the deserted red zone. I got a very clear view of the luxury cruise liners in the port, accommodations of the G8 delegates. The ships glittered with bright lights.

Once the convoy left the red zone, we soon reached a police camp at a place I think is called Genoa-Bolzaneto.

We were made to stand facing a wire fence. A policeman drew crosses on our cheeks with a blue highlighter. We were questioned as to name and nationality. The police wore paramilitary-style uniforms.

As dawn came, we were led into a building, where we had to stand spread-eagle against the wall while we were searched. One policeman kicked me viciously in the ankle I'd been limping on. They confiscated our remaining possessions, including my X-rays and shoelaces, which were put in envelopes. Luckily, they let me keep the sleeping bag.

Bent nearly double by a policeman pressing on our heads, we were led down the corridor with our arms behind our necks. They pushed us into a holding cell, about 20 x 20 feet, with a barred door and a large open mesh window.

Once again we were made to stand spread-eagle against the wall. This was very painful because of my damaged wrist. Any sign of arms dropping was met with threats shouted by police officers behind us. This went on for a long time. Paramilitary police gathered outside the mesh window to shout at us. I only recognized a few words, such as "Communist!" and "Intellectual shit!"

I was standing near the window. They spat on my face twice, but I kept my eyes downcast.

Eventually they allowed us to

sit. Perhaps twenty-five people were in the room, many with bandages and plaster casts. We all slumped against the walls, six or seven along each side. With no talking allowed, we stared at one another or the floor. Terrorized, basically.

It was intensely cold on the stone floor. I shivered uncontrollably. We had no blankets at all, so a few of us shared the sleeping bag from the hospital.

All attempts to ask the guards about our situation met curt refusal. After a while, they allowed people to go to the toilet one at a time. When my turn came, I was marched head down to the toilet. When I came out, a policeman dressed in gray fatigues threw cold water over me so my shirt and shorts were drenched. Sitting cold and wet in the holding cell increased my uncontrollable shaking. I was suffering from shock and blood loss.

I find it hard to remember the exact sequence of events in the holding cell. At irregular intervals, groups of police marched into the cell with lists of names. If our names were called, we had to jump to our feet and answer our nationality and date of birth. Police continued to shout threateningly outside the window. We were made to do another session of standing spread-eagle, which may have lasted an hour.

In between, detainees tried to catch sleep, lying on the stone floor or slumped against the walls. At no time did any police say anything about our situation—about any legal process or whether we had been arrested. Clearly, the police felt they could do what they liked, with no regard for rights or law, without danger of being held to account. I felt like we had been "disappeared."

During the day, we were taken in ones and twos to a parallel building for processing. Two plainclothes police wearing black leather gloves escorted me to a hollow concrete shed that contained sophisticated equipment like military-looking laptop computers. I was placed in front of a device attached to one of the computers, which had binocular lenses that shone directly into my eyes. I thought they might record retinal scans. I was photographed several times. My fingerprints were taken five times. I was made to sign several forms without understanding their contents. My questions about them went unanswered.

In the afternoon, one of the supervising police officers came in with a bag of ham rolls. According to an Italian prisoner, he said not to complain about this food. There were only twelve rolls for all fifteen of us in the cell. As many of us were vegetarians, we took the rolls apart and tried to share the bread evenly.

As evening came, the atmosphere became very tense. All the plainclothes police disappeared and we were left with the paramilitaries. From down the corridor we heard snatches of voices, banging, and crashing. Images of Pinochet's Chile flashed through my mind as people were removed from the cell and did not return. I felt I had been transported to another continent.

We were moved to another room, where we again had to stand spread-eagle. I heard a blow and a prisoner close to me cried out. (I found out later that he was struck on the back of the head.) We heard people being beaten. Norman was one of the first to be removed. A while later, I heard him yell in pain.

Blankets covered the barred door of the opposite cell, so we couldn't see who was taken in or out of it. I felt sure we were going to be interrogated and made to sign false statements, to excuse the police for their violent actions. In a whispered conversation with a German prisoner next to me, we exchanged thoughts about how best to resist a beating. I felt very weak from lack of food and sleep.

In a side room, I was strip-searched, photographed, fingerprinted, etc., again. As I was being marched back down the corridor, two paramilitaries in gray uniforms gestured that I should go into one of the side rooms. They had their sleeves rolled up and were wearing thick riot gloves. A superior officer behind me said something like, "No, *non identificato*." I was taken back to the holding cell. Norman didn't return. I worried about him.

In the morning, we were handcuffed in pairs and taken by a prison bus to a place I know now to be Pavia Prison. On the way off the coach, we were each given a plastic bag with a couple of rolls and a bit of fruit. We were processed, given a couple of sheets and a towel, and taken to cells. It was a relief to be part of some sort of official judicial process and out of the hands of the paramilitary police. However, the prison guards continued to refuse our requests to contact the outside world. There was still no explanation of our situation, just rumors among the prisoners about how long we could legally be kept incommunicado. Along with others I spoke with, my feelings turned to frustration.

On the second day in prison, I was placed in a cell with Norman. It was great to see him again. I found out he'd been struck by a guard while being strip-searched. That night I was denied sheets to sleep under. I'm sure they had loads of bedding, so it was just typical "screw" (prison officer) behavior. It was a major struggle to get vegetarian food. My eyes suffered from wearing the same pair of contact lenses since my arrest. Although they were daily disposable lenses and dangerous to wear for more than a day—because they can adhere to the surface of the eye—I didn't dare remove them because I wanted to see what was going on.

All of us insisted on our rights to see a lawyer (*avvocato*), to no avail. At lunchtime on Tuesday, I received six telegrams from family and friends, grudgingly handed over by a prison officer. This was a turning point—knowing that people knew about us and were outside working for us.

Later that afternoon, I was taken downstairs to meet Gilberto Pagani, the lawyer my family had nominated for me. I believe I was the first prisoner to get a legal visit, possibly the only one to see a lawyer before our judicial hearing. He explained that we would be taken in front of a magistrate, who would check whether our detention was correct. Gilberto made me feel hopeful that the injustice of our arrest could be successfully challenged. He also told me about solidarity demonstrations in Milan and other Italian cities. In the exercise yard later, I told the others about Gilberto's visit. We all felt that the sooner we got in front of a magistrate, the better.

• • •

Five minutes before being taken to a holding cell on our way to see the magistrate, prison officers produced new shirts for us to wear. I was determined to keep my bloodied shirt and not let them hide this evidence of my treatment. Among those in our holding cell, we had a broken leg with multiple fractures, three broken arms or wrists, seven head wounds that had needed stitches, a broken nose, and facial injuries. Two people's backs were literally black with bruising. One of the German men said that police officers at the school had sprayed CS gas in their wounds and their faces while they lay on the ground after being beaten.

We were handed our charge sheet—in Italian. We were clearly being charged as a group. Among the list of items the police claimed were found at the school was a T-shirt bearing the slogan "Stop the Police Violence." Whoever drew up the charge sheet clearly missed the irony. Dangerous items like "1 floppy disk" were listed, as well as black clothing.

The magistrate asked if I was a member of any organization, to which I answered, "A trade union." She asked whether I had seen any of the so-called Black Block in the school (no) or seen any Molotov cocktails in the school (again, no). She asked me to describe my arrest. After a few minutes, she threw up her hands and said, *"Non confermato, non confermato,"* which was translated to me as "arrest not legally correct." She said I was free to go. The guards returned me to my cell.

Hours later, I was given back my shoelaces and sleeping bag and processed out of the prison with five Germans and a Spanish detainee. The police refused to give me my medical records. Outside the front door, a group of uniformed police insisted we get into a police van. The woman officer said we were to be driven to the Italian border.

Our supporters had gathered at the prison gate. We insisted that we were free to go, which made the police very agitated. As we were arguing with the uniformed police, four plainclothes officers moved between us and the front gate and pulled on leather gloves. We were told we were subject to a deportation order.

Eventually we got in the van and were driven to the main Pavia police station. There we were detained in a small side room guarded by a detachment of carabinieri. Despite being declared free, we had to ask permission to go to the toilet. We were still obviously prisoners.

However, some really great volunteers from the local Genoa Social Forum brought us food and phone cards. One of them also gave me a T-shirt, for which I was very grateful.

Supporters and the media gathered outside the police station fence, but we couldn't talk to them.

Our lawyers came to the police station. They were mounting a legal challenge to our deportation order. The German and Spanish consuls arrived to talk to their nationals. Some time later, the British consular staff also arrived. They were friendly, but at no time did they attempt to debrief me or take any sort of statement.

The legal tussle went on all night. When we asked the authorities how we could recover belongings abandoned at the school, there was no answer. I'd lost my rucksack, clothes, and a mobile phone. Others left cars and vans in Genoa. I felt really bad for a German man whose girlfriend was still in the hospital in Genoa. He was going to be deported without being able to see her.

When we received deportation papers, they stated we were excluded for five years for being "a danger to public order and security." Given that more than sixty of the ninety-three people arrested at the school had injuries requiring hospital treatment, the only danger we represented was as clear evidence of brutal, repressive policing.

At four A.M. we were driven out of the station under guard in a police bus. Even at that hour, a crowd of local people waited outside the police station to cheer us and show solidarity.

We were dumped at the main entrance of the airport. The police formed a guard line on the pavement. After some milling around, we were told that it was our responsibility to deport ourselves. If we didn't, we would be re-arrested. When I asked how I could deport myself when the police kept my money and passport, I was given no helpful answer.

Norman and I were assisted by the consular staff to book a British Airways flight to Heathrow. However, we had to pay for the tickets with Norman's credit card.

On the plane home, I became agitated because my sweat- and blood-stained clothing smelled bad. Apart from swapping the shirt, I had been wearing the same clothes since the original arrest. A kind stewardess gave me a sample bottle of aftershave so that I could cover the smell and be able to meet my parents

and girlfriend with more confidence.

On returning to Britain, I visited the hospital to have a proper record made of my injuries. It may be used in any action against the responsible authorities.

I believe that there was a systematic attempt to intimidate, brutalize, and unlawfully imprison me. One unintended effect has been a huge outpouring of support and care from friends and strangers to me, my family, and the other detainees. Many have said that this incident has woken them up to how bad things have become. There is a broad sense of determination to oppose global injustice. Despite having had a painful and frightening experience, I feel inspired and strengthened to stand up for a better world.

One of the Genoa Social Forum slogans was "Another World Is Possible"—a world based on justice and harmony, rather than profit and exploitation. While in custody, however, I felt a great fear—for Italy and the rest of Europe—that another, even darker world is possible: a return to fascism. I have seen that pockets of this world exist within the Italian state. How far are we going to allow it to spread?

GENOA AND ANTI-GLOBALIZATION

by George V. Neville-Neil

People who have not been involved in the anti-globalization protests remember only two of them: Seattle and Genoa. Seattle has the honor of being the first large protest against globalization; Genoa, the first such protest at which someone was killed.

The four names that come up most often in relation to the anti-globalization movement are the International Monetary Fund (IMF), the World Bank, the World Trade Organization (WTO), and the Group of 8 (G8). The G8 is made up of the United States, Britain, France, Italy, Germany, Japan, Canada, and Russia. These countries have a strong say in the actions of the other three organizations. The World Bank is a body that lends money from the large, industrialized nations to poorer developing nations. The money comes from the IMF. Contributor nations control the funds. The United States is the biggest contributor and has the largest single vote of all countries. Votes are measured by a percentage: the United States has a seventeen percent vote, three times the next largest contributor—Japan, with six percent.

A single paragraph of this stuff is enough to make your eyes glaze over. So why have hundreds of thousands of people come out to speak their minds about these groups?

The WTO's power comes from its ability to impose financial penalties on countries not in line with the agreed-upon trade treaties. The WTO is not an elected body and is therefore fundamentally undemocratic. Its members are government-appointed bureaucrats with no need to keep the needs of the people in mind. The stated goal of the WTO is ". . . to ensure that trade flows as smoothly, predictably, and freely as possible." Although to any consumer this seems like a noble goal, it leaves little room for human concerns. These facts bring out the protesters.

The anti-globalization movement jumped into the media spotlight on November 30, 1999 (N30 in protester parlance), as tens of thousands of protesters shut down Seattle. Their goal was to prevent the meeting of the World Trade Organization (WTO). The world press took notice, but what they noticed was the occasional spurts of violence (the breaking of windows and burning of garbage cans) and not that a large number of people cared about a subject that makes most everyone change the channel. Who cares about a bunch of bureaucrats discussing trade?

Anti-globalists come from a diverse set of groups, but are labeled by the mainstream media as progressive. The main groups in the movement are environmentalists, labor unions, and anti-capitalists. Environmentalists are concerned that decisions of the WTO will degrade the environment by overriding treaties and laws meant to protect it. Labor unions are worried about the movement of jobs to countries with poor working conditions and a cheaper workforce. The term *anti-capitalist* is a catchall for groups such as socialists and anarchists, who oppose the capitalist system on the humanist principle that it degrades people and society.

After Seattle there were many other protests: Philadelphia and Los Angeles during the 2000 U.S. presidential election, as well as other World Bank and IMF meetings.

The G8 decided that their next meeting would take place in Genoa's Ducal Palace on July 20–22, 2001. Protesters decided their next meeting would be in the same city on the same days. Dubbed J20 (for July 20), the protest drew a very large crowd.

In the week before the meeting, Italian authorities decided they would not allow protesters to shut the city down. They erected a fence that was more than twelve feet tall around the entire conference area (called the red zone) and militarized the city of Genoa. Large numbers of untrained police conscripts were brought in to maintain order. One of these conscripts killed Carlo Giuliani.

On the afternoon of Friday, July 20, two to three hundred thousand protesters converged on the red zone. Running battles ensued with the police, who attacked protesters with tear gas, rubber bullets, and beanbag guns. The protesters fought back with bricks, bottles, and anything at hand. During one of these isolated battles, a group of demonstrators cornered a jeep containing several police conscripts. The protesters attacked the car with boards and bottles. In the moments before his death, Carlo Giuliani can be seen threatening the vehicle with a fire extinguisher. A twenty-year-old conscript shot him, then backed over him with the jeep. Twenty-three-year-old Giuliani died at the scene.

This propensity for violence spilled over into the police attack on the Independent Media Center and the Genoa Social Forum on July 22. The IMC is an organization that provides media coverage of the anti-globalization movement. The GSF hosted several of the protesting groups. Both spaces were used as sleeping quarters by the protesters.

At two A.M. Sunday morning, a large number of police, military, and agents provocateurs attacked the offices of the Italian IMC and the Genoa Social Forum, which were across the street from each other. During the attack, which lasted forty-five minutes, police sealed off the area to the mainstream press. A helicopter was brought in for support. The attack began with provocateurs, dressed in jeans, bandannas, and T-shirts stenciled with "polizia" overturning garbage cans in front of the buildings in an effort to draw the protesters into a confrontation. When this proved fruitless, they entered the school hosting the GSF and began to beat people indiscriminately. While the provocateurs worked over the GSF, uniformed police and military personnel moved into the IMC—where Dan McQuillan's story took place.

By the end of the night, more than five hundred people were reported missing, ninety-three were arrested, and sixty of those had to be treated at hospitals for broken bones, head trauma, or both.

In the attack's aftermath, the Italian government defended its actions. Amnesty International and other groups called for investigations. The police repression sparked more than two hundred protests worldwide, thirty in Italy alone. The legal wrangling and finger-pointing continues to this day.

As does the fight against globalization.

(Sources: www.indymedia.org, BBC OnLine, ABC News, alter.net, and personal e-mail from friends at the scene.)

Tracking the Zodiac

by Darren Mckeeman

I spent many lonely days in San Francisco when I first fell in love with her. She always sent some new adventure winging my way, just a little something to remind me that life with her would never be boring. So far, I've been able to keep up with her, even when she threw a life-threatening situation at me.

I had only one book to guide me through the Bay Area while I was contracting for IBM. The book was *Zodiac* by Robert Greysmith. It's a pretty good read, but I loved it because the author was a stickler for accuracy. Even today it haunts me: just last week, Eliza came back from the library with a copy of it. "I wasn't sure if you'd read it or not," she said.

My first free weekend after moving to San Francisco, I took a side trip up to Vallejo. Vallejo is the community where the Zodiac Killer got his start on December 20, 1968. He killed two teenagers that night out on Lake Herman Road. I stopped the car and took pictures of the spot, then I went back up the road to the parking lot of Blue Rock Springs Park and ate a bag lunch from McDonald's. It was pretty fun. I saved the outer casing of a pack of rolling papers I found in the park, wondering how many teenagers sit in that lot to this day to get stoned. Is the Zodiac watching them? He was never caught, you know.

The Zodiac was a true bogeyman, someone whose normal life we can only guess at. He appeared out of nowhere with a pistol and shot the teenagers out on Lake Herman Road. The same thing happened the night he killed two kids at the park. That time, he used a rifle that he had attached a flashlight to, sighting the bullet in on the black spot in the middle of the beam of light.

I visited the site on Lake Berryessa where his third encounter happened on September 27, 1969. People had been out on the lake in boats. On an isthmus into the lake, a young couple debated something madly that day—so madly, they didn't notice that some weird guy in a black outfit with a square hood had walked right up on them until he stuck a gun in their faces.

He ordered the girl to tie up her friend, then tied her up and stabbed both of them in broad daylight. I stood on the isthmus in the spot where the girl bled to death and traced the route the boy crawled back to the road as I returned to my car.

The Zodiac liked to send taunting letters to San Francisco's and other newspapers. I bought the font some person on the Net made out of the Zodiac Killer's cipher. I'm a sucker for merchandising.

He wasn't a stupid man, but he was fixated on rather a lot of things. His costume was a reproduction of a costume worn in a movie called *The Most Dangerous Game,* which featured the character Count Zaroff. Count Zaroff hunted down his hapless victims one by one. It was pretty much the same thing the Zodiac Killer did.

The Zodiac Killer wasn't the sexual sort of predator most serial killers turn out to be. He was in it for the thrill, of course, but he was by nature a person obsessed with outwitting the police and killing as many people as possible. He was teaching himself how to kill and not get caught.

The notion began to cross my mind that maybe it wasn't such a good idea to go to all the sites in succession. The Zodiac has still never been caught; maybe he was watching. A worse fear built in my head, anyway. It was the fear that by going to each of the sites in succession, I would be unlocking some kind of nasty curse or something.

I decided to skip the next site in the chain and made plans to go to Santa Rosa to see the spot where the Zodiac Killer lost a girl he was going to kill. After he picked her up, he accidentally drove up a freeway on-ramp the wrong way. She jumped out of his car and hid in a field until a trucker stopped to see what was going on. The Zodiac drove away in his white Chevrolet with the messy interior and baleful headlights.

Luck was not going to be with me.

One evening before my Santa Rosa jaunt, I was coming back from some club or another–I was always going to clubs. I had a bad tendency to drive through the worst parts of the Tenderloin. My apartment building stood in the heart of it, close to the hotel where Fritz Leiber wrote *Our Lady of Darkness.* I was always looking up at my apartment window–usually at three o'clock in the morning–hoping to see some malevolent entity waving at me from up there.

I was cured of that pretty quickly. I had just finished dropping off a friend and had forgotten to lock my car door. As I sat at a red light, looking at the windows of the apartment high-rise two blocks away, a manic-looking crack pimp opened the passenger-side door, sat down next to me, and pointed what looked like a .22-caliber pistol at me.

"Drive, motherfucker," he said.

A gun is a gun. Many people would laugh at what a .22-caliber would do to you. Ronald Reagan wouldn't; neither would James Brady. Then again, there was a time when Reagan might laugh at just about anything. I sort of resigned myself to dying and drove. I decided I could be a Republican, if it meant I could get Alzheimer's and forget this shit was happening to me. I was very tense for about six blocks.

"Do you often take people out to the sea and kill them?" I asked cheerfully. Since I was coming back from the club, I had on a very nice velvet jacket. I also wore some leather bracelets with rings

on them. I think he had just noticed. I thanked Jesus, Buddha, and J. R. "Bob" Dobbs that I hadn't been painted up like Bozo the Gothic Clown when he'd caught me, that I'd die without makeup on. I didn't want to be found and have the cops automatically assume I was trying to imitate *The Crow*.

"Shut up and drive," he said.

"Yes, sir!" I barked.

"Shut up!" he said.

"I'm only being polite to you!"

He considered for a moment, then said, "Okay, I can accept that."

This guy's not even gonna kill me, flashed through my mind. He was just trying to get away from

"This Is the Zodiac"
by Kimberlee Traub

wherever he had come from. Probably didn't even have any bullets in the gun. I bet he had just held up a liquor store or something. He'd be a professional then. No bullets.

I began to get very angry, but decided to see if I could find a cop. I drove up into one of the rich neighborhoods.

"Where are you going?" he asked.

"I dunno. I have only been here a week," I lied.

The guy must have gotten that all the time. I thanked "Bob" again for good measure. There are some times when San Francisco's tourism pays off. No criminal in San Francisco wants to kill a tourist—the cops think tourist-killers are just ahead of cop-killers on the "need to shoot first" list.

When we crossed the magic street corner at Washington and Cherry Streets, I realized where I was.

"Oh, my god," I said.

"What?" asked my passenger.

"This street corner, I recognize it from a book about the Zodiac Killer," I said.

"The what?" asked my crackhead.

"The Zodiac Killer. He was a serial killer in the early seventies."

The guy didn't say much. I think he got scared of me. I rambled on, idling the car. He listened in rapt attention as I rattled off facts about the Zodiac Killer. The place in Vallejo I visited where the killer shot them with a pistol very similar to his automatic .22 pistol. The stabbings at Lake Berryessa. And the last known Northern California victim, cab driver Paul Stine. The Zodiac had hailed his cab in the theater district, pretty close to where I had been car-jacked. He'd used the .22-caliber pistol on the cab driver, too, I told my passenger. He was looking more and more like a frightened rabbit.

"Do you know why the .22-caliber handgun is the weapon of choice among professional assassins?" I asked him. "The Zodiac knew. He knew it was a sure kill if he could just push the gun up to the back of the head of the cab driver and pull the trigger. The bullet would go through the skull and bounce around, turning the brain into a big pureed mess."

The gun went up to my head.

"Put your head on your lap," he ordered me.

Oh shit, I thought. *This is the part where I miscalculated and freaked out the crackhead so bad he shot me anyway.*

He put the gun to the back of my head and said, "Don't look up or I'll shoot you."

I did as he said, with a smile on my face.

• • •

I reported that to the police. They said there wasn't much they could do unless he used my credit cards, which he hadn't actually taken from me. I prefer to think that he got scared out of his wits and leave it at that. It makes for a good story, too.

I never visited Santa Rosa. I decided that maybe it wasn't such a good idea to be following the Zodiac's trail. I also think that I won't stop for very long if I do find myself in Santa Rosa. I've heard stories about people being followed there by a mysterious man in a white Chevrolet late at night. He flashes his headlights at you. If you flash back at him, he follows you and tries to kill you. It seems too much like tempting fate.

Gainful Employment:
The Morbid Things
People Do for Money

"The Trio" by Kimberlee Traub

Hell on Heels

by Dana Fredsti

The club is dimly lit. Clouds of cigarette smoke hang in the air like smog in the L.A. Basin. Scantily clad females wearing "fuck me, but don't ask me to walk" heels are seated on barstools or at tables, talking to the customers, all of whom are men. The women take dainty, controlled sips of expensive, watered-down cocktails. Like the B-girls of old, their job is to stay sober while encouraging the customers to spend as much as possible. Conversation vies with the music blaring over the PA.

A lushly figured brunette occupies a small triangular stage in the back. Her luxuriant hair whips back and forth as she writhes for the pleasure of several men seated nearby. She's trying to simulate ecstasy, but looks more as though she's trying to claw her way out. Or simply can't keep time to the music.

Up on the central stage, a hard-bodied girl with silicone breasts gyrates expertly. Two gold Lycra triangles barely cover her 38D hooters. A third triangle does its best to cover her nether regions. A black Lycra skirt and gold lamé top lie where they were discarded during her first dance. This is her third number. Sweat glistens against her orangey tan-in-a-bottle. The seats rimming the stage are full, men of all ages watching with varying degrees of interest and lust. Some place dollar bills on the edge of the stage. One enthusiastic businessman shells out $10.

The music builds to its climax. She grasps the pole that stands center stage and slides up and down, her groin thrust against the metal. Head thrown back with calculated abandon, she slides down the pole as the music fades in an unintentional parody of the dying Odette in *Swan Lake.*

To scattered applause, the dancer retrieves her clothes and makes her way around the stage to collect her tips. The bouncer/doorman, a hugely muscled fellow, watches to make sure none of the men tries to touch her.

I watch all of this from the dressing room door, nervously adjusting my top as the house DJ demands another round of

113

applause for Bambi, who rudely pushes past me. The DJ then announces the next main stage dancer: Gypsy.

I thread my way through the tables, hoping that I don't break an ankle in my three-inch heels, that my wig and/or my top doesn't fall off, and wonder, not for the first time: What the hell am I doing here?

The answer was deceptively simple: an actress "between jobs," I was sick of doing temporary secretarial gigs to pay the bills. I wanted something creative. Waitressing was out of the question. Bad enough that I'd done some modeling.

Katie, a fellow unemployed actor, landed a job at a bikini bar on Sunset Boulevard, running the sound system and introducing dancers. Several girls had recently quit, so the bar was looking for replacements. Three to five sets per six-hour shift, three dances per set: was I interested?

I've always loved dancing. I've studied flamenco, ballet, belly dancing, and have been the last survivor on a dance floor at a party. I'd done a stint as an artist's model. While not an exhibitionist, I had no problem being partially unclothed in a room full of people. But dancing on stage in a thong bikini? My mother would spin in her grave—if she were dead.

Well, said Katie, it didn't have

to be a *thong*. But the girls who wore them generally made better tips.

I was young, stupid, and broke. I took the job.

I met JD, a friend of Katie's who managed half the dancers in the club. In exchange for seven percent of my earnings, JD's management meant slightly better hourly wages, exemption from chatting with customers between sets, and the privilege of being five minutes late without having my paycheck docked. While JD struck me as a low-key pimp, the thought of being forced to socialize with customers was incentive enough to accept his management. Besides, I didn't have to audition to get hired. JD's word was good enough.

Katie took me shopping on Hollywood Boulevard. An aspiring go-go dancer required a bikini or two-piece equivalent; high-heeled shoes, preferably bone-colored to make the legs look longer (according to Cyd Charisse); pasties (worn by most dancers in case their tops "fell" off); and interesting overgarments for my entrances. Those would be taken off during the first dance of each set.

As I browsed racks of glittery, tacky bathing suits, I felt like I was going for the "before" look in *Pretty Woman*. I hated everything Katie excitedly held up and decided to be inventive with what I already owned. I did, however, purchase two sets of pasties (one in black sequins, the other in silver) because I couldn't resist the novelty. Maybe I'd attach tassels and learn how to twirl my . . . Nah, I'd just put 'em on and giggle.

I also bought a long, curly, dark brown wig that made me look like I should wear gold bangles and dance with a tambourine, singing "Golden Earrings." The wig inspired my stage name. I'd wanted to avoid names ending in that long "e" sound—Bambi, Candy, Sandy, Randi—but Gypsy had a certain class the others lacked. Hey, I needed all the illusions I could muster. Looking at it as playing a part helped, even made the preparations fun.

For my "costume," I stitched silver chain mail and black crystal drops to a black pushup bra and chose French-cut black lace underwear in lieu of a thong. Years of costume collecting provided ample choices for my outer attire, so I put together several combinations that enhanced the *Gitana* image.

My last preparation was musical selection. Each girl made a tape suited to her personality and style of dancing. My tape ranged from "Wild Girls" to "Black Velvet" to the theme from *Heavy Metal.* There was some Prince,

some Robert Palmer, even some Fine Young Cannibals. The only requirement for me was a certain kind of beat, something steady and sensual.

I practiced dancing alone in my boyfriend's living room, combining belly dancing and flamenco with a modern twist. I did not want to be one of those dancers whose entire repertoire consisted of grasping her ankles and bending over with her back to the audience, or lying on her back simulating orgasm. According to Katie, they made good tips. I wanted to make money, but I also wanted to respect myself in the morning. Faking sex on stage was just not for me.

All the preparation in the world didn't prevent a major attack of jitters my first night. I tried to settle my nerves with a shot of whiskey. By the time my set rolled around, I was as ready as I'd ever be. Katie announced the debut of "Gypsy." As I passed the tiny sound booth where she perched on a stool, she gave me a thumbs-up and an encouraging smile.

With my stomach in whiskey-soaked knots, I reached the three stairs leading up to the stage. Could I do this? I looked around at the audience, perversely hoping no one would be paying attention. No such luck. Most of the men around the stage and the bar were looking in my direction.

After all, I was fresh meat. Was it too late to change my mind?

Yup. The opening chords of "Wild Women Do" poured out of the speakers. I had no time to do anything but get up on that stage and dance. Taking a deep breath, I successfully negotiated the stairs and strode confidently onto the stage, catching the rhythm of the music as I did so.

The strong lights brought a faint sheen of perspiration to my skin before the first dance was halfway over. The wig prevented my body heat from escaping. With a sigh of relief, I discarded my black chiffon-and-velvet top, revealing the bejeweled bra underneath. That allowed me to feel the breeze from the fans at the back of the stage. I grabbed the pole with one hand and spun around, sending my top wafting toward stage right. I caught the eye of a man sitting close by; his face was impassive as he nodded and put a dollar on the edge of the stage. Cool, I thought. My first tip. I gave him a distantly sultry smile and continued my set as the first song melded into "She Drives Me Crazy."

When the last song ended, my wig was still in place, my top had *not* revealed my pastie-free nipples, and the stage was littered with quite a few bills. Belly dancing and flamenco had stood me in good stead, allowing me to be sensual and sexy *without*

being tacky. And the biggest surprise? I'd had fun.

Famous last words . . .

At two A.M., three sets later—five if you count the two I did on the small stage—the rosy glow had worn off. As I limped out to my car, reeking of smoke, I came to several conclusions.

First: Support the new girl on the block? Ha! I quickly learned who would just as soon steal your pasties as look at you. I was confounded by the attitudes of many dancers who shared the long, narrow dressing room.

Second: If a dancer had invested in silicone, she invariably had teased (and dyed) blonde hair, a bitchy attitude, and tended toward the "screwing the pole" style of dancing. She gravitated toward other silicone sisters.

Third: Doing "fill-in" dances on the back stage sucked. Those dancers rarely got tips. Worse, they had to dance to music chosen by the main stage girl. I dreaded the back stage whenever Robbie, a sturdy little redhead with cropped hair, danced up front. Robbie was a fireball. She spent half her set whirling around like an aerobic Tasmanian devil and the other half literally climbing the pole to the ceiling, hanging upside down, and spinning around and around back to the ground. Robbie's exuberance was fun to watch, although it made me dizzy. Unfortunately, she favored eighties death rock—impossible for anyone but her to dance to effectively.

Fourth: You dance for yourself, not the customers. Sound perverse? Not at all. Oddly enough, the men don't concentrate on what's happening onstage. They're either trying to pick up the B-girls or staring morosely into their drinks. Trying to make them pay attention makes a dancer look desperate. Kara, possessor of thick chestnut brown hair, milky skin, and a Rubenesque figure, swayed on stage, happily lost in her own world.

Fifth: Not all men who come to these clubs like women. I'm talking downright misogynists. They sit at the very edge of the stage and stare at the dancers with a hostile expression that says, "I dare you to turn me on, you bitch." I learned to ignore them, but it was still disturbing. They never tipped. I saw one pull out a dollar bill and hold it while a silicone sister writhed in front of him for an entire song. When she finished, the man smiled and deliberately put the money back in his wallet.

Sixth: The wig was a great idea. I got more feedback on my "beautiful hair" than my dancing. Whatever got the tips.

I struck up on-the-job friendships with Kara, Robbie, and

"Tasha." She was half-Chinese, half-French, a deceptively fragile exotic beauty. Tasha was also "managed" by JD and so exempt from mingling with customers. Kara wished she'd known about JD when she was hired. She was tired of men trying to grope her under the table. Some girls made extra money *that* way, Kara informed me, but not her.

Tasha and Robbie found dancing to be the easiest job to hold with their class schedules. Neither of them seemed bothered by the men who tried to make us feel like whores.

Kara was a single mother of two who waitressed during the day to make ends meet. She was always on the phone between sets, talking to her babysitter, making sure her babies were okay. There was something very vulnerable about her and the jerks could scent it. Once, she abruptly left a table where she'd been drinking with a greasy little creep in a cheap business suit and came back to the dressing room in tears. She took a dock in her paycheck rather than go back out that night.

Myself? I lasted four nights. No matter how many times I told myself that it didn't matter what the men in the place thought of me, the combination of hostility, lust, and the assumption that we were all prostitutes began to chip away at my self-image. I felt vaguely disgusted with myself after the third night. Intellectually, I knew what was going on, but my emotions wouldn't listen.

The final straw came on the fourth night. I'd joined Kara on the floor for a drink, just to keep her company. A short fellow with an accent like Andy Kauffman's character on *Taxi* approached us. He said he was a Romanian businessman. I reminded him of women back home. What beautiful hair I had. Would I be available for the evening? Um, no, I was finished after one more set. No, he meant *after* I finished dancing. Would I be available? He had much American money. I explained very clearly that I was a dancer. Nothing else. Either his English was worse than it seemed or he played dumb, because he opened his wallet to show me his American currency. Or he had traveler's checks, he added. Resisting the impulse to say, "American Express?" I went back to the dressing room to await my third–final–set.

I realized that no matter what joy any of us found in dancing, there would always be men who refused to see it as anything but one step away from prostitution. Even sadder, our self-images could be destroyed by men with nothing better to do than spend their evenings in a bikini bar.

At least I still have my pasties.

Blood Gags

by Frank Burch

"In the end, everything is a gag."
–Charlie Chaplin

Sid tried to convey the idea that he was some sort of Carlos Castaneda of the flesh, that there were mysteries he could reveal regarding the charm of bondage that straight people either denied or were blind to. He expounded an arcane philosophy devoted to giving women power by tying them up. Because I'd had production experience working around studios, he offered me a job as a minor and part-time villain in some of his little movies. It would be safe enough: I knew that Sid wouldn't cross over into my normal life; I knew, too, that' none of the women I knew would ever be interested in working with someone like Sid. The technical term for this degree of innocence is *hubris*. (Within a period of six months, half a dozen women I'd previously met were working with Sid.)

It was barely the eighties. Reagan was president, Belushi and Lennon were freshly dead, disco and polyester ruled the club scene, and AIDS was still a novelty. In a darkened, sprawling underground warehouse at the edge of some unnamed city, I helped Sid make it look real. And for some people, if it *looks* real, it *is* real. There is a parallel to the audience reaction at the last turn of the century to *The Great Train Robbery,* in which the robber fires a pistol directly at the camera. That caused pandemonium in nickelodeons as people screamed, fainted, or leaped out of the way of the bullet. A perspective on bad boys in film from then to now makes this reaction seem quaint, but people here in the ass-end of the twentieth century still want to rewrite laws based on their alarmed guesses about what constitutes reality.

At some level, of course, it *is* real, since Sid's work was about sex and money, which are both real and abstract. Enough money can buy anything, no matter how twisted, perverse, or ostentatious. My provincialism let me be surprised that the girl-next-door would strip naked in a warehouse with a couple of men she'd never met before for $200. Now, jaded like everybody else, I realize there will always be a Bettie Page; there will always be an Irving Klaw; there will always be an Estes Kefauver with a gavel and a committee to keep them underground, where the real delicacies are found, like gold and truffles. It is a law as rigidly enforced as gravity.

During the course of our working together, Sid told me amazing stories about this industry whose eccentricities we serviced, about the appetites involved, about the money available to feed those appetites. Some of these seemed little more than fables designed to impress the unsophisticated novitiate, apocrypha one associated with the Illuminati or the Mafia or Arabs, all of whom figured frequently.

He told me about a woman that he couldn't work with because she was too close to the edge to maintain the illusion that Sid required for his work. This suggests to me, more than anything else, that she is real. She entertained violent rape fantasies and would permit almost anything to be done to her. She had eroticized brutality through some arcane mechanism that puzzled even Sid. In the performance of her violent but wholly consensual fantasies, she could only get off—as they say—by having her labia stitched together with a sailmaker's needle and heavy thread. I never met her, but I did see women who liked to impale themselves on heavy, polyurethaned wooden dildoes projecting upward from a chair seat, rocking back and forth in a slow, almost religious ecstasy, veins standing out on their neck, bodies vibrating as if machines worked beneath the flesh, fluids puddling in the chair and scenting the room with an aroma that was similar to the burning flesh one sometimes smells at fiery freeway accidents.

I was aware I was watching a profound pathology only remotely connected to sexuality and Sid knew it, too. All the same, with Sid at the rudder, we pressed deeper and deeper along this narrowing river into the moist jungle where Kurtz lived and I began to understand that we were operating in a dimension that was only marginally adjacent to the one I was familiar with, a world that could only be illuminated and understood in fitful bursts. It was like war, neurosurgery, and rock-and-roll, all at once. We looked upon it in our masks as the women swung before us in their webs of nylon ropes, glistening like great spiders in a dream. Well . . . maybe it's not quite the same hallucinatory experience when one just reads about it. You had to *be* there to understand it, like walking across hot coals, to see that it's possible to come into intimate contact with fire, to feel great heat and not be burned by it.

This was a world unknown to me, except for its theatrical aspects. *That* was the real world to me. But I was endlessly fascinated by Sid's ability to mix the two, creating realistic backgrounds in a low-rent basement. Sid could toss off a couple of weeks' work with two-by-fours, sheet rock, cheap paint, Styrofoam, PVC pipe, and furniture

on short-term rental, and produce half a dozen sets that looked like the backlot at Universal. Venetian blinds and drapes hung against blank walls and, because you expected a window to be there, you'd never know there wasn't one. "No Smoking" signs in three languages and foreign editions of a couple of newspapers produced that *Mission: Impossible* feeling of being in some unnamed South American dictatorship. With Sid's attention to detail, you'd never know you weren't on the island of *El Molestiado.*

Sid even created an urban diorama, meant to be casually visible from the balcony of an apparent high-rise in some vaguely familiar metropolis. He sketched a skyline in false-fronted buildings lit with strings of Christmas lights, foamcore pretending to be steel and glass, cardboard pretending to be Chicago or Istanbul. There was a hyperreality to it all, like wandering backstage at the *Pirates of the Caribbean* on acid. Especially since, two hours later, I would be back at my apartment, living my utterly ordi-

"Deeper Than the Forest Would Permit" by Timothy Renner

nary life, drinking coffee and learning lines for another Neil Simon comedy, where the illusion of reality was never as critical nor so well achieved.

In pursuit of said illusion, Sid granted me perks that I wouldn't have gotten in a straighter workplace. As Sid's sorcerer's apprentice, I got to tear clothing to shreds and flog women with a doubled belt. The raw-looking stripes were applied with makeup rubbed on the belt and then rubber-stamped across thighs and buttocks and breasts: Sid always did the makeup since he was invariably better and faster at it than the women were. Needing to keep his hands clean to do makeup and costumes, load the cameras, tend to the paperwork and script logs, Sid let me rub the naked bodies of the day's talent with mineral oil to make them seem sweaty, although we usually kept heaters running during a shoot in the cavelike warehouse.

Since this was a science project, not particularly a fantasy of mine except for the naked girls, I was never aroused by any of it. I was half roadie, setting up a stage, laying out the tripods and heavy orange electrical cables for the lights, and half lab assistant for this curious class in physics, setting out ropes and pulley systems. Sid and I worked with the same disinterested efficiency as any news crew setting up for a press conference with the mayor.

I was a geek now, inside the tent; sweaty-handed excitement was for the rubes who had never seen it before and thought it was real. I mean, even though my back was to the camera, anyone could tell I was unzipping my pants; the telltale masturbatory jiggle of elbow with head tilted back, that little shudder: those must surely indicate an orgasm. My hips moved out of the shot and the camera saw only the victim's face, frosted with cream like a cinnamon roll.

Surely it must be real, except that you can forget it, Jake: this is, after all, Chinatown. Bullets or pain or blood or jism, it's just a trick. Geeks know that; rubes don't. There's the difference between being a geek and being a rube, half-blind from the chaser lights and loud music, stumbling over power cables buried beneath the sawdust between the tents, intoxicated by the awful perfumes of terror, adrenaline, and pussy, where it *has* to be real because it means *something really important* to him. *Must* be real, because it *looks* real. In this case, we used Tame cream rinse, a perfect substitute for semen because it's pearlescent and creamy, always available with a squeeze and a squirt. The manufacturers probably have some subliminal thing going, making it look so exactly like ejaculate.

Sid wasn't doing his act for the local market. He had a national, even an international, reputation to uphold, creating work nasty enough to be smuggled in from Europe as an example of how really depraved people can be—especially people in places other than the United States, where we wouldn't do such things. Smuggling, I learned, was a two-way street: Sid produced his work in 16mm and smuggled it, in a manner of speaking, out of the country—into Switzerland, let's say. Producers there duped it to 8mm or dubbed it over to video (PAL format, of course, to make it seem a local product), then sold it to depraved American (or English) tourists with a taste for "the real thing, the hard stuff, heh heh, you can't get at home." The tourists hid this sinful contraband inside their luggage or taped to their chests as if it were a chunk of hashish like in *Midnight Express* and really smuggled it, in the opposite direction, back into this country.

While all this subterfuge was playing out at Customs starring sweating middle-aged bankers and lawyers and fundamentalist ministers—your basic pillars of the community, the primary market for Sid's work—Sid enjoyed the sybaritic delights of Amsterdam, where the four-hundred-year-old Rembrandt canvases are filled with exactly the same sort of light and shadow and meticulous attention to detail that so defined Sid's oeuvre. Your ordinary pornographers like to flood the scene with light to show everything; Sid knew the value of chiaroscuro and lit at a forty-five-degree angle, giving shadows and a sculptural quality to his films. Sid among the immortals, sort of.

I remember a call from Sid one afternoon for what he liked to call "one of the special projects." After the heavy door to the warehouse was bolted shut, I was on my knees next to a woman I had been introduced to only an hour earlier. She now stood naked with her legs spread, making small talk about airline food. In her real life, six hundred miles away, she was a librarian. Here, she was the slut who flew in to work with Sid, traveling first class like a Mafia hitman, in and out in two days, a job to do—and then back to the Dewey decimal system, as ordinary as any librarian in the country.

The dildo Sid had made was spiked with rubber nails that looked real but could not cut. Just out of frame, I held a plastic aquarium tube in my lips. The other end of the tube ran invisibly along the back of the dildo's shaft. The dildo was inserted in a close-up shot no wider than the librarian's hips, with the awful tool twisting in Sid's hand. The finished film cut to a shot of the woman in terrible pain, screaming in obvious agony. Then the finished film cut back to another shot of a (another, shorter) dildo, apparently stuffed further inside her, tearing at her with the spikes.

My cue from Sid, since the gag was self-explanatory: "Go when you hear the camera rolling." I heard the gears engage and began blowing the same stage blood used by rock groups like KISS: your basic Karo Syrup and red food coloring, which oozed from the top of the tubing, pushed along by air pressure, flowing over the top of the dildo and down over the torturer's hand. Cut to the woman's face, her outstretched arms and legs tied in place (except that she wasn't because we were doing, no pun intended, "insert" shots, so she could just stand there), screaming, except that she had no need to because she wasn't in real pain, or even in a great deal of discomfort. Our subterranean studio was chilly so her nipples would be erect and her goosebumps would show, but the screaming was all MOS (a term derived from émigré technicians in early Hollywood, German for "mit out sound") and done purely for the visual effect that the viewers would be able to extrapolate into the sort of under-the-counter material that's scary and nasty,

that they'd never show to their wives or even their closest friends. That they'd vote against if a politician brought it up. That they'd never admit to liking, *needing,* even in a confessional. Something that they'd have to search for, maybe for years, to key precisely into that little notch in their brains that needed something like this to get them off.

With my pedestrian tastes, this odd little interlude working for Sid wasn't something that changed or converted me. It didn't get me off. It was just a job that other people can masturbate to. A woman who is helpless and at my mercy is entirely too retro for me. Been there and done that. As a geek, I understand the trick of it. But naked? Just for the hell of it? Yeah, naked is still good.

Ultimately Sid isn't an easy figure for analysis, as I may have suggested, or as complicated as he'd want you to believe. He wasn't an Ed Wood Jr. or an Orson Welles. It's like John Waters's observation about Russ Meyer: "He makes industrial films, about breasts." Fifteen years after, looking at pictures of myself in my trench coat, playing a bad guy to a woman tied to a chair, I feel like the drunk who stumbles up out of the subway and says to his friend, "I've just been down in this guy's basement and, Jesus, does he have a set of trains."

The Jumper and the Crabs

by Kalifer Deil

At seventeen, I joined the Coast Guard. My first assignment in 1954 as seaman second class was in San Francisco at Fort Point Life Boat Station. It was a two-story structure with the mess hall and galley on the ground floor and a recreation room, offices, and dorms upstairs. Behind the building was a long pier with a boathouse and dock at the end. Charles Van de Voor (Van) was the cook. He came from a Midwest butcher shop family and was a pretty good cook. I was assigned as his helper.

Only two weeks out of boot camp, the alarm sounded. Van and I ran to the back of the station where everyone mustered on such occasions. The rest of the crew was already committed to other missions. One picket boat and both rescue vehicles were gone.

Warrant Officer Black, the station's commanding officer, appeared. "You're it." Black directed his attention to Van. "We've got a floater near Sausalito, about a hundred feet from shore."

Van motioned me to follow. We piled into the remaining forty-foot picket boat, threw off the lines, powered up the twin diesels, and took off. We almost instantly reached thirty knots. This was fun!

I was the definition of green and had no idea where we were going or what we were going to do. "What's a floater?" I had visions of a large log or other flotsam and jetsam one might find in the Bay.

Van shouted over the engine noise, "A dead body! Probably a jumper. There was one over a week ago."

I had never even attended a funeral. I had no idea what death looked like, except in the movies and on TV. "Jumper?" I remembered an earlier dinner conversation, when they complained they couldn't find the jumper when they went out on a call.

"A bridge jumper! There's about one a month!"

"Really?"

"Yeah, really! I'll show you when we get back."

We came up on Sausalito fast.

Van noticed a dark patch bobbing in the water on the starboard side. He pulled alongside and cut the engines. "Grab the other end!"

It dawned on me what the body-length metal mesh basket was for. Following Van's lead, I grabbed one end, unhooked it off the cabin wall, and lowered it into the water by its attached ropes. Van maneuvered the basket under the body with a boathook. We hauled the body on board the stern of the boat. As the basket caught a spar and tilted sideways, two Dungeness crabs—one fairly large and the other medium size—scuttled out. Van grabbed them and put them in a red fire bucket in the engine room.

I was transfixed by the dead man face up in the basket. His blue suit was tattered and torn. His skin looked highly bloated and soapy. I later learned this was due to a process called saponification.

Van looked me straight in the eye. "See if he has any ID."

His words echoed, rebounding off my disbelief that I would be asked to stick my hand in the dead man's pocket. "Ya gotta be kidding?"

"No. Do it!"

I patted the outside of the right pants pocket lightly. "No wallet here!" I caught a whiff of the rotting corpse and had an almost overwhelming impulse to puke.

"See if there is anything in the pocket."

I approached the corpse again, holding my head back as far as possible, upwind. As I gently worked my hand into the pocket, Van pushed the throttle full forward. My hand darted into the rotting flesh. I yanked it out with a start. It was not pretty.

Van laughed so hard his tears were flowing freely. I hung over the side to dip my hand in the water, then puked all over my arm.

We pulled dockside at the Fort, secured the boat, and hauled the basket onto the dock. It was an unusually hot afternoon with a five-knot breeze coming from the north. The smell of the putrefying corpse was well beyond description.

Van faced the boathouse and pointed to a long line of little men stenciled on the wall. "Those are all the Golden Gate Bridge jumpers. Now we have to add another." There were hundreds of these little figures, but I was no longer interested. I just wanted to get off the dock so I could resume breathing.

Van brought the bucket of crabs into the galley. The smell of the body seemed to follow us.

I looked at Van with suspicion. "What are you going to do with them? You know where they've been dining."

"I'm going to make a giant

crab salad for dinner. What's the problem?" He put a large pot of water on the stove. I knew he was serious.

"Hey, then you don't need my help!"

Upstairs in the recreation room, I shot a game of eight ball. The rest of the crew joined me when they returned from their various missions. The slight breeze blew the smell of the baking cadaver from the dock into the room's open windows. Black got on the phone to plead with the coroner to come as quickly as possible. I was getting used to the smell, but the others were gagging.

Another really bad smell came up from the galley. "What the hell is Van cooking?" Black inquired.

I responded weakly, "Dinner?" I had learned not to volunteer more than I was asked. I'd seen Van spit on the griddle when cooking something for the CO. There were things you didn't talk about.

Black persisted. "What's for dinner?"

"Crabs."

"He didn't order any crabs. Where the hell did he get the crabs?"

"He caught them."

"Where?"

"Ah, you'll have to ask him."

"Don't you know?"

"Can we talk privately?"

"Don't tell me that they were fished up with the body. Jesus Christ!"

Two of the crew headed for the men's room. They obviously had lost control.

Van rang the dinner bell. No one showed. Black went down ten minutes later to find Van obviously enjoying his crab salad.

Black told him, "You can have it all, you fucking cannibal!"

Van smiled. "There wasn't enough for everybody, anyway."

I think of Van often as a pioneer in recycling.

Illustration by Kimberlee Traub

CRAB LOUIS

Medium head of iceberg lettuce
1 pound of cooked crab meat, chilled
2 large tomatoes, cut into wedges
2 hard-boiled eggs, cut into wedges
Lemon, cut into wedges

Line four plates with a lettuce leaf. Tear remaining lettuce to bite-size pieces. Reserve four large pieces of crab and shred the rest. Arrange shredded crab and torn lettuce on plates. Add tomatoes and eggs, then salt lightly.

LOUIS DRESSING

1 cup mayonnaise
¼ cup chili sauce
¼ cup diced green pepper
¼ cup finely chopped scallions
1 teaspoon lemon juice
Dash of salt
¼ cup whipping cream

Combine ingredients, except last. Beat cream to soft peaks. Fold into mayonnaise mixture. Add 1/4 cup dressing to each salad, top with the remaining crab pieces, sprinkle with paprika, and serve. Bon appétit!
—Editor

A Night in the House of Dr. Moreau

by R. N. Taylor

> "To this day I have never troubled about the ethics of this matter. The study of nature makes a man at last as remorseless as nature. I have gone on, not heeding anything but the question I was pursuing."
> –Dr. Moreau, *The Island of Dr. Moreau* by H. G. Wells

It began as just another night in a seemingly endless succession of jobs spent crawling through nightmare mazes of heating ducts and air shafts. For what it was worth, the occupational title was "duct crawler." It was a title we certainly earned, if we earned much at all. The hours were long and unpredictable, the pay was lousy and seldom on time, the work itself dirty and demeaning. Few people with any real option lasted long. The turnover in personnel was fast and furious.

This particular December night was bitter cold. They were calling for fifteen below. The company dispatcher had phoned during the afternoon and instructed me to meet TJ, one of the company foremen, at eleven P.M. at the usual gathering place, a twenty-four-hour greasy spoon.

"At least we'll be working inside," TJ said. He fumbled in his shirt pocket with cold fingers and came out with a folded worksheet. "Some research lab out northwest of town. We're supposed to have a double crew on this one. We have to finish it off in one night."

"I hope this lab isn't like that Argonne job. I'd sure hate to be sweating blood on a night when it's fifteen below," I joked, referring to a place where we were up on scaffolds cleaning some ductwork in 110-degree heat last summer. As a result of the chemicals used in the lab, sweat actually beaded out blood red—a rather unnerving experience, to say the least.

TJ seemed considerably more intelligent and sophisticated than most of the others employed by the company. He had recently been released from prison after serving six calendars of a twenty-year sentence for armed robbery. Outside of a diamond stud in the lobe of his left ear, he looked straight. He was clean-shaven. His crisp dark hair was neatly cut and combed. He always wore the dark blue service uniform that the company issued to its foremen, right down to the white oval name patch that said "Ted" above his left breast pocket. Most of TJ's criminal activities stemmed from his junk addiction over the past fifteen years. He had gotten the proverbial monkey off his back in Soledad Prison. For whatever reason, he gravitated to the Midwest after his parole. Much about TJ posed questions rather than provided answers.

Shortly after TJ's arrival came Puerto Rican Dave, a balding Latino with a goatee. Dave's eyeballs sort of floated around freestyle behind his thick horn-rimmed glasses, giving him a deranged appearance, not incongruous with his volatile personality.

Next through the door glided Solomon, his large ghetto blaster up on his right shoulder. A nod of his head was his greeting as he slid into the booth behind us. Solomon was one of the few truly black people I had ever seen, with jaundice-yellowed eyes and purple gums. He lived in the violence-permeated Cabrini Green Housing Project. The few occasions that Solomon did speak, it was to describe getting high on the weekends with his bros and engaging in recreational sniping at police cars.

Solomon ordered a Pepsi, but after just a couple of swigs, TJ consulted his watch and announced: "Drink up, fellows. We've got to get going." After paying for our drinks, we all strolled out to the parking lot behind the restaurant where the company van was parked. I sat up front with TJ. Solomon and Puerto Rican Dave climbed into the back. Once we were in the fast lane on the expressway, TJ—driving with one hand—began to stuff a flat white onyx pipe with reefer. He clutched it shakily between his dentures and lit it. He passed the pipe to the rest of us as he explained that the place we were going had real tight security. Once we were inside, there would be no chance for smoking any more pot. Solomon grumbled incoherently and Dave shifted uncomfortably in his seat.

The pipe was quickly

exhausted. TJ filled it again as he drove down the tollway at an eighty-mile-an-hour clip. After a surrealistic hour's drive with the eight-track pulverizing our senses, we pulled off on an exit ramp and drove down the sleepy streets of suburbia. Finally we arrived at a complex of brown brick buildings surrounded by high chain-link fences topped with three strands of loose concertina wire. Large mercury-vapor lamps glowed from high poles, illuminating the entire compound.

At the only entrance was a narrow wooden guardhouse. A burly black man dressed in a dark blue security uniform stepped out, scowling, with a clipboard in hand. He came up to TJ's window to ask what we wanted. TJ showed him the worksheet and explained our business.

A mixture of arrogance and distrust played upon the guard's face as he looked at the worksheet with his long black flashlight. He seemed to be a slow reader. He handed the worksheet back and announced that each of us would have to sign in on the guest sheet attached to the clipboard. The clipboard made the rounds. I scrawled in "Emperor Jones" when it came to me. We were allowed to pass through the gate and headed for a parking space near a large steel security door we were told to use. When we got out of the van, I glanced

back at the guard. He was still reading the guest list.

After a number of trips to the van for extension cords, vacuum cleaners, brooms, solvents et al., we gathered in a nearby glass-enclosed office off the main hallway to stage our operation for the night. We put on our coveralls, tied rags on our heads pirate-style, and duct-taped the hems of our pants and sleeves to keep dust out.

While we made these preparations, a dark-haired man in his middle fifties entered the office. He wore a starched white lab technician's smock and glasses. After rigorously washing his hands at a wall sink with a green antiseptic soap and hanging his smock on a coat rack, he sat down at one of the desks and began writing notations on a form, paying no attention to us. Several minutes later, a young Malaysian couple entered.

"Oh, Doctor!" chirped the small Malaysian woman, bouncing up and down on her toes, looking up at the doctor, who was much taller. "We are so sorry to miss the operation. We've been looking forward to it for months, but we will be gone over the Christmas holidays."

He said, "We'll be doing two more triple bypasses in the coming months, so you should be able to observe one of them

131

when you return. I'll certainly notify you both when that has been firmly scheduled."

"Oh," she said, clasping her hands together and swaying back and forth. "I'm so happy we will be able to be there for the triple bypass."

I gathered up my equipment. The doctor was back at the sink, washing his hands again. I noticed a single red spot on the seam of his smock as I left the room.

The four of us congregated in the main hallway. TJ climbed an aluminum ladder up to the duct-work suspended from the ceiling, took a chisel and hammer out of his tool pouch, and began to cut a three-sided opening. He folded the jagged metal down and back.

"I need a volunteer to do this duct," he announced. Since I was closest, I agreed to do it. As TJ steadied the ladder, I climbed up to the newly cut opening with my hands straight over my head, to narrow my shoulders. Once safely inside the duct, I reached down to get the orange extension light and a small industrial vacuum cleaner that TJ handed up. Both ran off one-hundred-foot extension cords. I began my crawl down the duct, carefully bringing up the extension cord's slack since there was always the possibility of snagging it on the sharp edges of the opening and

shorting it out or electrifying the sheet metal around me. I crawled over the sharp machine screws that protruded through the sheet metal at each of the duct junctions. Rarely did one emerge from a duct unscathed by punctures to one's hands or knees.

As I began to crawl, a cool rush of air hit me full in the face. It wasn't a pleasant breeze, but one that carried the stench of decay. Twenty-five feet down the duct I encountered the mummified remains of what had once been a white laboratory rat. Little remained but the furry outer shell of its carcass, literally a husk with empty eye sockets. I pulled a rag from my pocket, took the object by its hard tail, and swung it back in the direction of the opening. I hit on my vacuum cleaner and cleaned up the spot where it had lain for who knows how many years. I proceeded down the duct. It wasn't long before I encountered another mummified rat. This one I left, along with the vacuum cleaner, and began my crawl back to the opening. On the way I grabbed the first rat and took it along in my free hand. I called down for someone to come to the opening.

It was TJ. "What's up?"

I flipped the rat carcass down to him.

"Goddamn. What the hell is that?"

"Lunch. There's another one up here, as well. I'm going to need a plastic bucket or something to put these things in."

"I'll get you one from the truck."

I lay there with my head protruding from the duct.

As I awaited his return, down the hall came Solomon with a vacuum cleaner and extension light. He didn't notice my head hanging out of the duct. He strolled up to a door in the hallway and went in. The door closed. The door immediately opened again and he slammed it shut, exclaiming, "Motherfucker! What kind of motherfucking shit is going on in here? That's a motherfucker!"

"What's the trouble?" I asked.

Solomon nearly jumped off the ground at the sound of my voice. "They've got some shit going on in there I can't even handle."

I swung around and climbed down the ladder. TJ was coming back with a plastic bucket. "What's up, men?"

Solomon pointed at the door he'd gone through twice in a split second and said, "Take a look in there and you'll see what's up."

TJ opened the door. "Damn. That is really something."

I walked over to look. Solomon craned his neck nervously over our shoulders. Inside the room was a long stainless steel table holding twenty or more rabbits with their heads trapped inside what looked like a colonial stockade. Plastic tubes hung overhead. Some solution that looked like dense liquid detergent dripped down their faces, making their pink eyes tear as they stared off into space. The whole room smelled of rabbit scat mixed with soap. Solomon piped up, "I ain't working in that motherfucking room. No way!"

TJ looked pretty disgusted as well. He said, "We'll just save that for when Danny and his crew come. Leave it for them to do."

Everyone agreed. Just as I was about to climb back up the ladder to the duct, Dave came out of another door further down the hall.

"Hey, man, you guys checking out the rabbit room? That's a trip, isn't it?"

Solomon was the only one to answer. "It's a motherfucking trip."

Dave ignored Solomon's lack of enthusiasm. "You guys ought to see the dogs. They got some great big dogs in that room I was in. Let me show you." Dave, playing the proud tour guide, led us all to a room at the end of the hallway.

Sure enough, there were six large dogs: a mastiff, a few rottweilers, several retrievers. Each was in a separate cell with bars and a drain in the floor. The entire place was painted institutional green. We walked down the cells, looking in. The dogs didn't bark but jumped up on the doors. When I reached out, TJ stayed my hand. "You better not stick your hand in there."

I did anyway and the dog licked my hand like I was some long-awaited liberator. I noticed a patch on the dog's right rib cage where the hair had been shaved off. There was a scar about ten inches long. "Those bastards. This must be one of the dogs I heard them talking about doing triple bypass experiments on." I related the story of the Malaysian couple and the doctor. Everybody agreed this place was a torture chamber for animals. Only Dave seemed to be enjoying the spectacle.

The big yellow dog was still licking at my face and hands as I talked. I saw a bunch of bones lying outside the cages. I figured the least I could do was to toss the bones into the dogs, which I did. TJ finally said we had better get back to work. I went back up into the duct and began my long crawl with the bucket and extension light.

Dave went back to work in the dog jail. TJ went down the hall looking for something to employ Solomon with, other than the dreaded rabbit room. I crawled back to the last white rat carcass, flipped it into the bucket, and vacuumed around the area, then continued down the duct, dragging everything along with me. By the time I reached the end of the duct, where it dipped down to a return, I'd collected eleven dead rats. My bucket was nearly full of rat carcasses. "Here's the catch for the night," I called down to TJ, who was wrapping an extension cord in a roll. "Eleven prime specimens." I dangled the bucket down for him to take.

"Oh, God. This is really disgusting. I'll be happy when this night is over with," he said.

Danny and his crew came in the door. Danny was complaining about all the nonsense they had to put up with coming through the gate. He had several others with him: another foreman named James and some Slavic-looking kid I'd never seen before.

After several minutes of conversation between the new arrivals and TJ, Dave reappeared with a demonic look on his face. "You gotta check out this room I was in. This is really a rush!"

We followed him down the hall. Dave was acting like a kid left to roam a toy store afterhours. "Do you guys know why none of those dogs bark when you go in their room?"

"I give up," someone said.

Dave continued, "It's because

they haven't got any vocal cords. They cut them out."

"How the hell do you know that?" TJ snapped back.

"'Cause I was teasing the big dog with his bone and I could tell he was trying to bark but nothing was coming out but a little squeak." Everyone shook his head in dismay as we approached the next Pandora's box Dave was about to open.

The small white sign on the door read LD50–AUTHORIZED PERSONNEL ONLY. Dave announced, "Welcome to the Monkey House, gentlemen," as

he hit the light switches. Glaring fluorescent lights flickered on. Inside were a dozen monkeys in cages that seemed almost too small to contain them comfortably. Several monkeys sluggishly climbed to their feet and hung from the stainless steel bars, chattering excitedly. Others roused themselves awake. One lay at the bottom of his cage. The only sign of life was his large moving eyes. Everyone gathered around the monkey cages.

Danny was the first to lose interest. He looked around the lab room and was quickly joined

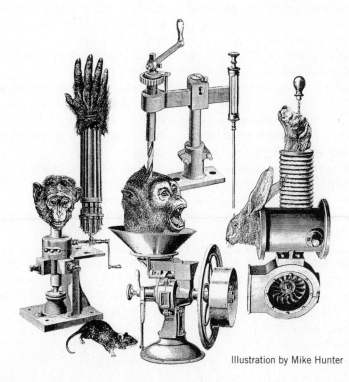

Illustration by Mike Hunter

by most of the others. It never failed, whenever the company was let loose in an unattended business, the first thing they did was to spread through the place, searching the drawers and desks and closets for anything worth palming. It was an unspoken reflex that they always acted upon. Out of curiosity, I joined Danny at a large metal desk. The surface of the desk was cluttered with various sheets with notations on them, no doubt in some way connected with monitoring the progress of the experiments. On the desk was the classic sculpture of three monkeys sitting in a row: see no evil, hear no evil, speak no evil. There was something twisted about this effigy's presence, considering the surroundings. Another small bronze-like statue depicted a monkey contemplating a human skull.

Danny pulled out a small black paperback book titled *The Story of O* and began flipping through it. "Hey, this is a fuck book," he said. It disappeared into his back pocket, as did a book of JOB rolling papers he found in the same drawer.

Dave attempted to elicit a reaction from the monkey prone at the bottom of the cage. I saw him poking a pencil into its side. Nothing happened. It continued to lie there, panting. "Leave the poor thing alone, you asshole!" I shouted.

Dave snapped back to reality. "I was just trying to see if there was any life left in it." He went over to rummage through a metal cabinet at the back of the room.

TJ, who had joined in the treasure hunt with the rest, finally said, "Okay, fellows, let's get out of here before someone comes by and catches us all." Slow but sure, everyone began to exit. TJ turned off the lights and left the critters in peace. The rest of the crew began to wander off down the hall in different directions, opening doors and looking around the place. I headed back to the dog jail. The dogs were still hunkered down on the bones I'd tossed in. I've always had a fondness for canines. Looking at these imprisoned creatures, their obvious fate was heartrending. I began to think: if nothing else, I ought to let these dogs out the door. What worse fate could they encounter out there?

TJ and Danny entered the room. TJ looked over at me with a smile and said, "Don't do it. They'll only get run over by a car on the highway or something."

"Yeah, but at least they'll die a natural death rather than the slow death they're dying in here, one day at a time."

Both Danny and TJ expressed similar feelings and sympathy for the dogs, but felt we'd all get into some hellish trouble if we did anything like letting the dogs out of the building. I agreed, reluctantly, that they probably were right. Slim chance the dogs could get out of the compound alive, past the armed guard and all. We all left the dog room with heads bowed. TJ turned off the lights and closed the door.

The night wore on, as we continued to clean the heating system in the crawl spaces of the building. The other members of the crew related stories of white lab rats in the various rooms. Finally TJ looked at his watch and said, "It's time we wrap it all up and get the hell out of here. The morning staff will come in about forty-five minutes, so we better have the place cleaned up and be gone."

We swept up our mess, wrapped up the extension cords and lights, put our tools back in their boxes, and loaded everything up into the vans in the parking lot. As we went out of the glass-enclosed office, I noticed the drop of dried blood on the hem of the white lab coat hanging on the coat rack. It had darkened to maroon. For me, the image of the blood spot somehow epitomized the entire evening we spent there.

Danny rode with TJ and me. We signed out at the gate and headed for the highway. Danny rolled a joint, lit it, and passed it around. Conversation was minimal during the ride back to the city.

When I arrived back home, it was early morning. My wife greeted me. Karen asked if I was hungry and proceeded to heat up my supper. Our small black terrier, Balin, came to greet me with tail wagging. As I sat at the table waiting for my food, I ruffled the fur on her head, thinking about the dogs at the lab. Then, as I related the night's horrors to my wife, tears welled up in my eyes.

NO SPILL BLOOD

by Loren Rhoads

I was straight out of college with a journalism degree. The most important thing I learned at the university was that I did *not* want to work at a newspaper, calling strangers to ask how they felt about the latest accident or emergency. I'd never held a real job, other than making sandwiches. I didn't have any self-confidence. The only skills I could offer were fast typing and a grasp of the finer points of written English.

So I applied for a job in a lab at the university's dental school. I'd be required to type papers for the doctor who ran the lab, as well as for his five graduate assistants. I'd have to keep his files, do occasional research, and answer the phone infrequently. It seemed very low-key. I'd have a lot of time to do my own writing—which I was welcome to do—as long as I was available forty hours a week to jump when Dr. Brandon required me. After four years of school, the money seemed exorbitant. I accepted the job.

Then Brandon asked if I had any trouble with the concept of animal testing. His focus was on the degeneration of taste that came to humans with age. His lab explored the subject by tracking the neural pathways from taste bud to brain in sheep. I would be working in the lab while the grad students operated on live animals.

It was all phrased grandly, in terms of improving the quality of life for the elderly. An appeal was made to my fondness for my own grandmothers. I was young and very innocent. I'd grown up on a farm and had no problem with the subservience of animals to human needs. I started the next day.

At first, they sheltered me. I'd worked there nearly a month before the animal experiments began. Bob, Brandon's postdoc, worked in the darkened lab, a bright white lamp blazing down on the opening in a sheep's skull, glistening off the pink folds of brain. I can't forget the sharp smell of cauterized flesh, when Bob sealed the blood vessels around the scalp so he could see inside.

It took a long time for me to realize that the sheep could not recover from having their skulls cracked open, their cranial blood flow blocked. Eventually, I wised up enough to ask Bob how he killed them. He increased the anesthetic until their breathing stopped.

I never asked what they did with the bodies.

Outside the lab, Bob smoked a lot of pot. It was his coping mechanism. We sort of got to be friends, I think, because he had so few people he could tell about what he did. He worked hard, trying to please Brandon. He killed two, sometimes three sheep a week.

Mark, a doctoral candidate and one of the other lab assistants, dropped out of school halfway through the semester. He decided he would rather hike alone in the Colorado Rockies than slaughter sheep in the darkened lab. Perhaps his departure was acrimonious, but again I was shielded. All of a sudden, he was gone.

My job changed then. One of Mark's duties had been to look after the lab animals. Bob had finished collecting data on elderly and adult sheep and needed to begin the third phase of the experiment. Brandon told me to bottle-feed the lambs.

It was the first time I was allowed into the locked end of the floor. The tour fell to Bob, of course. I peeked into a room filled with monkeys, but Bob warned me that they bit and threw feces. White rats filled another couple of rooms. All of the animals were merely housed back behind the locked door. I suspect, now, that none of them survived their tests.

Bob showed me where to get the bottles, how to mix the formula, and left me to it. The lambs were hungry. Only half a dozen of them lived in the room, each in its own wire-mesh cage. They understood what the bottle was for and jostled against the wire, eager to feed.

I held the bottle for the first one. It looked up at me with big heartrending eyes, trusting and childlike. Poor thing. It loved me for feeding it, for keeping it alive to be anesthetized, its skull plundered, its tongue stung with electrodes.

For the first time, I understood my complicity in the horror going on in the lab. I had been able to rationalize it before, when I had no interaction with the animals. But now I wondered: how many animals had been killed to produce data? How many had been killed in the time I'd been there? How many more needed to die? Was increasing the pleasure that old people took from eating worth so much death?

I cried as I fed the lambs. Then I washed the buckets and bottles, put everything away, and took a long lunch. A very long lunch.

When I came back, I told Bob, then Brandon, that I wouldn't feed the lambs again. If they required me to, I would quit.

● ● ●

I quit anyway. I couldn't tolerate what was happening any longer. I couldn't pretend it was helpful or good. Smoking pot wasn't enough to deaden me to the torture and death of so many helpless animals. I didn't last a year in Brandon's lab, but I worked there a lot longer than I am proud of.

Brain Salad Surgery

by Seth Flagsberg

I heard him before I saw him. The clink and clank from the metal chains around his ankles announced his arrival. When he turned the corner, the fluorescent jail lights reflected off the handcuffs on his scrawny wrists. He was joking with the steroid advertisement in the blue corrections officer jumpsuit escorting him to me.

I was still shaking off the early November chill, standing to the right of the painted red line that ran the length of the linoleum floor. I leaned against the open doorway of one of the little attorney conference rooms—with the red panic buttons and the white plastic chairs—waiting to meet my new client.

I wasn't scared when the red metal door shut with a dull thud and I heard the latch locking us in. Ron Donsteel was the first murderer I was ever locked alone in a room with, but he looked like a retired accountant or high school science teacher or someone's grandfather. He didn't look like a guy who would use a ball-peen hammer to bludgeon a

sleeping man to death in the middle of the night while four other people, including a six-year-old girl, slept nearby.

Ron was in his late sixties, short and wiry, with a day's growth of salt-and-pepper stubble and a shock of grayish white hair sticking up from his head like a lawn whose owner had been on a lengthy vacation. He was dressed in a red jumpsuit, the usual garb for violent prisoners, which made his pale skin even whiter and his gray-blue eyes even shinier. The one idiosyncrasy was his fingernails. They jutted from his fingers like dirty icicles. He looked more like an elderly Howard Hughes than a cold-blooded killer.

Before I could introduce myself or give Ron the business card I'd been nervously shuffling in my pocket, he asked, "Why do American men prefer Mexican prostitutes?" (Not the first question I expected.) Eyes glinting, Ron cackled, *"Frijoles."*

For the next ten minutes, while Ron told a few more dirty jokes, I wondered if I'd chosen the right profession. Then he fixed me with those gray-blue eyes and asked, "You're my lawyer, huh? When are you going to get me out of here?"

Ron expected to be released soon. Very soon. Ron was adamant that he had no choice but to kill. Ron believed he was no different from a man who finds a burglar in his house and shoots and kills him. Ron had absolutely no doubt the jury would see that he was justified. He insisted on a speedy trial so he could get back to work. As I packed up my belongings to leave, Ron said, "I'd like to be out in time for Thanksgiving."

The police reports made it clear the case was no whodunit. At 4:19 A.M. on October 24, the 911 operator received a call from a

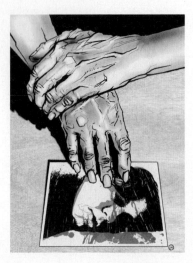

Denny's restaurant two blocks from Ron's house. A traumatized woman breathlessly reported that her landlord had attacked one of his tenants with a hammer, there was blood everywhere, and the tenant might be dead.

Officer Rausch arrived at 4:25 A.M. He found Ron in the driveway of the ranch-style house. Blood covered Ron's shirt and arms. When Officer Rausch asked what happened, Ron said, "I murdered him." Ron was handcuffed and Rausch proceeded to the cluttered living room. There he found a dead man with a smashed-in skull lying on the brown carpet in a circular pool of blood. More blood spattered the carpet, couch, and walls.

At the police station, Ron waived his Miranda rights. He told the homicide detectives who had taken over the case that the dead man was his boarder and former "business" partner Sonny Martino. Ron confessed he had used a ball-peen hammer to smash in the sleeping Sonny's skull because Sonny threatened to steal their business equipment and take it to Nevada in the morning. Ron said that he knew Sonny was serious and Ron faced certain ruin if it happened. Ron explained that, after Sonny went

Illustration by Erik Rose

to sleep, Ron stayed up thinking and thinking about how he could keep Sonny from ruining him. Ron could think of no solution but to kill Sonny before the sun rose. So Ron went to the garage, grabbed his hammer, and tiptoed into the darkened living room where Sonny and four other tenants slept. Ron squatted over Sonny and pounded on his head with the hammer. Ron estimated he hit Sonny at least fifteen times. He told the homicide detectives that no jury would ever convict him under these circumstances.

Shortly after word of Ron's arrest got out, a few of his former coworkers contacted me to offer help. Ron had worked at Lockheed as an electrical engineer for more than thirty years. He'd held a top security clearance and worked on sophisticated weapons projects. Ron's former coworkers were shocked to hear he was charged with murder. They all used to play cards together. They said that while Ron was a bit different, he was, as one told me, "An engineer, you know."

Ron's friends told me something he had neglected to mention: ten years before the murder, Ron had been in a coma following a serious auto accident. Because of the accident, Ron was forced to retire from Lockheed.

Ron's neighbor Frank Bernstein told me that after his retirement from Lockheed, Ron began renting out rooms and sleeping space in his house to augment his pension. Ron had six tenants—mostly lowlifes—living in the house the day Sonny Martino showed up looking for a room. Sonny was a middle-aged alcoholic hustler with a documented nasty streak and a lengthy misdemeanor record. Sonny immediately pegged Ron as a sucker to be sucked dry. Before long, Sonny convinced Ron to put $15,000 into a machine business. Sonny would handle the finances and bring in the business while Ron did the lathe work.

Sonny, however, had a competitor for Ron's money. Carmen was another boarder. A small pious Filipino woman, she always wore two crosses around her neck and carried a Bible. Carmen considered herself Ron's wife and was trying to get Ron to legally marry her. Carmen had already convinced Ron to give her $3,000 for her crippled daughter, whom no one had apparently ever seen.

After Sonny moved in, he and Carmen fought for control of Ron's remaining money. Sonny won.

After Ron forced Carmen to move out, Sonny printed up business cards for R&S Machinery. Ron bought a lathe that he put in the garage. On his last night on earth, Sonny got drunk, as usual, and got into a vicious argument with Ron. Sonny threatened Ron that he would take the lathe and all the money from the business. Sonny even went so far as to call his friend Patrick in Nevada to tell him he'd be arriving soon with a lathe.

During my visits with Ron, I realized that he was quite insane and a major cheapskate. Ron's thinking was so rigid, he truly believed he had no choice but to kill Sonny. He could not understand it would be traumatic for the six-year-old, who slept in Ron's living room with her mother, to have watched him hammer Sonny to death as blood spurted all over the room. The day I asked him about it, Ron said it was, "No big deal. She'll get over it." I looked in some psychiatry books and realized they might as well have put Ron's picture next to the diagnosis for antisocial personality disorder.

I decided justice would best be served if Ron went to the state mental hospital rather than prison. I told Ron I wanted to hire a shrink to examine him to see if he was crazy, because I wanted him to plead not guilty by reason of insanity (NGI). I couldn't enter this plea for him, because the law requires that a defendant personally enter the NGI plea.

Ron laughed when I suggested this. "I'm not crazy," he told me. "You folks are crazy to keep me locked up."

I told him, "Since you're not crazy, there's no reason not to cooperate with the shrink. If he says you're not crazy, I'll drop it."

Ron agreed, without asking what we'd do if the shrink said he was crazy.

I hired Dr. Lisett, who examined Ron and of course found him to be insane. Legal insanity, however, is not quite the same as medical insanity. You're not legally insane unless you can't distinguish between right and wrong and can't appreciate the nature and quality of your act. Dr. Lisett believed Ron could tell right from wrong, but not truly appreciate what he'd done.

Dr. Lisett and I came to believe that the car accident changed Ron from a strange engineer to a cold-blooded killer. I tracked down the medical records and learned Ron had been in a coma for fifteen days and had undergone two brain surgeries to repair his damaged frontal lobes.

By now, it was June. On a warm summery afternoon, I visited Dr. Fine, Ron's brain surgeon, at his office near Good Samaritan Hospital in Los Gatos. Dr. Fine appeared to be in his seventies, with liver spots on the outside of his very large hands–which seemed to shake a little too much for a surgeon. When I told Dr. Fine his former patient was now a murderer, the first thing he asked was whether Ron had killed a lawyer. Then he belly laughed. Dr. Fine absolutely hated lawyers. Over the next ten minutes, he made it clear lawyers were below murderers on his food chain.

I wondered just how many times Dr. Fine had been sued for malpractice. After I left, I knew that any jury who saw Dr. Fine testify would no doubt believe he had screwed up Ron's brain operations.

Luckily for Ron, no one seemed overly upset by Sonny's death. As the prosecutor readily conceded, Sonny was bad news. Police reports documented that he had pushed his pregnant ex-wife down a flight of stairs, he never paid child support, and he was always causing trouble. It was silently understood that Sonny needed killing but that, alas, Ron Donsteel was not the man for the job.

I explained all this to Ron and told him that while there was a very slight chance he might be acquitted of murder, he would certainly be convicted of manslaughter, which carried a twelve-year prison term. Ron refused to plead insanity, so I was trying to figure out how to get this insane man to say he was insane so I could get him to the state mental hospital. Crazy people are often similar to tired kids. The crazier they are, the more vehemently they protest that they are no such thing. Ron thought it was funny I thought he was crazy. He continued to insist on a trial.

Help arrived from an unexpected source. A lawyer I knew filed a lawsuit on behalf of Sonny's ex-wife (the one he'd thrown down the stairs) and their two kids against Ron for killing Sonny. Since the murder happened in Ron's house, I got his homeowners insurance company to defend.

When I spoke to Neil Connors, the insurance lawyer, he told me the company would pay all damages *only* if Ron was found insane. If he was found guilty and sane, Ron would have to pay, because the policy did not cover intentional acts.

A 150-watt lightbulb lit up in my head. If I'd learned one thing about Ron, it was that he was even cheaper than he was crazy. I knew Ron's cheapness would prevail and he would agree to plead not guilty by reason of insanity because otherwise he might lose his house and all his money.

I made Connors, the insurance lawyer, come with me to

visit Ron in jail so Ron could hear this from the horse's mouth. It was the first time Connors had ever met Ron or been inside a jail; I don't believe he'll want to repeat either experience. Connors was a bit rotund, with apple cheeks. During our meeting, Ron constantly berated him about his weight. But Ron listened intently, picking at his fingernails, while we explained the financial benefits that flowed to Ron from a finding of legal insanity. When we were done, Ron agreed to enter the NGI plea.

With Ron now onboard the insanity express, I set up a meeting with Mick Avery, the tall disheveled head prosecutor, at his office on the sixth floor of the rusty-looking county building. I gave him a copy of Dr. Lisett's thirty-five-page psychiatric report. Dr. Lisett had determined that Ron's brain damage was organic. No way he would ever get better.

I told Avery that Ron would plead guilty to the premeditated murder of Sonny if the prosecution would let the judge find Ron not guilty by reason of insanity based on Lisett's psych report. I knew this was no sure thing. The prosecution rarely agrees to an NGI, because they fear some doctor might soon say the person was now fixed and sane and ready to be released. Should the released person then go and do

something very bad, the resulting publicity would not be of the type the DA's office liked.

I held my breath while Avery read the report. When he leaned back in his chair and said, "Well, it's not like this guy is going to take some meds and get better," I knew we were home free.

A week later, Ron Donsteel pled guilty to premeditated murder. The judge found him not guilty by reason of insanity. Ron was ordered to spend the rest of his life at Atascadero State Hospital.

After leaving the courtroom, I found myself still thinking about the case. I believed that losing his job was the beginning of the end for Ron. His work had been his life. He had no contact with his family. His wife of many years had divorced him. Neither she nor Ron's two grown children—a doctor and a pharmacist—ever contacted me during the case. It seemed so sad. I wondered what Ron had done to make his family write him off.

I also thought about how Sonny had made a fatal error in judgment. He had underestimated just how crazy Ron really was. Ron believed Sonny's threats and it cost Sonny his life. There was a certain poetic justice to Sonny's death. Sonny had reaped what he had sown. Ron's mental handicap attracted Sonny to Ron in the first place, so it seemed just that the same mental handicap had cost Sonny his life.

What goes around comes around seemed to be one lesson I could take from the case.

Before I got back to my office, I came up with two others: never underestimate the power of money and don't let incompetents operate on your brain.

THE LENGTH OF SENTENCE FOR NGI

"Once sentenced to a treatment facility as NGI, six months must be served before the patient becomes eligible for outpatient treatment. The maximum term of commitment for an insanity plea is the longest sentence possible for the crime, if the defendant had been placed in the criminal justice system. There is no plea bargaining. The inpatient treatment term cannot be reduced for good behavior. The NGI plea often results in a life sentence because of the strict application of the statutory scheme."

—the Office of Patients' Rights, a division of Protection and Advocacy, Inc., a California lobbyist organization

Another Day, Another Dead Guy

by Kimberly Poeppey-Del Rio

In my line of business, I see a lot of unusual things. Running across rodents, insects, filth, and stench are the least of my worries. The thrill of the chase makes me not notice the really disgusting things. I would smack a huge rat out of my way if it stood between me and something I could get a couple hundred bucks for. You see, I'm a third-generation antiques dealer. I've been doing this my entire life.

Last March, we'd had a good week of really nice weather, in the fifties. All the snow had melted and the ground was dry. My dad called to ask if I wanted to help him with an estate call. That's when someone calls you to come out to their home to see if you want to buy anything from their estate or, if you're lucky, to buy the entire estate. Dad had recently sprained his foot and wasn't able to crawl around in the attic with its low ceilings. Seeing that crawling around in attics is one of my favorite things. No, really. It's a lot like Christmas! Lots of boxes to open and you never know what you'll find.

Could be a dead rat, could be a Tiffany lamp—I said that I'd be right over.

Before he hung up, Dad suggested I wear old clothes, as this home was dirty. Par for the course.

A man was waiting for me outside. I said my dad told me the house was dirty. This guy laughed. "Dirty is one thing. Hope you don't mind dead flies."

I laughed and asked if there was a dead guy to go with them.

He said, "Not for two days now."

I started thinking that Dad should have warned me about the smell. I prepared myself for the stench of death. If you've smelled death, then you know how it sticks in your nostrils. It's sickly sweet and makes you gag because you can almost taste it.

I walked in through the back door and immediately focused on the carpet of dead flies. There must have been millions of them. As their little bodies crunched under my feet, I noticed not the smell of death but the smell of a disabled shut-in. The odor of poopy pants and old-guy BO hung heavily in the air. It's the same scent you get a nose full of when you ride a city bus and sit next to a street person. I hate that smell.

My dad smiled. "It's a good thing the men put out a bug bomb."

That day we worked only in the attic. I found lots of great antique toys! After a couple of hours of digging, I was told we'd come back to go through the rest of the house the next day.

The first thing I noticed was the moldy food on the kitchen table. Funny how the outside of a watermelon keeps its shape, while the inside turns black and seems to shrink.

We sorted through the closets, drawers, and cabinets in the living room and dining room. There were huge piles of stuff everywhere: hip-deep piles of newspapers and boxes stacked several deep in corners.

I was shown where this guy had died: on the couch in the living room. There was a permanent indentation where he had lain for years beforehand. It was a green couch, but the body dent was grayish and kind of crusty. Still, no dead-guy smell. I guess the bug bomb overwhelmed the stench of a week-old dead guy—

who just happened to croak during a warm spell, thus explaining all the flies. Fine gold powder dusted everything: bug bomb residue. Maybe I should have worn a mask.

As Dad and I looked at the couch, Dad joked that I should go through the cushions to find loose change. I declined.

The bedroom toward the front of the house had unusual notes taped to its door, things like, "Don't come in here, I'm sleeping" or "Keep out, I'm in the shower." We were told that this guy had a wife who passed on a few years before he did. They didn't get along and would communicate via little notes like the ones we found. She had her half of the house and he had his.

We opened this door and found the bedroom heaped to the ceiling with bags and boxes. Apparently, this guy was obsessive-compulsive. He would collect anything and put it into a grocery sack or garbage bag and throw it onto the bed. There were boxes of rocks. Bags of envelopes with the stamps cut off. Cans of food several years old. Tons of clothes. As I moved bags off the bed in hopes of finding something we could make a buck on, I spied what looked like a vintage Hawaiian shirt. My first mistake was opening the bag. I must have been momentarily stunned, because then I reached into the bag. The shirt was both sticky and slimy. I realized the repulsive stench was severe body odor. I let go of the shirt, gagging, and threw the bag across the bed.

There were a hundred bags just like the one with the Hawaiian shirt. I didn't open any more. We surmised that, instead of doing their laundry, they simply bagged their filthy clothes, went to Goodwill, and bought more.

The second bedroom was obviously the wife's room. It wasn't cluttered but was covered with years and years of dust. The couple of snow shovels leaning against the wall looked out of place. My dad sat on the bed,

"Azrael Errant" by Suzanne Dechnik

leaning forward to go through the dresser drawers. I said, "Dad, don't sit on the dead lady's bed. What if she died there?"

But it was clear by the dark three-by-two-foot area on the gray carpeting that she had died on the floor.

I'm a bit of a detective, in that I piece together the obvious, creating a scenario that explains what happened. It was clear to me that the wife had died on the floor in front of the closet. Since she and her husband didn't talk much, she lay there long enough to decompose, hence the shovels and the thick black stain on the rug. I pictured some guys hired to clean up the mess, using shovels to scoop up her decomposing fat and pouring it into big plastic biohazard bags.

Dad stood up and opened the closet door.

I said, "Dad, don't stand there."

"Why not?"

"That's where the lady died."

He looked down at his shoes and attempted to lift one toe off the floor. In a cartoon voice, he commented, "It's sticky!" Then he did a little dance, saying, "Look, it's all sticky," making squishy noises with his mouth

that were very similar to the sounds his shoes made. He laughed the whole time.

The man who'd called us came in behind me. He asked me to come into the hall. He opened the closet door and asked me to pick up a box on the floor of the closet.

I said, "No, thanks." I imagined an Ed Gein scenario, someone's severed head in a box or a mummified fetus. So this man reached down and picked up a box just a little bigger than a shoebox. The label bore the dead lady's name and the name of the funeral home that cremated her. Her husband disliked her so much he simply left her remains in a box on the floor of the hall closet.

I found it sad that no one loved this lady enough to pick her up off the bedroom floor, that both of these people had died alone. At the same time, I was repulsed that people could live like this.

But, as I'm addicted to the chase, I see past all these things. The anticipation of that next big find in a smelly, filthy, rat-infested basement or attic is what keeps me going. It's what I do for a living. I'm an antiques dealer.

Halloween Hell

by Mary Ann Stein

It seemed so perfect: a three-month gig, good pay, and a nice change from the office jobs I'd been working since quitting my managerial position at Barnes & Noble almost a year before. Temporary office jobs depressed me. I found it hard to sit still for even one hour, let alone eight. Getting back into retail for three easy months looked like a good solution.

I could manage a Halloween super-store. Halloween was a good holiday: no religious overtones, no compulsory gift giving. It was a fun time of year—my friend Kristin always dressed her cats in costumes for Halloween. Even cashiers in banks wore unusual outfits. My childhood memories were happy ones, too. One time I wore an old lady outfit with a gray wig. My parents' friends remarked that I would be a fine-looking woman someday.

The interview was a snap and I was hired on the spot. The two-day training session out at the Hayward headquarters was fun. Soon I was taking the 25 Bryant bus to downtown San Francisco to watch my store being built. From the beginning, I had a list of people who wanted to work this three-month job. Most of them had worked Halloween the year before. Many had three-to-five-years' experience. I had about ten good interviews before I hired my two assistant managers. Nothing seemed ghoulish or scary about this job and now I had two fine young women to help me.

Ours was the first of two hundred Halloween stores to open across the country. There were six cash registers to install, so I called Hayward. "Who will be installing these registers?" I innocently asked.

"You," was the answer.

This is *not* my strong suit. I do not like wires and cables and knobs and buttons. For two days, I struggled to set up the cash registers. There were no written instructions. Each register had six same-size black cords. I even had to go to Radio Shack to buy more cords and knobs. Somehow, in desperation, I was able to install the registers *and* credit card printers. Such a sense of accomplishment I felt! I knew these registers so well that whenever one broke down, I was able to fix it faster than a teenage witch could mount her broom.

Merchandise arrived by the truckload. The store had not officially opened, but we kept busy hanging hats, stacking costumes for adults and children, setting up tables to display all the rats, witches, owls, moving hands, bloody swords, skulls, skeletons, gravestones, ghosts, and gargoyles. I thought we'd never sell the ten $99 fog machines, but I plugged one in by the front door anyway. We reordered this expensive item time and time again. That was just one of the surprises awaiting this unsuspecting manager.

A lot of the employees were rehires, Halloween junkies who lived for October. They worked with us so they could get the thirty percent employee discount on costumes and Halloween merchandise. They loved horror movies, coffins, Freddy merchandise, and anything that looked like real blood. Coffins were cool to this small subset of strange people of both sexes and all ages.

They dressed in elaborate costumes every day. Nina was in her seventies but loved to dress like Cinderella. Roger walked the streets in the hottest weather in a heavy warrior costume with all the accessories. He carried a sign advertising our store and talked to everyone he met. Every day he added or changed some costume part and found me to show me. "Oh, great," I'd say, seeing nothing different from the day before. Liz was a Glinda the Good Witch aficionado. Debbie insisted on wearing three-foot angel wings, even when the store was way too crowded for her to move around. Taylor wore a different hat each day, but the blue velvet pimp hat was his favorite. I knew that Judi should not have been in the store in the skimpy French chambermaid costume, but she didn't see anything wrong with that very short black skirt, fishnet stockings, and X-rated décolletage.

Opened in mid-August, the store was successful from day one. Halloween is the second biggest retail event after Christmas. Our customers often came in two or three times a day to buy weird things.

Such nice customers, too. Lots were children, of course, but San Francisco is a Halloween city. Plenty of adults want to live in a fantasy world at least one day a year. I had no idea that so many people had parties or that they'd spend so much money on decorations. A $500 sale was not unusual. These were happy people, looking forward to entertaining and celebrating. There was excitement in the store every day.

I looked forward to opening the store each morning and setting the batteries in the rats and bats. Our toys would all be turned on. Screams, meows, yelps, and cackling filled the store. The fog machine sent a gentle gray mist out onto the street. "Who could it be now?" moaned the big monster hanging in the front window. What a fun job I'd found for myself this time!

My store had a separate section for masks, one area just for wigs, and four semiprivate dressing rooms with mirrors. At first, we were good about picking up costumes and repacking them. September rolled peacefully by. We were making money and keeping payroll in line. Once a week, I faxed headquarters to request merchandise. At this time, I communicated the problems in the store: assistant managers not getting along, a $60 shortage, more security needed, angel wings selling well, everything pretty normal.

In October, the lid came off the coffin. It became the month from hell in the Store from Hell. Employees forgot their schedules and just didn't show up. Customers were increasingly cranky if they couldn't find the right costume in the right size. Piles and piles and piles of costumes hud-

dled in the middle of the floor. None of us had time to pick them up, let alone put them back in the correct costume bags. Lines at the cash registers reached to the back of the store. Often I'd be the only cashier. I began to hate every minute of my working day.

Customers were stealing. Employees were stealing. The mound of loose costumes grew larger every day. I considered hiding out in the Darth Vader costume, but I put on the purple Mad Hatter hat instead, to try to keep my spirits up. Some of the managers caved and just didn't come in.

I stopped sleeping completely about October 15. My clothes hung on me as I turned into a skeleton. I counted the days, the hours, the minutes until this horror would be over. My friends tried to cheer me up with witch and ghost jokes, but there was no laughter left. I hated Halloween and all it stood for.

Finally it was over. Our store was very successful, number five in sales across the country. We had a half-price sale the day after Halloween, then waited for the inventory people to come and count. I donated thousands of dollars' worth of costume pieces to Delancey Street, a charity headquartered in San Francisco. Then we packed what little was left and I drove it over to Hayward to the warehouse.

I'd lost fifteen pounds. I was never so exhausted in my life. I felt I had walked through fire, but I was proud of myself and the few employees who remained at the end of this experience.

I received a nice fat bonus check, plus an invitation to return the next year. I declined the latter, but I'd earned the right to wear the Wonder Woman costume for the rest of my life.

Illustration by Mike Hunter

✧

Curious Behavior: The Morbid Catchall Category

✧

Ephemera from the editor's collection

Prelude and Fugue State for Roadkill (An Accident Report)

by William Selby

My moment of violence, followed by its expanding tableau of surreal horror, has over the years graced me with a kind of hindsight that borders enlightenment. In fact, my gratitude at escaping annihilation has made me feel downright lucky to be alive more times than I can count.

Of course, when the accident occurred on that sweltering summer Saturday in 1975, I hardly felt lucky.

I'd landed my first art job in downtown Columbus, Ohio, at Roach Studios, then the largest manufacturer of iron-on transfers and silk-screen T-shirts on the planet. No sane person works weekends on salary, unless his lofty yet simple goal is to be a great T-shirt artiste; in that spirit, with creative fire burning in my belly to prove my shit smoked, I asked for and was granted a key to the studio.

On this specific Saturday, I worked from ten in the morning until three in the afternoon. By the time I left, I was gleeful as a rug rat banging on a stockpot with a wooden spoon. I mention this merely to indicate my positive, happy state of mind as I climbed into my emerald-green 1973 Volkswagen Beetle (aka, the Green Goblin). My immediate plans were: drive back to my comfortable apartment, jog three miles, shower, see my girlfriend, cook stir-fry, consume stir-fry, have sweaty sex, cuddle up with a twelve-pack of Stroh's, and watch *Saturday Night Live.*

Cranking open the sunroof, gazing up at pure powder blue, I smiled. Two weeks ago, I'd made the final payment on my car. In fact, yesterday's mail brought the title from City National Bank. Now it was official: the Green Goblin was all mine. Hot damn! The artiste's life was good!

August dog days had slunk in, bringing stagnant air and high humidity. I slid an eight-track cartridge into the under-dash deck, rolled down the windows, eased out of the gravel parking lot as the Moody Blues' "Question" blared from Sears custom-installed auto speakers, turned onto Columbus' Main Street, and zipped east toward Interstate 71.

A huge red and gray flatbed lumbered forward one block ahead, in the oncoming traffic lane. It barely registered. No weaving or unsteady vehicular movement. No menacing visual cues. I had no premonition, no hint of danger—just an obscure notion that the truck was picking up speed when it pivoted hard left and plowed into my Bug on the driver's side.

"Jesus Christ!" I yelled, astonished that—as an atheist—of all available curses that could have popped out of my mouth, I had regressed, failing to seek refuge in a simple "Shit!" or "Fuck!" (This was probably the moment I turned agnostic.)

Split-second impact impressions: *humongo crash noise!*—forward movement stops—body levitates, violently hurled against driver's door and steering wheel—car's left side/roof crumple inward—glass explodes—car spins—body whips across center hump and gear shift, smashes passenger door—shoulder/head hit metal—neck twists/*snap!*—hot red-gold-green sparks, human Spin Art/lurid colors squeezed on white and revolved, blending, mixing in deconstructive chaos, centrifugal force drawing blood and bone toward extremities, away from whatever center I once had.

Then, pitch-black.

I forced my eyes open.

A raccoon stared up at me from the floor, baring pointy little teeth. That made no sense. I liked animals, but what the hell was a raccoon doing inside my VW? Head throbbing. Neck burning steadily. The world a blur. Where the hell were my glasses?

I'd gotten knocked unconscious . . . Wow. That was a first! How long had I been out? Sprawled on my right side across the bucket seats, noggin wedged against the passenger door, I felt rivulets snake down my cheek, bulb at the chin, plop onto my chest. I wiped blood from my eye and, attempting to rise, propped myself up on my elbow. Pain bolted through my left leg and hip, but at least I could move.

The Moody Blues played on. I hit eject, killed the music. A big engine coughed and rumbled somewhere. There was incessant buzzing . . . the Green Goblin's interior swarmed with bloated flies.

I really needed those glasses.

Black, brown, and gray furry shapes covered the lower half of my body. I wriggled away from them but more took their place, cascading like Tribbles down through the sunroof. What the fuck? A potent, familiar stench stung my nostrils: the odor of decay.

Squinting at the blurry fur covering me, I made out vague forms: pieces of rabbit, squirrel, skunk, possum, rat, dog, cat. The raccoon continued to stare blankly up at me. The back of its head was dented. I thought I saw tiny bugs burrowing in its pelt. My car was filled with dead animals!

Instinct trumped thought: get the fuck out of the car! Adrenaline surging, masking pain, I frantically gripped the passenger door handle, lifted, shoved. The door grated partially open, groaned, then stopped. Obstructed.

Heart thumping, dripping with sweat, I escaped from beneath the blanket of bristly body fragments through the gap in the door, flopping fish-like onto hot pavement.

Rising shakily, I braced against the side of the car. The scene was a surreal Buñuel/Dalí *Andalusian Dog* nightmare as rendered by Norman Rockwell, viewed through shock's hazy scrim: my torpedoed Volkswagen, pinned against the buckled abutment, covered with carcasses in various states of decomposition. Looming over the spavined Green Goblin was its assailant: a gigantic, battered, old open-top GMC.

Black smoke spewed like foul breath through gaps in the rotten, leering maw of the truck's pockmarked chrome grille—a wounded beast champing at the bit to eat me and my car.

Built up behind the corroded red cab were slatted wooden side panels, slathered in gray paint now cracked and peeling. Above the cab, a wooden panel had broken loose on impact, releasing an abattoir of foul furry Frisbees, flattened fauna, and road pizza. A few animals seemed to be sleeping, intact, but most were in pieces, repellent displays of crushed bone and entrails—pulped varmint viscera that had been run over repeatedly.

Twenty-eight years may have passed, but I've never been able to eradicate the smell of death from my sense memory. The smell has become a fugitive virus, dormant for a time, but recurring like a bad cold sore.

Death smells funny. Not ha-ha funny; more weird body-sensation funny. Picture that brief sinking or rising sensation deep in your guts, strapped into the Concorde as wheels escape runway and you leave your stomach behind, or watching a suicidal jumper take a skyscraper dive and spackle the sidewalk. You know, mortality-awareness funny, with a sauce of hot tar, blood, and gasoline, simmered on a spit over crackling flames.

The aroma could have buckled a butcher's knees. Sniffing diesel fuel and burned rubber, I felt my gorge and anger rise.

From far off, a police siren wailed. The assassin truck's engine stopped and the driver's door opened. Emblazoned on the door in faded, hand-painted script was "Columbus Cartage & Transfer." A herky-jerky figure staggered out, clad in grimy navy coveralls.

I wiped blood from my face and lurched toward the carter and transferrer, fists clenched, ready to beat the shit out of him. My left leg and hip screamed, but I didn't care. This cocksucker had ruined the very first car I'd bought off a showroom floor—and I'd just made the final payment!

As my mouth struggled to form suitable invective, I stopped dead in my tracks. The thing that had scuttled out of the truck wasn't a man at all. It was a demon who stoked furnaces for Satan.

The wiry creature had no hair, not even eyebrows or lashes. Its ears were missing, as were its lips and nose. Flesh was

marbled meat, a hellish patchwork quilt of shiny scar tissue. Open-mouthed, its greenish-yellow teeth were perpetually exposed in a repugnant rictus. Raising its arms in a "Why me?" gesture, the demon brandished former fingers that had been fused into claws. "I orry," it said.

What the fuck had happened to this guy? Had he been burned in the accident? How was this possible? Could I be dead?

Fear vaporizing anger, I backed away, stumbling over the decapitated, maggot-infested deer carcass that blocked the Goblin's passenger door. The world swam away from me. I sat down beside the deer and threw up.

Cherries spinning, a cop car screeched to a stop beside us and cut its siren. A black female officer emerged, approached the scene, hand on her holstered .38. She sized up the situation with a rookie's nervous deportment and radioed for fire and ambulance services. I forget her last name, but still remember her first: Gloria.

"I orry," repeated the demon trucker. He started toward us and Gloria instructed him to stop. She was almost as freaked out as me. I was spooked all over again by her concern. She assisted me up out of the puddle of leaked gasoline I'd been sitting in. "Help is on the way," she said, moving us over to the sidewalk, aiding me to lie down.

She returned to her prowl car, retrieved a fire extinguisher, gingerly negotiated a path through animal remains to the cartage truck, opened the hood, and emptied the whooshing extinguisher at the fuming interior.

Impressions while I drifted in and out of consciousness: the demon's garbled nonstop apologies and protests; Officer Gloria made the creature about-face, snapped shiny cuffs on him, locked him in the back of her cruiser; two ambulances and a ladder truck appeared out of nowhere; paramedics shined a penlight in my eyes, secured a collar around my neck, made me demonstrate I could wiggle my feet and raise my arms; people yelled at me to stay awake; me on stretcher; stretcher on gurney; gurney in ambulance; ambulance in hospital garage; me in hospital.

Oh, yeah: hospitals smell funny, too.

I spent the night of the accident in Grant Hospital with a mild concussion, cuts (one on my forehead required twenty-eight stitches), bruises, abrasions, but miraculously no broken bones. I took the first of many hot, lengthy showers to expunge the stink from my pores. Long after it was physically gone, the smell persisted. The hospital had placed my bloody clothes, which reeked of roadkill and motor fuel, in a plastic bag. I thought about making the bag's contents into a decorative cloth sculpture but wound up dumping them in the trash. In those days, I was more emotionally invested in forgetting than remembering.

Everyone who saw photos of the Green Goblin was amazed I was still sucking air. My grandmother held the Polaroids and burst into tears: the Volkswagen's entire driver's side—from hood to back door—was accordioned. An insurance investigator later proposed that, had I buckled up for safety, I would have been pancaked. Evidently, not wearing a seat belt saved my life.

That autumn, I obeyed the Columbus city prosecutor's summons to appear at the Franklin County Courthouse to testify against the demon truck driver, whose earth-bound name turned out to be Lamar Hardwicke.

Lamar Hardwicke was cousin to the owner of Columbus Cartage & Transfer, which had the contract to scrape up dead animals from Franklin County's highways and byways. Evidently, on that particular Saturday, Lamar and his relation went on a roaring bender and, when the cousin passed out, Lamar—great good-deed-doer that he was—decided to surprise his boss and drop off a week's worth of road-kill to the city incinerator. More important (to Lamar), he'd make a run for more beer. Naturally, the thought of going to jail if caught a fifth time for driving under the influence didn't faze Lamar. Neither did operating a Class 1 vehicle with a revoked license.

Before the trial, a short, portly public defender with greasy black hair tried to elicit compassion from me toward Hardwicke. My eyes kept darting to the dandruff flakes that clung to the part in the defender's pale scalp as he explained how unfortunate Lamar had been injured in an industrial accident involving hydrochloric acid and fire sixteen years before. Since that tragedy, Lamar had been in and out of hospitals and mental wards; Lamar was unable to reintegrate into society or hold down a job; Lamar, blind in one eye, was on disability. Severely depressed, Lamar had even tried to kill himself. (The city-appointed lawyer compassionately conjured up his client's name as many times as possible in the attempt to humanize him.) At last, the attorney pointed out Lamar Hardwicke, yanked from a holding cell, temporarily attired in a cheap, disheveled suit, head bowed, sitting alone on a bench in the hallway outside the courtroom and asked me not to testify.

I realized Lamar Hardwicke was not inherently evil. He was no demon. He was simply a guy with really bad luck and a catastrophic weakness for alcohol, which made him dangerous as hell.

Before I replied to the public defender, Officer Gloria arrived. She didn't recognize me without all the blood.

My testimony put Lamar Hardwicke behind bars for two and a half years.

January in Columbus, five years later: I'd quit Roach Studios and embarked on a career as a freelance illustrator. I was up late Sunday night, trying to meet a Monday morning deadline. The radio was tuned to WOSU-FM, the Ohio State University classical station, which had news on the hour. The ten o'clock report iced my spine.

"A collision resulted in two fatalities early this evening at Cooke Road and Interstate 71. Lamar Hardwicke, 56, of Columbus, was arrested and charged with two counts of manslaughter after entering the Cooke Road exit ramp in a truck and colliding head-on with a car driven by Thomas Zustiak. Zustiak, twenty-four, and his wife Carol, twenty-one—newlyweds married three months ago—were pronounced dead at the scene. Hardwicke, who was driving without a license and allegedly intoxicated, was unharmed."

That funny smell came back. It still comes back.

HOW CREEPY IS THIS?

by Mehitobel Wilson

First the critter's feet got screwed to the tree. Raccoon feet are badass. Their front paws look like gloved human hands.

Normal skinnings are performed after hanging the beastlet from a rod and tackle thingy, but my house isn't exactly Pelt Central. The job was much less gory than I had expected. There were no guts, no gouts of goop, no strings of connective tissue. I suppose Tony's knife might have sheared any stringy things off without my noticing.

The whole time the skinning was taking place, I was saying, "Aw, god, that's so awful. Oh, jeez, that's gross. Oh, yuck. Wait, don't move. I want a picture."

Photograph by Mehitobel Wilson

Thanksgiving at Bel's

by Mehitobel Wilson

This dainty carnivore endured an abscessed wisdom tooth throughout the month of November. As I write this, I'm trying not to suck on my sutures.

Despite my inability to chew, I went home for Thanksgiving. I did not want to. I wanted to hit myself in the skull with a liter of Jack. The thought of driving three hours only to be faced with succulent meats that I could not eat made me miserable. Last year I was in San Francisco for Thanksgiving, which made my mom cry, so this year I had to go home.

I took Tony with me. Tony has skills. He's the kind of jack-of-all-trades Southerner that nobody believes exists anymore. Imagine a punk rock good ol' boy in a Star Wars T-shirt hunting boars, and you've got the general idea.

I'd been in a backwoods cock-fight with him: "You think you were raised in the middle of nowhere? I'll show you nowhere, buckaroo."

"Oh, yeah?"

"Yeah."

"Oh, yeah?"

Yeah.

On the road to my nowhere, we passed a really choice piece of roadkill. "Raccoon!" I said. "Turn around!"

He did. He knows more about roadkill than I do, so I left the appraisal up to him. He approved and tossed the carcass into the bed of the truck. Thus began Thanksgiving Day.

Tony borrowed my dad's drill.

"Why do you need it?" asked my dad.

"There was a really nice dead raccoon on the road and Tony's going to skin it for me," I said. "He needs to screw its feet to a tree." My dad thought this was okay.

I wanted to stay up at the house and read, but Tony said that if he was skinning a critter for me, I'd damn well better watch. So I borrowed my mom's camera. If I had to watch, I'd damn well better take pictures.

Now, I'd never seen an animal get skinned before. It looked easier than I'd expected. Since then, I've been creeped out every time I pet another animal. The mental images of my cats' skins laid over my arms, their little eyelids empty, their faces flat, makes me very panicky.

I doubt people are as easy to skin as raccoons are, but still, I stare sometimes at Robert and wonder how much he'd weigh, emptied. Yargh.

I wanted the spine, too. Since dead critters are important to living ones, we chose the natural route. Tony cut the nape and tail of the skinned carcass and threaded an eight-gauge wire through the spinal column, then strapped the whole critter (well, not the whole critter, since its skin was in Mom's freezer) to a tree in the woods. By the time I arrive at my folks' house for Christmas, the buzzards and crawlies ought to have done all the meat work and I'll find a spine attached to the tree.

I recently sent a couple of raccoon penises to a friend of mine. Now I have photographic proof that those swooping bones really do come out of actual raccoon dicks. The dicks stick to trees. As far as I know, the dick is still stuck to the tree, because I forgot to retrieve it. Crap. I should call my mom and have her grab it for me. (She'll hang up on me.)

So this poor raccoon ran into a car on Thanksgiving morning and now he'll be remembered forever. The buzzards will be fed and the raccoon's fur will be petted often. And I'll grow fretful every time knife-packin' Tony pets my Hazelcat for more than a minute and I'll have unpleasant dreams about my friends walking around with their inside-out skins hanging from the tops of their flayed heads, trailing down their peeled backs.

Happy holidays.

Feed

by Katrina James

My mother took me to see Frank Langella in *Dracula* when I was nine. I don't recall a fear of vampires before then, but this was the first time I'd seen one portrayed as an attractive, romantic character. It changed my life.

At first, *any* vampire movie or novel would do but, as I got older, I developed a preference for the ones with strong romantic or erotic overtones. I even wrote some erotic vampire stories, most of which were eventually published in *Vamperotica* magazine.

In 1995, I saw an HBO special that featured an interview with San Francisco poet and sex worker Danielle Willis. Not only did she have a vampire fixation, but she'd also had her teeth capped in fangs *and* drank the blood of her lovers. I was smitten.

I found her book *Dogs in Lingerie* online and ordered it immediately. I also taped a rerun of the show and watched it obsessively. When you're stuck in a small Kansas town and your blood fetish is a joke even to those closest to you, discovering

that there are others in the world who share your kink is a Really Big Deal.

However, it wasn't until December 1999 that I actually managed to escape the Midwest in favor of San Francisco. By that time, Danielle had gone underground. Even a lot of people who'd once been close to her didn't know where she was. In fact, many of them assumed her lifestyle had caught up with her in a fatal way.

My girlfriend Sherilyn and I never gave up hope. A common appreciation for Danielle and her work was part of what had brought us together; we wanted to tell her that. For two years, every time we came across someone who'd known Danielle, we inquired about her. Once, while walking down Van Ness Avenue, we thought we spotted Danielle wearing an old army jacket and no makeup. We briefly considered calling out "Danielle!" simply to see if she'd respond, but shyness got the best of us.

In July 2002, the lead we'd been hoping for dropped in our

laps. At a poetry reading, I approached Jennifer Blowdryer with a pen and her Joker card from Annie Sprinkle's *Pleasure Activist Playing Cards.* Jennifer happily signed the card and struck up a conversation with Sherilyn and me. She invited us to a party at her friend Alvin's house that Saturday night and mentioned that Danielle might be there. The party had sounded interesting before, but this bit of information cemented our presence.

The party was pretty low-key. Although Sherilyn and I had a good time getting to know Alvin, Jennifer, and some of the other guests, both our hearts skipped a beat every time the doorbell rang.

After a couple of hours, Danielle's close friend and former partner-in-crime Violet Hemlock showed up. He chose a seat next to me and immediately struck up a conversation. While one half of my brain was listening to what he was saying and attempting to form coherent responses, the other half was squealing in an embarrassing fangirl way, *Oh, my god! I can't believe I'm talking to Violet Hemlock!*

Danielle showed up about an hour later and immediately wandered into the bedroom of Alvin's roommate Tyler. She spent most of the evening in there, though I did eventually get her to sign my copy of *Dogs in Lingerie.*

However, sometimes there's an advantage to being obvious goths in a room full of non-goths. Pegging us as kindred spirits, Danielle eventually invited us into the room with her, Tyler, and Violet.

The events of the night are something of a blur to me, smudged by cold medicine and excitement, but the most memorable moments were exchanging locks of hair with Danielle and wandering the streets of the Tenderloin with her in the wee hours of the morning.

We spoke with Violet, Danielle, and her boyfriend Ixe a few times after that, but then Danielle and Ixe moved to Cleveland and Violet grew quiet.

Nearly a year later, Sherilyn received an e-mail from Violet. Not only had he missed hanging out with us, but he wanted to let us know that Danielle was coming to town to do a few readings and wanted to see us.

Most of Danielle's "Back from the Dead" tour went off without a hitch. Friends and fans were thrilled at her reemergence into the world of prose. We spent quite a bit of time during her three weeks in the city getting to know her better than we ever thought we would.

Then, after a solo night out

with Danielle and Violet, Sherilyn wrote the following in her journal:

We discussed the comparative sharpness of Violet and Danielle's fangs. In the interest of science, they each bit me on an arm. Not hard enough to break the skin, but enough for me to determine that Violet has the sharper fangs. It makes sense, seeing as his are smaller, while Danielle describes her own as "chimpanzee fangs." Violet had been opposed to the idea at first, playing the adult as he so often must—I couldn't help but laugh when he said, "Danielle, you have to remember that not everybody is insane like you"—but when I agreed, his eyes practically widened. I can only imagine the willpower it took for him to go easy on me. I'd briefly considered telling him not to worry, but, quite frankly, a bleeding arm probably wasn't what I needed and I don't know the communicable disease factor in arm biting. Not to mention the pain. It would have left a helluva cool scar, though.

I was extremely jealous. Though I'd extended the offer of my blood to Danielle—who'd accepted with a smile and a gleam in her eye—we'd found it difficult to arrange a time for the actual bloodletting. Even if that hadn't been the case, being a donor is usually a very sterile process involving needles, not fangs.

A few nights later, as we were waiting for our friend Tristan to close up the comic shop where he worked, I turned to Danielle and Violet and said, "Hey! How come you guys have been biting my girlfriend's arm when *I'm* the one with the fang fetish?"

Danielle immediately turned and strode purposefully toward me. I started to pull up the sleeve of my jacket, but she had other ideas. Grabbing me around the waist, she bent me over and bit my neck *hard*—leaving behind, Sherilyn told me, a pair of bright red marks. Part of me wishes I'd been expecting it, but there was something wonderfully primal about the way things played out, including the step backward that the force of her body caused me to take.

"Happy now?" she tossed over her shoulder as she walked out the door.

"I think my panties are damp," I replied, only half jokingly. She laughed.

Tristan locked up behind us and we piled into the car, headed for excellent cheap sushi and even better conversation. My mood was high. I was out with some of my favorite beautiful, creative people and I'd just been bitten by a vampire who, later that night, was finally going to drink my blood.

After dinner we went to Violet's, where he prepared for the bloodletting. Danielle is handy with a needle herself, but she was too sleepy for any of us to be comfortable with the idea of her having a go at my veins with sharp objects.

Though I've tasted my girlfriend's blood a few times, this was my first experience as a donor, what some call a *blood doll.* Two weeks before, Violet had drawn my blood for the first time, but that had been for an art project I was working on. The only consumption at that point had been what little I licked off my fingers.

Violet had been very concerned about hygiene then. This time was no different—as a licensed phlebotomist and former junkie, he knows firsthand the damage a few germs can inflict. After he'd laid out the supplies, washed up, and put on gloves, Danielle wrapped a black leather belt around my right biceps.

I don't know if my veins were just being elusive or if the flow wasn't strong enough, but unlike the instant success we'd experienced the first night, Violet made two attempts to draw blood from my right arm with no luck.

He switched to my left arm and got lucky on the first try. Since, oddly enough, I have an aversion to needles, I'd been looking away as Violet slid the needle into my flesh. Once it was in place, I watched the syringe fill with 10ccs of my blood.

Throughout all of this, Danielle sat on the floor beside Violet, elbows on the couch, chin in her hands, watching the process like a hungry child watching her mother frost a cake.

No sooner had Violet removed the needle from my vein than Danielle grabbed it out of his hand. She opened her mouth slightly, slid the needle between her teeth, and—head tipped back—slowly depressed the plunger.

It wasn't until the syringe was nearly empty that a bit of blood trickled out of the corner of her mouth. I wanted so badly to lean forward and run my tongue over the crimson drop making its way toward her chin, but I was worried about overstepping boundaries—just because Danielle was

"Plasma" by Kimberlee Traub

drinking my blood didn't mean she wanted to make out with me– so I sat quietly and watched her wipe away the blood with a piece of gauze. (Sherilyn later pointed out that Danielle more than likely would have granted my request if only I'd asked. Next time!)

On a whim, I asked Danielle if Sherilyn could take a picture of her biting my neck. I expected her to simply lean over me. Instead, she sat down beside me on the couch and told me to lie across her lap. My heart sped up as I stretched out, head tipped back, throat exposed.

Danielle bit down over my windpipe, which was a bit uncomfortable and not as arousing as the bite she'd given me earlier, but I was somewhat grateful for that. When Danielle lifted her head, Sherilyn gasped. In the middle of my throat was a large, hollow hickey glistening with Danielle's blood-tinted saliva.

I've always wanted to incorporate blood play into my sex life, but in the few opportunities I've had, the amount of blood involved has been very meager compared with what was drawn from me that night.

Seeing Danielle so excited about the prospect of drinking my blood, then her teeth and lips covered in it, definitely turned me on, albeit in a somewhat frustrating way because she was a platonic friend.

The bite mark faded with surprising quickness, but a few physical reminders stuck around a bit longer: a tiny bruise on my left arm and two small puncture wounds in the crook of my right arm that almost looked like a vampire's bite.

In a way, that's exactly what they were.

The Black Mass

by Gravity Goldberg

On the eve of Halloween, I attended a Black Mass in Oakland, California. I had been invited by a man I was sleeping with who was trying to pry me away from my boyfriend. The Mass took place at a house where he was living with about ten other people in a warren of tiny rooms. In the back of the house, adjacent to the kitchen, were two rooms they used as a temple. The house had once belonged to the local chapter of the OTO and, although the Gnostic Mass was now held elsewhere, the temple was still up and running.

I arrived at nine P.M. I've never been afraid of new experiences; sometimes I think it's as much because I'm too naïve to fully consider the potential dangers as wanting to add adventure to my life résumé. As I waited in the antechamber/kitchen, I had doubts. I was a longtime vegetarian. What if animal sacrifice was part of the ritual? What if I was asked to participate in an orgy? Among the jars of grains and legumes on the kitchen shelves lurked bottles of strange unguents, sealed with red wax and labeled with alchemical symbols. The walls of the kitchen were covered with equal parts anarchist posters and colorful occult paintings. People continued to file in as I found a chair near the table and chain-smoked. My lover was nowhere to be found.

At 9:30, a "bishop" emerged from the velvet curtain draped across the temple's entrance. Holding up an inverted crucifix, he instructed us to remove our shoes before filing through the door. He told us to acknowledge the crucifix in some manner. Many chose to spit on it, then erupted in scandalized giggling.

The temple was plush and inviting. Candles and strings of holiday lights illuminated the room. Cushions covered the floor. On the walls hung beautiful paintings of Egyptian deities. Tapestries hid the windows so no one could look in or out. We'd been transported to some ancient sultan's tent.

In the center of the room stood a long table holding what

looked like a woman's body. Fabric draped over her revealed her curves. Her hair spilled out from underneath.

As we settled onto the floor, libations of the four elements passed around constantly. The sweet smells of opium and hydroponic weed mingled with willowy incense. Smoke choked the room. Congregants used one another as cushions. There was enough kissing and fondling that my fears of an orgy seemed grounded. Finally, a round of hushing silenced the last of the nervous and excited whispers.

A man appeared, hunched over and limping like a mad scientist's Igor. He delivered a preamble in a falsetto, rolling his eyes and sneering. Spittle came out of his mouth as he performed a banishing ritual. When he finished, the High Priest appeared.

He wore a black ceremonial robe, hands hidden by long sleeves and his face almost entirely obscured by a droopy cowl. After his solemn and commanding entrance, he removed his hood and lit a black penis-shaped candle. He pulled a book from his robes and used the candle to illuminate the pages as he read a passage from the Catholic Mass backward phonetically. It sounded like the ominous gibberish of a record played in the wrong direction. Apparently, this is a requisite of any Black Mass. The audience was encouraged to respond with the word *nema* (amen backward). Many also punched the air with a fist, pinkies and pointers unfurled—the well-known gesture of Satan's horns—while screaming, "Hail, Satan! Hail, Satan!"

The priest dramatically ripped off the cloth to uncover the naked woman. Igor limped out from the shadows and took the cloth away, then lit candles surrounding her body. The Priest held up a goblet and blessed the ceremonial wine. Next he held up a home-baked host and blessed (or cursed) that as well, before slowly walking around the room. He returned to the woman, leaned over, and inserted the host into her vagina.

He gestured that the audience should rise. We shuffled around in a counterclockwise circle. When we reached the Priest, we sipped the sacramental wine and then turned toward the rest of the congregation to yell "Hail, Satan!" or "There is no part of me that is not . . ." or whatever else struck our fancies.

We stumbled, laughing, back to our seats. My lover finally snuggled up to me on the floor cushions. He offered me a sip of some crazy intoxicant that smelled like burning broomsticks but made me feel delicious.

After we were all seated, the Priestess arose from the altar. She had a cherubic face and small white teeth like a Victorian doll. Her smile was lascivious and her body voluptuous. She donned a matching black robe and picked up an ancient-looking book. (At least, the outside was ancient. I spied Xeroxed pages within.) She read from *Al-Jiwah* (*The Revelation*), the most sacred book of the Yezidis, who were ancient Satanists. The Priestess read Shaitan's promise to those who follow him: "I was, am now, and shall have no end. I exercise dominion over all creatures and over all the affairs of all who are under the protection of my image. I am ever present to help all who trust in me and call upon me in time of need. There is no place in the universe that knows not my presence. I participate in all the affairs which those who are without call evil because their nature is not such that they approve." I obtained a copy of this text after the Mass. The entire text consists of five chapters. The rest continues in a similar manner.

After the Priestess finished reading, the Mass concluded. Her robe fell off her shoulder so that white flesh peeked out.

The Black Mass was different from what I expected. I didn't feel that my immortal soul was in danger afterward. It was more like a production by the Living Theatre than a church ceremony, although it did somehow convey sacredness; it wasn't serious, but it *meant* something. People had fun. The Igor performed goofy pantomimes of church acts whenever the mood threatened to get somber, cracking us up. Libations passed constantly and everyone participated heartily. (Thus I don't remember as much of the Mass as I wish I did.) The couple seated to my left kissed and fondled each other without a care in the world. As far as I know, neither Satan nor Shaitan made an appearance during the evening, although he may have come in disguise.

Apparently the Black Mass is

Illustration by Timothy Renner

not about invoking Satan. It has always been more of a parody of religious services, particularly the Mass of the Roman Catholic Church. In *The Satanic Bible,* Anton LaVey writes: "A Black Mass is not the magical ceremony practiced by Satanists. The Satanists would only employ the use of a Black Mass as a form of psychodrama."

The infamous mid-eighteenth-century Hell-Fire Club, to which Benjamin Franklin belonged, celebrated the Black Mass as part of their secret rites, invoking Satan as a symbol rather than as an actual deity. In his book on the subject, Daniel P. Mannix writes: "There are two theories behind Satanism. In view of all the evil there is in the world, Satan is really God and should be worshipped as such, since no merciful God would permit wars, disease, famines, floods, earthquakes, and all the miseries around us. The other theory is that Satan is the natural leader of all the rebels who rise against the injustices of king, church, and society. Satan is a heroic figure who refuses to be pushed around." Certainly America's forefathers, rebelling against England and all that it represented, would have embraced this later theory. The irreverent tone taken by the participants in the Mass I attended clearly belonged to this iconoclastic tradition.

Curious to know how closely the event I attended was to the traditional service, I did some follow-up research. Mannix claimed that little is known about the décor of the secret Black Masses, but he speculates that "the chapel was draped in black and there were missals on exhibition containing obscene parodies of the scriptures." These details sound similar to the one I attended, but then he continues with more lurid descriptions that I am relieved did not happen: "The Mass was celebrated on the body of a naked woman laid out on the altar and the congregation drank the sacrificial wine from her navel. The crucifix was inverted and black candles were burned. Lamps of lewd design were used. (One in the shape of a monster bat with an erect penis is still preserved in the Witchcraft Museum on the Isle of Man.)" Mannix muses on the variety of poisonous and intoxicating herbs burned in place of traditional incense and on various other debaucheries found within the temple. LaVey, who most likely had a personal encounter with a Black Mass or two, reported on the earliest Black Masses. (He claims the first took place in 1666.) His descriptions mirror what most think of when they conjure up a terrifying image of the Black Mass: "A defrocked Priest stands before an altar consisting of a nude woman, her legs spread-eagled and vagina thrust open, each of her outstretched fists grasping a candle made from the fat of unbaptized babies, and a chalice containing the urine of a prostitute (or blood) reposing on her belly."

After the ceremony I attended, we were all in an ecstatic mood. The revelries continued in another room of the house. If the chance ever came again, I'm sure I would jump at attending another Black Mass, just as long as I didn't have to be the woman on the altar.

The Pain of Art

vs.

the Art of Pain

by Christopher R. Bales

Rusty nails, blades, saws, broken glass, live bullets, power tools, glass-etching acid, industrial epoxy, mold, mildew, and layer upon layer of dust: these aren't the remnants of a medical waste facility or an abandoned munitions factory. They coexist with me in my one-room apartment, where I eat, sleep, and create my assemblage sculptures. This type of art involves compiling found objects (medicine cabinets, old frames, antique photos, miscellaneous bric-a-brac) into a cohesive visual statement in search of the truth buried in the dark corners of my subconscious. Because this line of work requires such a tremendous mass of "stuff," it forces me into this crowded and somewhat hazardous environment.

My first mishap occurred with an early sculpture, a five-foot-wide twelve-foot-long triptych. I began work by sawing a twelve-inch hole in the front section in preparation for an inset piece. Holding the heavy object in place with my left hand, I attempted to drill four pilot holes from the opposite side of the wood panel. Given the sculpture's top-heavy bulk, I found myself off balance as I pushed the button of the power drill and found my mark. I hit the concrete floor on top of the sculpture, my left arm lodged beneath it all through the front hole of the panel, the power drill spinning inches from my right ear. Each shift of my weight produced new levels of pain as I attempted to free my trapped forearm while carefully relaxing my finger off the button of the drill.

There was a nervous knock at the door of my studio, located at that time in the lower room of my parents' house. "Honey, are you okay in there?" my mother asked tentatively.

Thoroughly humiliated and not wanting to panic her into a 911 call, I squeaked, "I'm okay."

Following this incident I decided: I will make no sculpture larger than my own body.

Cyanoacrylate is a fast-drying glue, strong and crystal clear. It's also one of the only glues that clearly states on the bottle: "Bonds skin in seconds." Although I have managed to weld my fingers together on occasion, it's not as dramatic as it sounds. There is an activator used in conjunction with the glue for those impatient types who feel sixteen seconds just isn't fast enough. I first used the activator with a thin piece of etched plastic I was planning to set to the base of a sculpture. What happened when the activator made contact with the cyanoacrylate was an unwelcome revelation. The chemical reaction sent vapor into my face, causing temporary blindness. The thick layer of glue and activator instantly fused my hand to the small sculpture with the burning sensation of hot solder. I wobbled up blindly from my chair, the small sculpture still adhered to my palm. I had no choice but to wait for the blistering adhesive to cure before I could rescue myself. I take great pride that, despite my personal pain and injury, the sculpture was unscathed.

• • •

X-Acto knives: courier of torment for artists, craftsmen, and hobbyists around the world. The slightest distraction while performing a cut can produce devastating results. While cutting through a stubborn piece of chipboard, a miscalculation sent me to the emergency room with a small slice from my left index finger carefully placed inside a bag of ice. I had no insurance. When the nurse described the staggering price of seeing a doctor right away, I decided to visit the local pharmacy for a wad of gauze and some surgical tape. I resolved that it wasn't too horrific, living with a finger that was somewhat flat on one side. Even so, it was more than a year before I was able to play guitar without stinging pain in my fingertip.

The application of epoxy glue often involves unusual tools. On occasion, I find fourteen-inch wooden skewers the device of choice. I was holding two sticks between my fingers like long cigarettes. One applied a dollop of glue behind the objects being set into place; the other smoothed the glue evenly around the edges. It was a hot August day and I had been working for hours. I inadvertently dropped one of the objects through my sweaty fingers. Absently, I stooped to pick it up. It was a sharp, focused sting as the epoxy-laden skewer stabbed deep into my nasal cavity. Although the pain was intense, I had the sense to carefully withdraw the stick in hopes of leaving behind as little glue as possible. I closed one nostril while blowing gently out the other. Blood oozed down my lip, but a ball of cold epoxy blocked most of the air. Fortunately it was water-based epoxy, with a cure time of twelve hours. I got a cup of warm water from the bathroom. Lying on my back over the edge of the bed, I filled the contaminated nostril. Eventually the epoxy softened enough for me to blow it out in a couple of quick discharges, filling the bathroom sink with blood mixed evenly with gray epoxy.

I've saved the best story to tell last: a brainless, life-threatening bit of ignorance. I often use bullets in my sculptures, some shiny and new, some dating back to WWI. I was working on one of those whiny "I hate war" sculptures, cheerfully mounting a series of small bullets across the top edge of a wooden box. Things were going well, with the exception of one minor annoyance. The small flange at the base of the .22 caliber bullets was making it difficult to set the bullets cleanly. I tried filing the edges, but that took too long. I decided to use a strong pair of wire clippers. The first snip went well: clean and even. The second was even better, already halfway there. On the third snip, I realized the danger of working with live ammo and exactly what "rim-fire bullet" meant. A pop like a large firecracker sent my ears into high-pitched ringing. Blood covered my numb fingers. My first question was: "Am I shot?" Ears still muffled, I stumbled out of the room frantically patting my body in search of bullet holes. As my panic subsided, I concluded I would live another

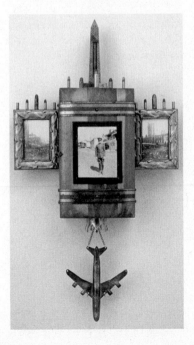

"Missing in Action" assemblage
by Christopher R. Bales

day. Heart still pounding, I went back to search the workroom. I found a benign cylinder of lead in the corner and the blackened bullet shell under the chair. All I could think of was how fortunate it was I hadn't been staring into the bullet on that fateful third snip.

Did I continue with my work after this? All I can say is that we (doctors, lawyers, teachers, auto mechanics) all have certain passions. Whether it's a crippling malpractice suit, a dangerously disgruntled client, a troubled student packing a gun, or a power tool gone mad, we all face dangers doing the things we care about. So I trudge on, inhaling dust and toxic vapors, going through box after box of bandages, gluing parts of my body together that were never meant to be—all for the love of something that has become so much a part of my life that even a speeding bullet can't stop me—at least not as yet.

Only eight lives left.

Be Careful
What You Ask For . . .

by Vance Yount

As I stood on the porch, I watched Orion descend below the redwoods, knowing that the otherworld abductions would slow. Their season was coming to a close. I almost felt as if I were losing a friend for a while, so telepathically I asked, "If you can hear me, I would like to see you tonight."

That was seven P.M.

I crawled back into bed to continue the book I was reading. Out of boredom, I decided to go to sleep. My friend, who had been upstairs, left to pick up his wife from work. I thought it odd that he didn't say good-bye, since he'd done so every night for the past few months while I'd stayed with them. I decided to get a glass of water before trying to go to sleep. I glanced at the clock: 10:50 P.M.

Back in bed, I lay there, slowly falling into relaxation, but definitely not asleep. For some reason, I opened my eyes and looked out the window near the foot of the bed. I saw a tiny red light far off in the distance, where small planes usually go by, but a bit off-course. The red light wasn't blinking. Excited, I jumped out of bed to go outside for a better look.

Once outside, I found the tiny red light again. It was still not blinking and most definitely off the usual course for planes. I wondered: *Could this be a UFO?* With the tiny light so far in the distance, I did not want to come to a complete conclusion. I would just allow my mind to be open.

It disappeared from my vision, blocked by the treetops. I was so terribly excited that I danced around on the porch. I needed a cigarette *immediately*. So I ran inside, found the package of cigarettes and my trusty lighter, and danced outside to smoke. I felt tremendously elated. I could have possibly witnessed my second UFO. My heart beat out of my chest, filling me with adrenaline, both out of excitement and a bit of nervousness.

I had the distinct sound of a swarm of bees in my head. At least, I thought it was in my head, because the sound was extremely dull and low. It sounded familiar to me, but where had I heard it before? Then I realized that the sound grew louder, though still dull. It came from my left.

I turned, almost as if this were normal. Thirty-five feet above the trees, something very surreal approached. The small disk looked far too much like the UFOs found in comic books and cartoons. It had three large round lights evenly spaced around it, two red and one blue, although the colors were not stationary in their placement. On the front of the disk was a large rectangular headlight shining an intense white light, lighting its path in the air. On the underside were four rounded-corner rectangular cut-outs, like frosted glass with a hazy white light behind them.

I had the distinct impression that there were two beings present in the disk. Before my eyes, the disk transformed into a spherical shape. My heart clogged my throat. I became very aware of the intense chill in my bones. My brain tried to be more rational than it had ever proven to be in the past and tried to make the

ship into a helicopter, without the presence of a propeller or a tail.

It was very clear to me what I saw. I watched the small ship pass above the house and slowly over the trees, out of my line of sight. The humming sound didn't go away. The craft seemed to be hovering where I could not see it, perhaps over the trees about fifty feet or so away from the house.

I paced around, very excited, but anxiety gained momentum. I smoked again. I went inside and wanted to call someone to tell them what had just happened, but decided that it was too late and my excitement might not drag them to the phone anyway. I tried to calm myself down enough to write about what I had just seen. I grabbed my journal and sat on a cushion in front of the fire, all the while poking my head outside about every thirty seconds to see if the ship would return. Could I still hear the humming or was it echoing in my head? I pulled out my pen. Warmth went through my body, quickly, ever so soothing. I wrote only one sentence, but my vision was rather foggy and I had no comprehension of the words on my paper. Instantly exhausted, I needed to go to bed at once.

Feeling warm and almost drugged, I thought, *They heard me.* I drifted into the introductory levels of sleep. I heard a two-legged, flat-footed something running up the wet driveway. I thought it odd that a child would be barefoot on such a cold night. Then it hit me that the closest child lived quite a bit away. My brain, in its new mode of rationalization, tried to think what animal would be about three feet tall—as I imagined this thing to be from the sound of its footfalls—and also flat-footed and running curiously up to my window. Strange, I couldn't think of even one.

I sprang out of bed to get the light switch. My heart, once again beating ferociously, nestled in my throat. The feeling of warmth was gone; cold had settled into my bones. I left my room quickly and grabbed my cigarettes in the living room but, if I went outside to smoke, whatever I heard would be out there as well. I paced around, trying to calm myself down. I noticed that everything in the house looked very crisp and surreal. The masks on the wall seemed to have personalities, as did everything else. Everything in the living room seemed alive. I felt like I'd walked in on a private conversation. The reflection in the windows seemed to be not a reflection at all, but an entirely alternate dimension looking in on mine. For some reason, none of this seemed out of the ordinary.

I was disappointed: How could I be so afraid of something that I have wanted for so long, something that I held so dear? I decided to be brave and face the fear and go outside. Besides, I was desperate to smoke.

I poked my head out the door. In my head, I heard, *Hello. Welcome, Vance.*

To which I replied meekly in my head, *Hello.*

This had to be a product of wishes and imagination. I lit my cigarette and dragged roughly on it.

Standing there, I noticed that everything outside had an intensely surreal look to it, too. Everything looked very crisp and more alive than I had ever noticed. I could feel the life of the trees that had given their wood to make the deck. I felt vibrations from all around—from the house, the trees, the grass, everything. I sensed this was not the same porch I had walked out onto before.

I had the impression I was not alone. As I turned my head slowly to the left, "he" spoke in a telepathic and booming acoustic language that sounded almost mechanical. It was the loudest sound I've ever heard. Veiling this being from my eyes was a triple-tiered pyramid outlined in a frosty blue-white light.

I was horrified because I instinctively understood this multifaceted language. He spoke with emotions, those of love and understanding, yet also of sadness because I was so afraid. The cigarette dropped from my lips as I threw the pack of cigarettes and my lighter in his direction, as if trying to hold him off. I threw myself back toward the door. I was screaming, "No, no, no, no, no."

I shot inside, slamming the glass door so hard it should have broken. I started running in circles, screaming the most absolutely horrified primal sounds.

They can't do this, I thought. *I thought I was ready, but I'm not.*

I was so afraid I hoped my accelerating heart would explode and kill me. I begged and pleaded for him to go away, to let me be because I could not handle this. The experience was much more than I had expected. I just wanted to at least lose consciousness to escape this unbelievable event, but I did not. I felt like a very small insect in a jar, watching the child to see if he was going to pick up the jar and shake me. But he didn't.

Maybe I was being shown

that what I thought I could handle, I wasn't ready for—but that next time might be easier.

I have no conscious memory of the being, but certain things trigger an image in my head, as well as fear. I'm sure I saw the being, because it was impossible to even look at any of the four cats in the house for the next few days. Their eyes tried to reveal a subconscious memory that I had put there for a very good reason.

I'm not sure if I went into shock that night, but if not, I had been extremely close. My heart pounded for more than an hour and I was freezing cold and petrified. I was also riddled with guilt for not being able to function at a moment that I had wanted my entire life and which turned out to be the most terrifying moment of my existence. I know there is no backing away from my relationship with them any longer. I asked for the knowledge that their presence is real. Now I have to accept it.

The Bomoh

by A. M. Muffaz

My uncle blushed. Youngest Uncle is very pale and very tall and blushing makes him look cute. Uncle had flown in from Kota Kinabalu for the weekend. His visit wasn't a social call. Youngest Uncle was here because Mom ordered him to come.

Mom's cell phone rang. She was using Dad's cell, the one with the snake charmer's song as a ringtone.

"Hello?" Mom yelled into the phone like we were stuck in traffic. Really, we were the only ones in the restaurant. "Yeah, yeah. We'll be there soon. Okay. Give us five minutes." Mom snapped the cell shut and looked at me. "Hurry up, Myra. They're here."

I stuffed more noodles into my mouth. The sauce was still blistering hot at the center of the dish. No amount of pickled chilies would cool it down. I wolfed down the last of the noodles and forced myself to finish my tea. By that time, Mom had already paid the bill. We walked back across the street to our apartment.

Lucky for us, they hadn't arrived yet. Mom did some last-minute sprucing up, Uncle sat down to read the paper, and I put the kettle to boil. The intercom rang a few minutes later. I was sent down to meet our guests. Meeting them always made me nervous, although the skeptic in me would say there was nothing to be afraid of. Still, Tok was supposed to have the skills to detect evil; evil was always afraid of good. My constant failures at *good* must have been the reason she made me feel jumpy.

I met them at the guardhouse. Auntie Em, the woman who usually accompanied Tok and served as translator for the bomoh's Kelantanese dialect, greeted me with a hug.

"How are you, Myra? Are you okay?" Auntie asked. Her gold chains glittered madly in the sun, burning low when we reached the shade.

"I'm fine, Auntie." It was the politest thing to say. Auntie is what we call any older woman and Auntie Em would probably be insulted if I upped her rep to Granny.

Tok shuffled slowly behind

her. Both women were round and jovial. Tok was only about my mom's age, but she looked older, with tired wrinkles around her eyes. She was wrapped conservatively in her scarf and *baju kurung*. The full, two-piece dress hung loosely over Tok's bulk. Like Auntie, she accessorized heavily in gold.

"Ah, this female child is pretty." Tok reached out to touch my face. She always greeted me that way. I bowed my head, embarrassed by her compliment. That's when I noticed the thick strands of crystal wound around Auntie's wrist. Large squares of citrines, sapphires, and rubies sparkled against her dark skin.

"Auntie"—I peered at her hand—"they look so pretty."

"Ah, if you want bracelets like Auntie's, afterward we can see them. I brought some jewelry from Myanmar." Auntie held up her handbag.

I led them to the elevator. Within its four walls, I felt distinctly more choked. It was a blessing I only lived five floors up.

Mom was ecstatic to see them, coming to the door with open arms. Youngest Uncle, as the stranger in our midst, greeted them with care. Tok told us that before she was called to see us, strong winds picked up around her house. She was meant to help us.

Auntie got straight to the point, nodding toward Uncle and whispering to Mom, "How is he?"

Mom put on her meanest look—that is, her normal face—and spat, "That woman took his ATM card and credit card. Now she refuses to let him see his daughter, so he's forced to go back to her."

"Eh, don't. He must not go back to her. She's using his daughter as bait." Auntie wrung her hands in front of her face. "Maybe Tok can find a way to bring the daughter back."

"Yeah, we were thinking that way, too. You know, Em, that woman made my mother suffer *so* much. When my mother was dying, she told my brother to leave the woman. That was her last wish for him. A mother's wish is the most powerful thing." Mom kept a sober face. "My father also prays that Tok can help my brother. Once he's cleaned spiritually and everything is finished, at least we'll know he'll go back to Sabah with a clear mind. After that, everything is up to him. There is nothing more we can do."

Auntie glanced at the living room, where Uncle stood in a daze. Tok said nothing. "Okay," Auntie said. "We should start now, get all his problems sorted out first, then we can talk some more, yeah, Nur?"

Mom nodded her approval enthusiastically.

A mat was laid out in the living room, upon which Tok settled her great weight and called Uncle to sit with her. Mom and Auntie followed suit. I sat away from them, behind the sofa in the middle of the floor. The isolation helped my nerves. All became quiet as Tok entered her trance.

A moment later, Tok was no more. In her place was her spirit guide, who saw everything. Her trances weren't scary eyeballs-rolling-back-into-the-head trances. They reminded me of a meditation, like monks in a deeper state of consciousness. With her spirit guide in charge, Tok's presence felt calming.

Tok laid her hands on Uncle's shoulders. She kneaded his flesh, her sausage fingers peculiarly flexible, cathartic beyond their calluses. As she moved her hands from his shoulders to the back of his neck and up across his skull, she swayed, groaning utterances in a *jinni*'s tongue. Uncle gasped at the pain, for Tok's hands are very strong. Mom encouraged him to shout if he felt the urge, while Auntie told him it was okay to cry.

From this spiritual foreplay, Tok began her visioning. It is not required to tell Tok's spirit guide anything about your wants or needs. Indeed, she usually knows what they are. She said,

"This man has problems with his woman."

Mom and Auntie were delighted. "Yes, he does have problems with his woman right now," they exclaimed, almost in unison.

Tok's brow furrowed deep into her nose. She had a real Malay face, with a low nose bridge and little cheekbone. Her nose was shaped like an onion, her eyes were large and black, her lips pronounced. She might not have been pretty in her youth, but she was certainly homely now. Tok resembled the ideal wife of her generation—the same as Mom's—although Tok's environment was the simple life of the village. Her hands pressed into my uncle's skull. Now he really did break a tear. "His woman is a foul woman," Tok said. "She is one of the Bidayuh, the native peoples. She feeds him unclean things and bathes him in unclean things, things I'm embarrassed to name. Is she a Muslim?"

Mom said, "She claims she is Muslim, but we aren't sure. She burns incense and does not pray."

"What kind of Muslim is that? No, she says she is Muslim, but she also prays to other things: statues, like the native tribes. She's a mix of many different tribes. Many different people run in her blood," Tok declared.

Mom leaned forward to whisper to Auntie, "Yeah-lah, that's

right. That woman is a Kadazan. Her face looks just like the Kadazan yokels from the jungle there."

Auntie whispered right back, "Tok is saying this woman worships statues." She raised her voice. "Tok, do you know what kind of religion this woman really has?"

Tok closed her eyes, pinpointing a hidden key in my uncle's head. "I don't know. She prays to statues and stones and trees. This is not Islam. She is not a Muslim."

"Ah, must be a tribal religion somewhere," Mom concluded sagely.

"She is far away. Far away over the sea. Tok can see the water." Tok tapped her fingers against my uncle's spine. "He has been tied in seven places." Tok opened her eyes. "She tied him in seven places so she could control him." Tok then showed us various points on her wrists, arms, and legs. "We must give him a bath and get rid of them quickly."

Mom had prepared for this while I was meeting Tok and Auntie downstairs. She made my uncle strip down and led him to the bathroom wearing a towel. Auntie cut up limes while filling a pail with water. As she sliced, she addressed Mom. "I brought some salt because I knew you wouldn't have enough time to go

and buy salt while you were running around."

Mom took the unprocessed salt from Auntie and poured it into a colander. The limes were thrown into the pail with the water. Tok came to pray over the bathing implements. She praised Allah, thanked Him, and threw the salt at my uncle's back seven times, once for each knot in his body.

We left my uncle so he could wash himself. Tok went back to the mat and called out to me. I went to her unsteadily. She reached for the back of my head, pressing those tough fingers on my collarbone and knocking her knuckles against my skull. I forced my face straight, trying to stop myself from wincing. I guess it showed, because Auntie said, "If you want to yell, just yell. Let all the bad things get out."

No, I didn't need to yell. This was good training, after a fashion. Mom always complained I was too sensitive. Anyway, I liked the pain. It helped me focus. Tok didn't say a word while she massaged me, only told when she was done. She did the same for Mom. Auntie told me in a low voice that it might be that Tok saw something on us but it was too minor to mention. Honestly, the massage gave me a headache. When I told Auntie this, Tok immediately declared that she had accidentally spread Uncle's poison to me when she touched me. Another massage and my head still rang, but I thought it was better I didn't tell them that.

Youngest Uncle came out of the bath. Without his shirt, he had ribs like a xylophone, straining against his skin. When he turned around, we saw red spots on his back. The spots were tiny, like chickenpox in dimension, crimson to bursting. They speckled Uncle's back as we watched, mosquito bites sans mosquitoes.

"Ah, that's the poison coming out of his back now," Mother declared, with the kind of emotion some people have for praising God.

"Yeah, those are the bad things coming out of him," Auntie chirped.

Uncle seemed weak, shuffling toward the mat where Tok awaited him.

"How are you feeling now?" Auntie asked.

"Okay." Uncle managed to crack a smile.

"Are you feeling any better than before you took the bath?" Auntie smiled gleefully as Uncle sat down.

Mom offered her dauntless opinion before he could. "He looks much better now. Don't you think his face looks better, Myra?"

Uncle's complexion did seem

"Lost Wax" by Cybele Collins

191

healthier than before the bath, a little pinker, less pale. Everyone has the right to be flushed after a bath.

"His face is glowing now," exclaimed Mom.

I watched Uncle as he was massaged again. Perhaps his muscles had relaxed. He didn't seem so much in pain now when Tok laid her hands on him.

"She's holding your child." Tok stated this firmly. "She took away your money, and took away . . ." Tok pondered. "Rectangles. She's putting the rectangles in a machine. Tok doesn't know these new, modern things." The bomoh shook her head.

"Ah, those must be the ATM machines-lah." Auntie laughed.

Uncle addressed my mom in Cantonese, using her familial rank: Eldest Sister. "*Tai Ka,* how do I get back my daughter?"

Mom posed this question to Tok in Malay. "Tok, how can he get his daughter back?"

Tok took a deep breath, rubbing into my uncle's shoulders. "That child is raised by her mother. She is under the influence of her mother. He cannot get his daughter back at this time."

"It's probably not a good idea to get his daughter back at this time," supported Auntie. "The courts wouldn't allow it, because his daughter is too young. On top of that, it was so difficult to get

him to get away from his wife's influence. If he goes back to her now, we might not be able to save him again."

"Yes, and his daughter's a whore, just like her mother." Hate returned to Mom's voice, deep hate I could taste as bitter bile. "Do you know, Em, when my mother was sick with cancer, that stupid woman taught her daughter to make fun of my mother? The girl used to stick her tongue out at my poor mother. They didn't even have that kind of courtesy."

I saw the pain in Uncle's eyes, not from Tok's fingers, but from somewhere deep within. He would be too polite to be ungrateful and Mother was his *Tai Ka*. Even so, there were things better left unsaid.

"We must get out the bad things his wife fed him. He must eat clay." Tok turned to Auntie. "Where is the clay?"

"Clay?" Mom exclaimed loudly, laughing.

"Yes, clay." Auntie took out a little plastic bag from her handbag. Inside were three clumps of white earth. "This isn't the clay you see at the construction sites, Nur. This is the clay they use to make pots."

Mom took the clay from Auntie. "Oh, that type of earth. *Aiya,* what is it now? Myra, what kind of earth is that, that white one?"

"Kaolin?" I suggested.

"Ah. Yeah. That." Mom passed the clay to Tok.

"This clay here, if you have been poisoned, this clay can get rid of the poison in your body." Tok spoke to Uncle. "Eat a bit of this clay three times a day. You must finish all of this to get out the poison inside you. If you vomit, this is all right, because the clay is helping you get rid of your poison."

"He should take the first dose now-lah," Auntie told Mom.

Mom turned to me. "Myra, go get some water for your uncle."

I got up from the floor. When I returned with the water, Uncle gagged the chunk of earth down. "Imagine it's *batang buruk,*" I told him. I doubted that a chunk of clay could taste anything like the powdery sweetmeat, even if they looked similar, so I handed over the water as soon as he reached out.

Tok asked Mom, "Do you have any Sunkist?"

"Sunkist? *Aiya,* no-lah. I just juiced the oranges yesterday." Mom frowned. Sunkist was one of the first "branded" oranges to arrive in Malaysia, so older Malaysians tend to call all oranges and things orangey Sunkist.

Tok nodded her head. "He needs to drink Sunkist to make him stronger to resist his wife's doings."

Auntie clapped her hands in surprise. "Nur, do you have any orange juice or syrup?"

"No, but the Korean supermarket downstairs sells it." Mom called on me again. "Myra, here. I'll give you fifty *ringgit.* Go down to the supermarket and buy some orange cordial."

Cordial in Malaysia refers to flavored syrup drinks, like Kool-Aid in America. "What if they don't have Sunkist?" I asked.

"Must it be Sunkist?" Mom chirped.

Auntie grinned. "No, no. Any brand will do, so long as it's orange."

"Get two big bottles of water too," added Tok.

So I was sent to wander outside on my own. At the supermarket, I scanned the shelves for orange-flavored cordial. It seemed they only carried one brand of cordial in an orange flavor and it certainly wasn't Sunkist. I took a couple of one-liter bottles of mineral water to the checkout counter, too. On the way there, I saw some large cartons of Sunkist Orange Juice in the chiller. Did Uncle's ghosties take freshly squeezed citrus, or would they prefer cordial? Since I was already at the checkout counter, I stuck with the cordial.

By the time I lugged the bottles home, Tok was blessing our last bag of black peppercorns. Mom bought those peppercorns in Vietnam; the pepper ground from that stuff was lovely. Now I'd never get to grind it on my eggs again.

"There," said Tok, taking her hands off the bag. "You must grind this pepper and mix it with rough salt. Then you must sprinkle this around your house. This will fight your wife's spells."

"If you pass by her house," Auntie added, "you must throw a little bit of this at her door. So you will fight her magic with the salt. When she steps on the salt, she will feel the pain. Like this, *prap prap prap prap prap*." Auntie squeezed her fingertips together, like she was picking up rice, and jerked her hands up and down, making firecracker noises.

We laughed, as Tok blessed the water and the cordial. Finishing her last prayer, she told Uncle, "Take this water and this cordial once a day. When you are running out of water, add some more into the bottles. The cordial will protect you from harm."

Auntie asked, "Does anyone else have a problem they'd like Tok to see?"

Nobody did, so Tok massaged her own feet and shoulders with Auntie's help, to get out the poison she'd absorbed from Uncle. She closed her eyes. Upon reopening them, her spirit guide had left her. She said to me once more, "This girl child is pretty."

Behind my back, I heard Mom explain in Cantonese to Uncle that Tok doesn't know what her spirit guide says to people, that if you asked her what she said during her trance, she wouldn't be able to tell you. Auntie took out another bag from her apparently bottomless handbag and laid its contents on the floor. I watched gold and semiprecious stones appear in filigree piles. The same rubies, sapphires, amethysts, and citrines I saw on Auntie's wrist glittered gaily against the raffia mat.

"Nah, Myra, this is the jewelry I was telling you about," explained Auntie, as Mom served tea and cakes.

I poked into the pile of jewelry. There were chunky rings, dangly necklaces and earrings, three or four bracelets. Almost immediately, I found a linked gold and ruby bracelet I liked. "This is pretty."

"It looks beautiful on you," said Tok. "Put it on."

I did. I found an anklet and cute necklace to match it, too. By the time the encouragement grew to teatime chatter and most of the tea was downed, Mom was convinced to purchase these items for me. Auntie Em gave us a fair price for three, not inclusive of the token Mom gave Tok. An honest bomoh only made so much from consultations and it was the least we could do. Uncle sat away from us, quietly reading the paper. He still seemed wary of Tok, but none the worse for wear.

Weeks later, I found out that he did eventually leave his wife, moving out of their house upon his return to Sabah. He never regained custody of his daughter.

I was never able to ask him how he felt about that. It seemed no one else in the family cared either way. Mom was only glad she'd fulfilled her duty as the eldest sibling. There were things, I guess, that no amount of magic could foresee.

PRACTICAL SUPERSTITION

by A. M. Muffaz

Malaysians are largely a superstitious lot. My country is still a place where people consult numerologists before purchasing lottery tickets, where auspicious license plate numbers are auctioned off at a premium, and where romance—and its fallouts—can be caused by witchcraft.

Magic as a reason for anything carries more weight in some parts of the country than others. The northern states of Peninsular Malaysia, like Kelantan, are the spiritual equivalent of the American Deep South. The people are prouder there, their ties to their ethnic heritage stronger, their love for their religion—predominantly conservative Islam—greater. And yet, this is the place one is likely to find the most powerful bomohs and their most ardent believers.

Malaysian magic reflects my country's greatly multiracial heritage as much as it does the different races' mistrust of one another. *Bomoh* is a Malay word that means shaman. Each major ethnic group in my country, whether Malay, Chinese, or Indian, possesses their own form of bomohs, with magical systems based on their individual ethnic and religious traditions.

As told in "The Bomoh," my uncle—an ethnic Chinese—married a Malay lady. My Chinese relatives came to the conclusion that he was under his wife's spell, which was why he could not let her go even after they'd separated. However, because his wife was Malay, they decided they needed a Malay bomoh to dispel her magic.

Interracial exchanges of magic don't only meet in times of war. The numerologists I mentioned above could be Indian and their clients Chinese; the auspicious license plate numbers could've been bought by Malay practitioners of Feng Shui.

My reason for telling this story was to share some of this land I come from, which often seems to have advanced into modernity too quickly for its people to keep up. We have a long way to go. Until then, our stories need to be told.

◇

Medical Adventures:
Morbid Medicine

◇

Illustration by Erik Quarry

Killing Max

by JD

At 8:30 P.M., the phone call I'd been awaiting arrived. I was not ready for it since I was, quite frankly, as stoned as I could get. At the other end of the line, J told me, "Max has said some things that make me think this is the night. D (Max's lover) is out to dinner and will be back here around ten P.M. Why don't you come by at the same time?"

I started some tea and took a bath, where I had a bit of a cry. Then, after steeling myself for the evening ahead, I went over to Max's place. Max was lying in bed in the same spot where he'd been earlier, drugged to near-unconsciousness. D was there, as was J. In a few minutes, G came down from the apartment upstairs. The cast was now gathered.

J explained that Max had been coherent earlier and had requested that we help him end his life this evening. We all knew that he wanted to do this, but weren't ready for it at this point. We wanted him to confirm his desire to everyone in the group independently. G and I went in to speak with him first.

It is hard to explain the pain I felt in seeing my best friend in this state. Though he used to weigh one hundred sixty pounds, he now weighed about seventy. AIDS had eaten him away. He was thirty-three years old, but looked like an old man. A *dying* old man.

Max realized who we were and quietly greeted us. We asked him whether he really wanted to do this. He agreed that this was what he wanted. We asked to see if he really understood what we were discussing. He agreed again. Finally, we explained that we would give him some pills that would make him sleep and not wake up. Did he want that? Max said that he did.

The only drugs that Max was still taking at this time were his painkillers. The heart drugs had been stopped several days earlier. The antibiotics and the anti-fungals had been stopped several days before that. D, Max, and the doctors had agreed that taking these drugs was rather pointless. Max was going to die within the next few weeks, whether or not he decided to take control.

His doctor had prescribed two different barbiturates. In addition, we had morphine and Dilaudid, a synthetic heroin.

We started to look through the only reference book on the topic, *Final Exit*. Though we did not have a lethal dosage of any of these drugs, we had three-quarters of a lethal dosage of a number of them. We decided that by giving a mix of all the barbiturates, with some help from Dilaudid and the morphine, we probably had what we needed.

One of the things that *Final Exit* has to say is how you should administer these drugs. The suggestion is that you take something to calm the stomach, then take half of the drugs. The other half should be mixed in pudding or some such thing. While D went in to spend some time with Max and give him some drugs to calm his stomach, J and I went into the Castro to buy applesauce.

On the walk to the Castro, J and I made small talk to keep our spirits up. As we were paying for our applesauce, the people behind us put applesauce and milk on the counter. J and I started to giggle uncontrollably. This was just too much. Was it Suicide Night, or what?

We headed further into the Castro to buy J some food, since he had not had dinner yet. I put the applesauce in my pocket. J asked, "What does applesauce, left signal?"

"Euthanasia, top," I replied. Again, we giggled a great deal.

Given our state of mind, Castro Street on a Friday night around eleven P.M. was a rather strange place to be. I felt like I was wearing funeral clothes to a Grateful Dead concert. Everyone was wandering around looking happy, looking for sex, and looking for fun. It did not jibe with our feelings.

When we got back, we found out that D had had a touching conversation with Max and that they had gotten to say good-bye. Max asked his lover if D had any messages for anyone. D told Max to say "bye" to D's mother, who'd been dead for a long time. Max clearly knew what was happening.

The preparations began. First, we put all the hard pills in a shot glass. Then we broke up the capsules and mixed them into a spoonful of applesauce. There was a bit of discussion about what to do with the rest of the applesauce. J insisted that it was bad juju to do anything other than dispose of it. No one argued.

Finally, the time came. D did not want to be the one to administer the drugs, so G waited with him in the back of the house.

J and I went to Max's room

to find our first problem awaiting us. Max was asleep—out like a man who is pumped full of morphine. We succeeded in waking him enough that we knew he understood what was happening and could cooperate. After I fed him each small handful of pills, J gave him sips of water. I will never forget the feeling of Max weakly nuzzling the pills out of my hand. Before we were even halfway through, Max tried to lie back down. We told him that we were not done. He propped himself up in a better position and we gave him all the rest of the pills in one mouthful. I then took over water responsibilities as J fed Max the applesauce. We then had him wash down the applesauce. With a final hit of the morphine pump, I said, "Good-bye, Max. I love you."

J and I left the room. We told D that he should go lie down with Max.

As this happened, R and C, G's lovers, walked into the house from the apartment upstairs. J and I promptly—perhaps discourteously—chased them from the house. G, J, and I had a hug.

We moved to the sitting room in the front of the house. The three of us sat and talked while D held Max in his arms in the next room. We talked quietly at first, but eventually moved on to any number of other topics, getting more and more boisterous.

After an hour and a half, D entered the room. He said that he thought the concept of having Max die in his arms was romantic and all. However, Max was not any closer to dying and D had to get up.

Max was sleeping, someone pointed out, the sleep of the dead. We knew at this point that Max was not going to regain consciousness. As far as Max knew, D's promise held true.

Time continued to pass. We played computer games, watched Max's cartoons on laser disk, scanned the channels, talked. After about three hours, D said, "Why did I have to marry the Ever-Ready Bunny?" This led to some moments of hilarity. For the rest of the evening, whenever someone went to check on Max, he would return clapping his hands like the bunny from the commercials, signaling that the "rabbit" was still marching on.

We discussed how our tasteless humor was appropriate to Max's life, since he had been the originator of much black humor concerning his own condition. I had been trying unsuccessfully to come up with a "Dead Max" joke. Now, with the time upon us, all the bad jokes came pouring out.

At four A.M., we realized that something was not working. Max was still around. His heart was still pounding. Max had not taken his heart medication for two days, which we thought would be sufficient. However, we looked it up in the *Physicians' Desk Reference* and found that it had a biological half-life of two days. It seemed that we were fighting a drug, not Max. We went back to *Final Exit* to see if there was anything we could do.

Our next solution was going to be morphine. Since Max was on a morphine pump, all we had to do was to take the pump off and empty the current bag into Max's veins. With the rest of us in the room, D started to do this. He had completely forgotten his desire not to take part in Max's death. After half the bag, D curled up with Max. G took over the bag. When it was empty, we all left the room, but continued to return to check Max's breathing.

By this time, we were all completely exhausted. Our patience was beginning to wear thin. At 4:45, we were discussing what our next plan was going to be. D said he was going to spend some time with Max. He went into the room. A couple of minutes later, J followed. I suspected what was going on. When I went back to check, J kicked me out of the room.

Then he came running and told me to get the guys upstairs to turn down the stereo, which was "loud enough to wake the dead." I sent G up to do it.

A couple of minutes later, J came out to say that Max was dead. We had a hug.

When G returned from upstairs, he joined the hug, followed by D. I later had my suspicions confirmed that D had blocked Max's nose and mouth and had helped him to stop breathing. It was over shortly before five A.M. We sat in silence, all our humor gone.

I wish this was not a true story.

CALIFORNIA PENAL CODE

Section 187–193—Abridged

187. Murder is the unlawful killing of a human being with malice aforethought.

188. Such malice may be express or implied. It is express when there is manifested a deliberate intention unlawfully to take away the life of a fellow creature. It is implied, when no considerable provocation appears, or when the circumstances attending the killing show an abandoned and malignant heart.

When it is shown that the killing resulted from the intentional doing of an act with express or implied malice as defined above, no other mental state need be shown to establish the mental state of malice aforethought. Neither an awareness of the obligation to act within the general body of laws regulating society nor acting despite such awareness is included within the definition of malice.

189. All murder that is perpetrated by means of a destructive device or explosive, knowing use of ammunition designed primarily to penetrate metal or armor, poison, lying in wait, torture, or by any other kind of willful, deliberate, and premeditated killing, or which is committed in the perpetration of, or attempt to perpetrate, arson, rape, carjacking, robbery, burglary, mayhem, kidnapping, train wrecking, or any murder perpetrated by means of intentionally discharging a firearm from a motor vehicle at another person outside the vehicle with the intent to inflict death, is murder in the first degree. All other kinds of murders are of the second degree.

To prove the killing was "deliberate and premeditated," it shall not be necessary to prove the defendant maturely and meaningfully reflected upon the gravity of his or her act.

189.5. Upon a trial for murder, the commission of the homicide by the defendant being proved, the burden of proving circumstances of mitigation, or that justify or excuse it, devolves upon the defendant, unless the proof on the part of the prosecution tends to show that the crime committed only amounts to manslaughter, or that the defendant was justifiable or excusable.

190. Every person guilty of murder in the first degree shall suffer death, confinement in the state prison for life without the possibility of

parole, or confinement in the state prison for a term of twenty-five years to life.

190.5. In determining the penalty, the trier of fact shall take into account any of the following factors if relevant:

(1) The circumstances of the crime of which the defendant was convicted in the present proceeding and the existence of the prior prison term for murder.

(2) The presence or absence of criminal activity by the defendant that involved the use or attempted use of force or violence or the express or implied threat to use force or violence.

(3) The presence or absence of any prior felony conviction.

(4) Whether or not the offense was committed while the defendant was under the influence of extreme mental or emotional disturbance.

(5) Whether or not the victim was a participant in the defendant's homicidal conduct or consented to the homicidal act.

(6) Whether or not the offense was committed under circumstances that the defendant reasonably believed to be a moral justification or extenuation for his or her conduct.

(7) Whether or not the defendant acted under extreme duress or under the substantial domination of another person.

(8) Whether or not at the time of the offense the ability of the defendant to appreciate the criminality of his or her conduct or to conform his or her conduct to the requirements of law was impaired as a result of mental disease or defect, or the effects of intoxication.

(9) The age of the defendant at the time of the crime.

(10) Whether or not the defendant was an accomplice to the offense and his or her participation in the commission of the offense was relatively minor.

(11) Any other circumstance that extenuates the gravity of the crime even though it is not a legal excuse for the crime.

After having heard and received all the evidence, and after having heard and considered the arguments of counsel, the trier of fact shall consider, take into account, and be guided by the aggravating and mitigating circumstances referred to in this section, and shall impose a sentence of life without the possibility of parole if the trier of fact concludes that the aggravating circumstances outweigh the mitigating circumstances. If the trier of fact determines that the mitigating circumstances outweigh the aggravating circumstances, the trier of fact shall impose a sentence of confinement in the state prison for fifteen years to life.

192. Manslaughter is the unlawful killing of a human being without malice. It is of three kinds:

(a) Voluntary—upon a sudden quarrel or heat of passion.

(b) Involuntary—in the commission of an unlawful act, not amounting to felony; or in the commission of a lawful act that might produce death, in an unlawful manner, or without due caution and circumspection. This subdivision shall not apply to acts committed in the driving of a vehicle.

(c) Vehicular.

193. (a) Voluntary manslaughter is punishable by imprisonment in the state prison for three, six, or eleven years.

(b) Involuntary manslaughter is punishable by imprisonment in the state prison for two, three, or four years.

THE LAST WORD

"A dying person should not have to do it alone."
—The Hemlock Society Credo

"Remember that assistance in suicide, no matter how compassionate and how sincerely requested, remains a crime for now. True, it is rarely prosecuted, mainly because the authorities never hear about it. It is the secret crime of our times.

"The actual helping of the person constitutes the crime by demonstrating intent. Intent is necessary for successful prosecution. So it is preferable if the person wanting deliverance does it alone."
—Derek Humphrey, *Final Exit: The Practicalities of Self-Deliverance and Assisted Suicide for the Dying*

"No decent human being would allow an animal to suffer without putting it out of its misery. It is only to human beings that human beings are so cruel as to allow them to live on in pain, in hopelessness, in living death, without moving a muscle to help them."
—Isaac Asimov, in praising *Final Exit*

Slippery Little Devil

by T. M. Gray

I'm a horror writer, but nothing could prepare me for the real-life horror that occurred when I was thirty-two.

At midnight on March 10, 1995, I went to the emergency room with severe stomach pain. No cause was found, so I was sent home untreated. Five days later, the pain had not subsided. I made an appointment to see my family doctor, who sent me to another hospital the following day for a sonogram.

The sonogram found an unidentifiable mass in my abdomen. I was prepped for surgery at 5:45 P.M. An hour later, I met with the surgeon and the nurse anesthetist. I signed a paper stating that I understood the risks of general anesthesia: rarely, a patient might die, go comatose, or experience strange dreams, etc.

"What's on tap?" I asked, eyeing the needle being poked into my IV.

"Thiopental," the nurse replied. Known as truth serum, thiopental is a barbiturate used to produce sleep during surgery. It causes unconsciousness and loss of feeling throughout the body. Within moments, I became drowsy, gave the doctor a thumbs-up, and closed my eyes.

I had no idea that, during surgery, I'd face a worse horror than I could ever imagine writing about. The first sensation was sound: I heard voices close to me. " . . . trocar," a female voice said. *Trow car? What the hell was that?* I assumed I was dreaming.

" . . . forceps," the same voice said.

Forceps? I had a pretty good idea of what those were. *Okay, so I'm waking up in the recovery room and they're cleaning up their equipment.* I tried to open my eyes. Couldn't. I'd had my tonsils removed in my twenties; I remembered the recovery room. Major grogginess; upset stomach. I expected to come to at any moment. I heard a sound like a water sprayer, the kind a dentist might use.

That's when I felt it. Hard to describe: it was incredibly hot and icy cold at the same time. My guts felt like a freezing, boil-

207

ing pit of burning agony. I realized I wasn't in recovery. I was on the operating table!

I screamed loud and long.

And made no sound at all.

I tried to twist away from the onslaught. Couldn't even wiggle a finger.

Something cold and hard pinched my guts and pulled upward. Screaming inside my head; I was in *so* much pain. I felt straps on my arms. I could even feel the tape securing my eyelids shut. I felt something lodged in my mouth and throat, preventing me from swallowing or taking a decent breath of air.

A reprieve: the forceps released my guts. I thought, *Great, phew, it's finally over!*

This was answered by another brutal flood of white-hot pain exploding in my stomach as the pinching and pulling resumed. This time, I begged for my life: *No! Stop doing this to me. You gotta put me back under. Can't you see I'm awake? Oh God, why won't you stop?!*

Another brief reprieve. When the tugging paused, I felt something slide back inside me— something that felt like it belonged there.

"Slippery little devil," the surgeon muttered, then the pinching/pulling resumed. By that point, my terror was beyond words.

I was no stranger to pain; hey,

I'd had a near miss with kidney failure in my teens, given birth twice by C-section, had a tonsillectomy, and developed dry sockets when my wisdom teeth were extracted. True, all these things hurt, but they couldn't begin to compare with the sheer agony I endured on the operating table that cold March evening.

I knew I was going to die. Something had to give. My mind and body couldn't stand it much longer. The pounding in my head slowed to a dull, intermittent thud. As the voices of the doctor and her team faded out, I felt myself shutting down, retreating to a very cold darkness where I faced the fact that I'd never see my husband and children again. That really pissed me off. My husband had been working—I'd called him from the hospital to let him know what was going on—and he'd promised to come as soon as he could find a replacement at work.

Thing is, he never showed up. We'd been together fifteen years and, aside from work, I could count on the fingers of one hand the times he'd actually been on time for anything. His being late for my surgery came as no surprise, but the lack of closure . . . It was so freaking unfair to die without saying good-bye!

Clinging to life with every ounce of strength I had, I visualized the faces of my children.

More than anything, I wanted them to know how very much I loved them.

I could have given up, sinking into the pain, letting it overtake me. Cardiac arrest might have been swift—but I was moving to the other end of the spectrum. *This must be what it's like to freeze to death,* I thought. *Hurts like crazy at first, then you get exhausted, and, after that, you just don't give a damn anymore.*

Finally, the anesthetist nurse said, "My God, she's awake!" What a fucking relief. Someone finally noticed. The pain slowly faded, then the voices went away.

The next thing I knew, I was waking up in ICU. I'd been in

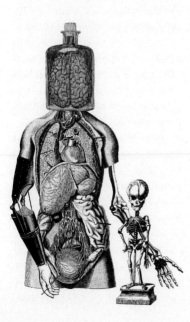

surgery two hours. Bob was there waiting for me. I gave him a shaky smile. "Hi. I gotta pee. Bad."

He slid a bedpan under my ass so I could take a piss. After I relieved myself, he kissed me and I fell asleep.

The next morning, I woke up in a regular hospital room. The surgeon came in to check on me, explaining that I'd had a ruptured ovarian cyst. (This caused the pain that sent me to the emergency room a week earlier.) The fluid from the cyst settled over my appendix, inflaming it. The surgeon said she cleaned the site and removed my appendix.

"You had trouble getting it out," I told her. "You called it 'a slippery little devil' because it kept sliding back in."

Her face went the color of sour cream. "You *never* should have heard that! I'm sending someone in to talk to you." She hurried out of the room.

An hour later, the chief of anesthesiology came in. He assured me, "It's very, very rare for anyone to wake up during surgery. It never should have happened, and I'm very sorry this happened to you."

I think the surgeon and anesthesiologist were more upset than I was. I had no inkling of

Illustration by Mike Hunter

the hell I'd stepped into, assuming the hard part was over. Little did I know it had just begun.

I was discharged on March 18 at 2:30 P.M. Incredibly tired, I spent the next five days on the living room sofa.

The first nightmare came on March 21. I was back on the operating table, wide-awake and paralyzed, trying to move, trying to scream, trying to escape. It happened all over again—and just like before, I was sure I was about to die.

I woke up, drenched in sweat, shaking all over. My heart was pounding way up in my throat. I glanced over at the alarm clock: 1:45 A.M. *Lovely*. I'd been asleep just a little more than two hours.

The next two weeks, I was plagued with recurring nightmares. I dreaded going to sleep. Some nights, I wouldn't go to bed, doing anything to stay awake so I wouldn't have those terrible dreams.

By April 5, I was at my wits' end. Lack of sleep was catching up with me. I called a psychiatric hospital at 4:30 A.M. but the night nurse said they couldn't act immediately unless I was suicidal. She asked me to call back later that morning. Fearing sleep, I didn't want to be alone, so I went to my best friend's house, where I called the psychiatric hospital again. They referred me to a psychiatrist. I called and got

an answering machine, left a message, and hung up.

That's when I suffered a panic attack, the first in a long line of demons that had climbed out of hell with me. My best friend helped me take slow, deep breaths, assuring me that everything was going to be fine. She urged me to call my family doctor.

He prescribed Xanax and secured an appointment for me to see a psychiatrist, the same one I'd tried to call earlier.

Thus I began therapy, combined with medication. Much of it was behavior modification—learning to recognize panic attack triggers: the smell of antiseptics, the sounds of running water, or the snipping of scissors. Watching doctors on TV could set me off. Good-bye, *General Hospital.*

My nightmares became more bizarre. I'd dream about camping: being pulled out of a tent and forced onto an operating table where bears ripped my guts open.

Bob and I tried to resume our sex life, but even that failed. I felt so cold inside, physically and emotionally. Every time I looked in a mirror, I saw a victim who'd been gutted. I feared everyone else could see it, too.

Then I learned that the surgeon and anesthesiologist were saying I hadn't actually woken up on the operating table, that it was all "just a bad dream"—or better yet: that I was "remembering things from the recovery room." (I was never in the recovery room; I'd been taken to ICU.)

Their denial of the hell I went through made recovery more difficult. Something had to be done, and done soon; I didn't know how much more I could take, so I contacted a lawyer who obtained copies of my medical records. The hospital took a very long time to release my anesthesia documents. According to the chart, I was awake for approximately half an hour and had been going into shock. My blood pressure spiked from a normal 120/70 to 140/80 then plunged to 90/40. Records show I was given more thiopental some time after the drop in blood pressure, which gradually returned to normal after that. The surgeon's report indicated, "Appendix was passed out with some difficulty due to its size." *Slippery little devil.*

How could they deny I was awake? All I wanted was for them to cover my psychiatric bills and to help pay for medica-

tion, about $140 per week total. They refused. If they'd agreed, you see, it would have been an admission of guilt. That's why the hospital said I was lying—careers and reputations were at stake. I abandoned the lawsuit when I understood that I could never win. I lacked money and clout. I could only hope I instilled some fear into the hospital—they knew I had woken up—so perhaps they'd do whatever it took to prevent it from ever happening again.

How did things turn out? Well, I faced my demons and went under the knife again. In September 1995, mine was the first hysterectomy conducted while voluntarily awake, thanks to a spinal and a strong dose of Valium. Near the end, I was told they had no choice but to put me under because they had to cut deeper than planned. I agreed to general anesthesia but only after assurance that they'd monitor me very carefully.

I awoke in the recovery room and not a moment before.

ANESTHESIA AWARENESS

by T. M. Gray

Two out of every one thousand surgeries (of 40,000 to 200,000 surgeries per year) result in patients experiencing some degree of anesthesia awareness (waking during surgery).

Prevention/lessening the severity is possible if hospitals:

1. Inform patients *before* surgery that they may wake up and feel mild to severe discomfort during an operation. They already tell us dying is one of the risks of general anesthesia, so the additional information should not be a problem.

2. Use brainwave monitors during surgery, so the medical team can respond *before* patients' adrenal systems have a chance to disrupt their brain chemistry (which is what happened to me and why the nightmares went on so long).

3. To prevent secondary wounding, if a patient recalls pain during surgery, he or she must not be discredited.

4. If a patient shows signs of post-traumatic stress disorder after anesthesia awareness, then the hospital must provide the patient with prompt psychiatric care.

5. Don't assume your doctor knows about anesthesia awareness. Because it's so unpleasant, it remains one of the most heavily guarded secrets of the medical profession.

For more information, see:
www.anesthesiaawareness.com
www.anapsid.org/cnd/drugs/anesthesia2.html
www.anesthesiapatientsafety.com/patients/ss/default.asp
www.aana.com, publishers of *Waking Up During Surgery* by
   Jeanette Liska

DIY Urology

by Geoff Walker

My urine sprayed all over. It spattered the wall to my left, my pant leg, and my blue prison loafer. It did not, thankfully, get on the inmate at the urinal to my right.

Something had to be done to correct this. I simply could not risk pissing off the people I lived with by pissing on them.

I secreted myself in one of the stalls and pointed my pecker up at my face. Yup. The little bit of skin that had formed over the opening of my urethra had gotten bigger, occluding almost half the hole.

This had happened before. Then, the telltale sideways corkscrewing of yellow liquid had gotten to be too much of a mess. It was more than I could compensate for by simply turning the head of my cock this way or that. Piss came out in a six-inch-wide fan. At the same time, it dripped from the tip in big yellow drops. Worse than that, the restricted flow stretched the skin flap to its limit. It hurt.

I'd been considering how to approach my problem, about the best way to rid myself of this pesky nuisance, when the skin broke one day during urination. It just gave way, leaving this ragged flap of flesh at one end of my urethral opening.

That had healed enough, then it healed too much. A month later, I was sitting in the stall with the same problem staring me in the face. I didn't exactly want to wait and hope for it to rip itself free again.

In prison, they didn't do any of what they called "cosmetic" surgery. No quality of life surgeries there. One fella I knew walked around with a distended hernia for several weeks. He showed up for his duties, swept up sand and put it in a truck to be dumped on the ground the next time it snowed. Weeks, this guy carried his gut around with him. I knew they weren't going to do anything for me.

Not to mention the fact that the *moment* I went and reported my little aberration to the cop doctors, my social life would have been over. The population would happily chime in, "You got the AIDS, don't you, faggot." I could just hear it. Who knew where that would have led? There was no way I was going to let anyone know what was going on with my dick.

What if I woke up with it totally closed? My stomach felt uneasy.

I knew what I had to do.

I went back to my cell and broke open a safety razor on the floor with my boot. After carefully extracting the small blade, I borrowed a contraband cigarette lighter from Randy, a middle-aged coke dealer who was getting out soon, to sterilize the blade. Like a good con, he didn't ask what I was up to.

Down the hall, I borrowed some triple antibiotic cream from the Baby-Faced Bandit. Around the corner and back into the bathroom, I waited my turn for a stall. With the door closed behind me, I undid the front of my camo pants.

Sitting on the toilet with my dick in my left hand, I ever so carefully inserted the edge of the blade into my urethra. I sliced upward toward the top of the opening, stopped, and looked at my handiwork. I hadn't cut it at all.

I reinserted the blade and pulled a little harder. It slid right through the skin. At the sight of a drop of blood, I felt just a hint of queasiness, but pushed it down

deep in my gut and smeared some antibiotic cream on the head of my penis.

I sat and breathed for a minute—until someone banged on the door. "What the fuck, yo, get up out that bitch! I got to go!"

I flushed the toilet, buckled my pants, and pushed through the door.

The whole scenario occurred twice more while I was incarcerated. It happened more frequently after I was released. I decided finally to go see a urologist.

He asked how long I'd had this condition. I lied to him, telling him this was the first time. In the Midwest, doctors have a tendency to lock you into your room while you're waiting, if you tell them you were in prison.

He explained that, while it could recur as often as every six months for the rest of my life, it wasn't going to be hard to deal with in the short term. It would require surgery, he said. He told me I'd be put under general anesthesia and that it was a good thing I had insurance, because the whole procedure would cost around $7,000.

The doctor left the room for a moment. I asked one of the residents he'd had in tow if this was something that could be done in the office. More specifically: If and when it recurred, was it the sort of thing that a person could take care of on his own?

He laughed out loud at my question and shook his head. "Oh, no. No way. Impossible." He laughed for a good fifteen seconds, until the doctor opened the door and came back in.

I laughed, too. It was not that long ago that I would have thought it ridiculous to attempt penile surgery on my own. I wouldn't have, had it been under almost any other circumstances.

Luckily, I haven't had to sterilize any more razor blades. The opening is slightly occluded, but I haven't felt the need to do anything about it in some time.

Donating My Body to Science

by Wm. Rage

It was a unique period of my life, to say the least. I needed to make some easy money, so I called up friends who had participated in medical experiments. I asked them a million questions. Two days later, I was in the experimenters' offices, filling out forms and being verbally prepped for what I was to undergo. Somewhat nervous, I showed up at seven in the morning at University of California San Francisco Hospital a week later.

Having spent too much time in hospitals dealing with one ugly situation or another, my view of them was negative. But there I was, willingly submitting myself to some gruesome unknown. The first experiment that I would do involved anesthesia and body temperature. I would spend the better part of six hours under heavy sedation while the doctors did tests. I was apprehensive. My friend who had undergone these same tests said it wasn't anything to really worry about. Still . . .

Once inside the study room in the surgery wing of the hospital, I was put on a table in nothing but my underwear. The doctors moved around me, prepping everything for that day's test. I asked a lot of questions. They answered even more that I didn't ask. It was obvious that they had done this many times before and knew the worries people have when submitting themselves to medical experiments.

As we talked, a nurse inserted an IV needle into my arm and taped it down. Next, she plopped sensor pads all over my chest and on my ticklish feet. She taped more on my back. She clipped an uncomfortable cotton-swathed inner-ear thermometer in place. Soon everything faded to black.

That test was the first of three over a two-week period. Two of the all-day tests had me under anesthesia in full experiment mode. On those days, needles—an inch to an inch-and-a-half long, wired to the machines in the room—were inserted all over my arms and legs while I was knocked out cold. The third was a control day, where they hooked me up and conducted the tests without anesthesia to determine my readings as a normal, functioning human. They didn't insert the thermometers that day.

After the first test, I felt heavy from the effects of the drugs used to keep me unconscious. When the anesthesia wore off that night after a long nap at home, I discovered the needle sites while in the shower. A multitude of small bruises dotted my arms and legs. I was shocked. What else could they have done to me? Then I vaguely remembered them telling me before I went under that they would insert thermometers into my body to record the core temperatures. I'd forgotten all about it.

Over the next nine months, I underwent more or less the same battery of tests. They put me under and either raised or lowered my body temperature to the point that I would sweat or shiver, then tried different means to bring my body temperature back to its proper level. Under anesthesia, the body has a farther threshold before sweating or shivering begins. The time it takes to return to normal can be critical in the midst of a delicate surgery. The tests were to find the safest and quickest way to obtain control. I was one of many guinea pigs relinquishing their bodies in the name of science and a quick dollar.

Some people could never sub-mit to being experimented on, no matter how much they were paid. A lot of variables govern what could happen while you're under anesthesia, and no one is ever truly certain how they might respond to the drugs. One of my friends reacted extremely badly and freaked out as the doctors began the experiment, thereby ending the test. She got paid only a small amount of money for her time.

Most of the tests that I did paid in the range of $300 to $450 for two or three days. I arrived at seven in the morning and would, under most circumstances, be home by 3:30 P.M. The doctors themselves gave me rides home to make sure I was okay until I got there. I had to struggle to keep awake until I got into bed, where I slept for a few hours. Eventually I would wake up–still drugged-out–take a shower, eat something, and then doze while the television glowed. A couple of times, the effects of the drugs lasted into the next day, and I felt as though I was mildly stoned. It wore off as the day passed, so it was never much of a hindrance. Surprisingly, it also never got in the way of my normal sleep schedule. All in all, it was very much like taking a sick day, except that I got paid for it. Must be nice to have a job where you get paid for being sick.

•   •   •

From the first anesthesia test to the last one, they used a drug called propofol to put me under. It's a good sedation drug and did a mighty fine job of knocking me out.

When propofol entered my blood system through the IV, I could feel it creeping up my arm, across my chest, through my heart, and into the darkness. It had a slight pulling feel to it: like the way a cobweb gives as your hand passes through, only the mildest tension to slow you down. It was a strange sensation, but I usually liked it, because as it reached my heart, my vision darkened and started to pixilate. I felt the warm floating sensation of sleep sinking in. I went under comfortably, only to awaken later feeling groggy and sort of drunk.

Throughout the months that the tests progressed, the drug started having a different effect on me. The first time it happened, I was stunned. I felt so helpless. From the moment the propofol met my bloodstream, it started burning. It crept up inside my arm, burning white-hot on its evildoing path to my heart. It hung in my chest cavity as I let the doctors know that it was hurting me badly. I was terrified. There was nothing I could do as the drug worked through my arteries. I suppose that might be what a junkie feels as he realizes

what he just shot up is death, when it's too late to do anything but die. The sedative did what it was supposed to do and, within thirty seconds, I was unconscious. I'm quite positive that, given the noise I was making about this new sensation, they monitored me more intently during this test.

The next time I went in for a study wasn't as bad, but I still felt a slight burning. I also experienced a new side effect from the drug. Normally after the tests, I would awaken in a fuzzy state. I would lie on the table for half an hour, slowly regaining consciousness until I felt awake enough to get up, get dressed, and go home.

On this occasion, though, I didn't feel fine when I awoke on the table. I felt more drunken than usual. Nausea was waiting for any opportunity to make me feel like pure hell. I thought I was going to vomit, which to me is one of the worst feelings. I got home and tried to go about my normal post-study routine, but lying in bed was the only thing that made me feel any better. I figured the nausea would pass. It didn't.

Later that evening, I positioned myself on the couch and tried to shake the nausea. Because I wasn't allowed to eat or drink for a minimum of eight hours before the tests, I figured that I was feeling sick from not having eaten. My roommate made me some chicken noodle soup, but the noodles were too much of an effort to eat. After I drank the broth, I tried to get up to go to the bathroom, but that movement was too much. I succumbed and vomited.

I called the study team immediately. They said that this happened sometimes and not to worry unless it continued for more than a few days. It dragged out another day before I felt better. They compensated me well for this negative reaction. When I had the check in my hand, it didn't seem any worse than having had a normal case of the flu. But the incident did make me start to think more about what I was doing to myself.

Once I began learning a trade,

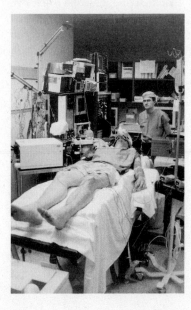

Photograph of the author

I had less need to do the tests to make money. I found less and less time to be a guinea pig. Occasionally, though, a test would come by that seemed unusual or worth my time in money.

The last study I did is one of the weirdest, wildest experiences I have ever had. The few times that I've spoken of it have been met with shock and near disbelief. I thought it was fascinating and an extremely beneficial experiment to participate in. Besides that, it paid $400 for just one day.

The test involved having roughly two-thirds of my blood removed and simultaneously replaced with a sterile saline solution. It was a proven-safe study: the tests had been going for two years at that point. I would be the thirty-fourth person to participate.

The option to have the majority of my blood, the very lifeforce within me, removed in a safe, medically controlled situation for the good of medicine was a rare opportunity. Given my morbid curiosity, how could I pass this up? It couldn't be any worse than the anesthesia experiments I'd already done. I signed on.

What followed was not all

that gory or as exciting as you might think. I sat in the same room where all the anesthesia protocols had been performed. Over roughly eight hours, a small army of doctors sat with me while the blood drained out of my right arm, punctured with an extremely large-gauge needle. Saline flowed in through an equally large needle in my left arm.

At every pint removed, the coordinator came in and performed a battery of mental aptitude tests that involved remembering fifteen words she told me, immediately followed by a series of eye-hand coordination games on a computer, and then trying to list back the words from the beginning of the test. Each test had different words and eye-hand combinations. The computer games were uncomfortable to play since I had a needle in each arm. In between tests, I watched movies I'd brought in and talked with the doctors.

They were studying the use of saline to replace blood for heavy trauma victims. Saline is a major component of all blood types; it can be used for everyone. Saline can carry oxygen through your system, supplying your organs and, most important, your brain. Saline also keeps the pressure up within your blood system so that your heart and other organs aren't taxed into working harder.

This gives paramedics crucial time to get accident victims to the hospital, where better facilities exist to replace the blood loss. From Type O Negative to A/B Positive, there are too many blood types for ambulances to carry them all, but ambulances can easily carry enough saline.

I watched whenever they changed the bags collecting my blood. At first, the bags were filled with a deep, rich, dark hue of red–blood-red, as it were–but as the test progressed, the color weakened so that pint #11 was a pale, almost transparent version of blood, like five drops of blood in an eight-ounce glass of water. As the blood removal progressed, I felt all right, albeit weaker and more tired, but at that final pint, I felt the worst I've ever felt in my life. I felt hollow inside. I could barely move. Even breathing was difficult, as though a huge weight pressed on my chest. Every fiber of my being felt something missing. My mind raced recklessly, unable to grasp any thought long enough to be coherent. I lay in this state for twenty minutes as they observed me, running through the tests while monitoring and recording my vital signs. Finally they started the process of putting all my blood–considerably spun clean in the blood lab upstairs–back into my body.

The first pint administered to

me was the first pint that they removed: the richest, healthiest blood. It felt so good as it returned into my system. My body responded immediately. The sick feeling subsided and my mind slowed down. I could breathe again.

They monitored me throughout the night and into the next morning, when I was discharged. All the saline that had been in my bloodstream was now passing through my kidneys, and I spent a large amount of the next two days in the bathroom pissing it out. Overall, I felt extremely healthy, having had my blood removed and cleaned. I also felt really good about having done something for mankind.

After this experiment, I pretty much stopped doing them. I was working full-time and had less desire to subject myself to the bad experiences with propofol. I had also begun to wonder what the long-term effects of undergoing such large amounts of anesthesia in a short period of time might be. There is only so much that I will do to myself in the name of curiosity.

Strangely enough, in the year and a half following my medical tests, I did not get sick. I watched everyone around me succumb to flus and colds of varying severity. Not once did I feel ill for more than half a day. It's only been in the past two months that I've experienced both a cold and the flu. I've wondered many times if all the tests strengthened my immune system. I think I'm back to normal now.

Looking back, I'm glad that I subjected myself to the studies. It was definitely very interesting. The tests helped me to survive monetarily while transitioning from one existence into the next. They also gave me new insight into mortality. Most people avoid being hooked up to machines while doctors and nurses try to figure out the best course of action. I put myself into the direct line of fire so that the next time you are in a critical medical situation, the medical professionals might save you more quickly. With time, I have become more aware of this aspect of the tests. Its importance far outweighs the money I earned.

Plus, it's great to be able to say, "I sold my body to medical science!" The reactions are worth it all.

ADVERSE REACTIONS TO PROPOFOL

(freely adapted from the *Nursing93 Drug Handbook*)

In the central nervous system, propofol can cause headache, dizziness, and twitching.

In the cardiovascular system, propofol can increase or decrease blood pressure and/or slow the heart to fewer than sixty beats per minute. Its chief effect in patients who continue to breathe on their own is a drop in arterial pressure of up to thirty percent, with little or no change in heart rate or cardiac output.

In the gastrointestinal tract, it can lead to nausea, vomiting, and abdominal cramps.

In the respiratory system, it may cause cough or apnea (temporary cessation of breathing). Life-threatening apnea might persist for longer than sixty seconds and require "ventilatory support."

It may make the skin flush.

At the site of injection, propofol can cause burning or stinging, tingling or numbness, pain, and a sensation of cold.

Postoperative fevers have been traced to contaminated solutions of propofol. The drug is intended for a single use. Any unused portion should be discarded.

—Editor

MALE RESEARCH SUBJECTS NEEDED

Research Study: Which Sedatives Best Facilitate Core Cooling?

Purpose:

The Outcomes Research Group is studying the thermoregulatory effect of several sedatives. The purpose of this study is to identify a combination of drugs that reduces body temperature without triggering excessive shivering.

Eligibility:

To participate, you must be a male, in good health, between the ages of eighteen and forty-five years, a non-smoker, drug- and medication-free, and be of average weight for your height.

You must abstain from alcoholic beverages, caffeine, smoking, and drugs for twenty-four hours before the study.

Study Protocol:

This study will require four separate days that include three sessions of sedation lasting about three hours on each day, plus a control (non-drug) study day. The sedative study days will take about five hours total time, including setup and recovery, and the control day will be about three hours total time.

During each study session, your core body temperature will be decreased, by as much as 7–9°F, by an intravenous infusion of cold fluids. This temperature change is similar to that occurring during surgery and is not harmful. An anesthesiologist will administer drugs.

Major Procedures:

1. You will be given a combination of two or three drugs, at a normal sedative dose. Sedation will continue for about three hours. The drugs being tested in this study are FDA-approved drugs believed to influence temperature regulation.

2. Following a local anesthetic injection, a thin plastic tube will be

placed into one of two veins in your arm to allow fluid and drug administration. The tube is one-tenth of an inch wide and seven inches long, but only five inches will be inserted into your vein.

3. Up to four quarts cooled saline solution will be infused through the tube in your arm. The fluid will decrease your body temperature up to 7–9°F and make you shiver. A short time after the saline administration starts, you will need to urinate and will be provided with a bedpan if necessary.

4. You will be given drugs and therefore should not drive or ride a bike until the next day (with the exception of the control "non-drug" study day). On sedative study days, you are expected to stay home and not return to work until the day after the study.

Reimbursement:

You will be given $600 for the full four-day study. Payment will be in the form of a check, mailed after a delay of about four to six weeks.

Needles in the Spine

by Dalton Graham

All the usual chores and little events that happen on a typical day have been swept off the table for my partner Jewel and me, so a sacred time-space has been created. I have gathered ritual healing materials: the new David Sylvian CD; books, primarily sex-oriented, to keep me from being miserable about being trapped in bed; two boxes of See's chocolates. I cleaned the highly organized cubbyhole by my bed so that everything I could ever need is within reach. I washed the ritual clothing, my own personal hospital gown (size 3X to accommodate my voluptuous frame), and packed it in the ritual bag–"My Personal Belongings," the generic heavy-duty plastic hospital bag recycled from the last trip–along with my own large-size blood pressure cuff and a slim volume to keep me occupied in the down-time. I am as prepared as possible for my selective nerve block injection series, which will decrease the pain from my herniated L5-S1 disk. In other words: I'm ready to get shots in my back.

Since I awoke, a couple of hours before the alarm went off, I've been inhaling deeply off and on as nerves required. The deliberate breathing takes me back to the last BDSM scene I did, where my ex-Dom had to keep reminding me to breathe. I masturbate after the alarm goes off.

It's a freakishly hot day in Daly City, California. The temperatures are predicted to reach ninety degrees in an area that rarely sees anything as high as seventy. The heat is well on its way to achieving a record as we walk through the glaring mid-morning sunlight to the building that houses the office of Doctor S, who sticks needles in my spine.

The first time I came here, I was terrified. The second time, I was prepared. This time I'm giddy. We breeze into the office; the receptionist knows me and hands me the paperwork with abbreviated instructions: "You know the drill: sign, initial, and fill out."

I dutifully complete the paperwork. Yes, I have a copy of the silly *Patients' Rights* handbook. No, I haven't had anything to eat or drink since last night (and I'm thirsty as all fuck because of it, thank you very much). No, I haven't taken any aspirin in a week. I don't *ever* take aspirin. No, I'm not allergic to any drugs, although I get every side effect known (and some unknown) to Western medicine and I really hate Demerol and don't you *dare* give me any anesthesia.

What are my medical conditions? How long have I got? I answer this one studiously, managing not to have to wrap around to the back of the paper.

There is the usual reductionist diagram of an unrealistic male body on which I am supposed to mark my symptoms. I wonder again how they read my small black-ink marks on the smudgy black-ink diagram, or if they bother to read it at all.

I get this foolish grin on my face thinking about the altered state to come and about how horrified the staff would be if they understood how much I mean it when I say, "I don't want anesthesia, because then I'd miss all the fun!" I'm enjoying this in a very sick way. Each time I think about how I'm about to have needles put in the very place that was pounded by a flogger a few days before, I feel a thrill in my clit. You actually *can* eroticize just about anything.

I start to stress about flatulence. The signals a few inches from my anus become increasingly insistent; I know I'm not going to be able to use willpower to keep from ejecting right in my dear doctor's face. A trip to the restroom, then I am fresh and clean and ready for action. The nurse takes me to the wee dressing room where she wraps the requisite plastic hospital ID band around my wrist and teases me about having brought my own gown. It amuses the staff to no end that I come equipped. I skin off my shirt, shoes, and pants, leaving on socks and underpants, and pull on my soft, familiar gown. A walk through the recovery area into the room where it all happens, a hop up onto the bed, and it's showtime.

A different nurse gives me a hard time about having brought my own blood pressure cuff while she starts IV heplock, butterfly-style, on the back of my left hand.

"She'll bring her own heplock next time!" she calls out to the other nurse. *Ha, ha*. She drapes a thin blanket over me. I am so practiced at this that I don't even glance up at the fluoroscopy picture left over from the last patient, showing her spine in X-ray vision, along with the telltale needle silhouette. The first time I was here, with a high level of fear and no book, there was nothing to look at but that picture. It was all I could do not to faint from the sight. This time I am boldly reading *Backpacking Basics,* which shocks the nurses because that is plain whistling in the graveyard–a back patient, who can barely sit, who can't lift even five pounds, reading a book about backpacking?!

Now it's time to wait. I try to value the pain in my hand from the IV needle, doing its small part to kick my endorphins into flowing. I'm well past reading about air mattresses and into a comparison of tents when Doctor S sneaks in and sits down. After a brief discussion of the procedure we're about to do–I'm a veteran, so there's no need to get elaborate–he shifts his focus to the book. "That's ambitious."

"Yeah, it's a goal. I don't necessarily want to do backpacking, but I do want to learn to camp." My already high and vulnerable state makes me stumble right into the next sentence: "What I eventually want to do is go to Burning Man."

Shit. I just outed myself as being alternative. Daly City is conservative; its shared border with San Francisco is evidently culture-impermeable.

"Burning Man, eh? There are some pretty *interesting* people who go there." Good euphemism, Doctor S.

"Yeah. That's the fun part."

He smiles. "That's out in the desert, right?"

"About an hour outside of Reno . . . I've never camped before, and I don't expect to be able to go this time, but I'm aiming for next year."

Surprisingly, he gives me some tips on air mattress solutions. He asks for the URL for Burning Man.

I have moments of severe discomfiture because he looks remarkably like my ex-Dom. Having him look down at me, so calm and compassionate, flusters me. Good thing he doesn't ask anything about my sexuality, because I would blab everything.

Instead, he goes out to look for our tech. Then it's time for me to roll over onto my stomach. The tech puts a pillow under my abdomen and hikes my ankles over a wedge pillow. He hooks up the blood pressure cuff to the dreaded Auto Blood Pressure Machine of Torture and puts the funny little heartbeat clamp on a finger on my other hand. He unties my gown in the back– luckily, modesty is not an issue for me–and tucks the waistband of my underwear below my buttocks.

"Now some soap," says Doctor S as he swipes something cool across my lower back. The blood pressure cuff fills, squeezes, strangles, and finally *pops.* I hear the noise and look over to see the stupid cuff expanding, a metal band gouging into my flesh, and the machine, aware only that it hasn't hit that horrific "ideal" level of resistance, continues to force air into the situation.

"Ack," I whimper, as the pain ramps up and my arm turns blue. "We have a problem with the cuff."

God knows where the tech is, so Doctor S himself has to rescue me. He unhooks the hose first, untangles me from the vile cuff, then turns to mess with the machine and force it off.

"I'm sorry, Doctor S. Now I've got you doing *blood pressure cuffs.*"

"All part of the service, ma'am," he says in his best cowboy-hero voice. Finally the tech realizes there's a tech-y kind of problem and comes over. The two of them figure out that my wonderful brought-from-home

cuff *broke.* I'm too high from anticipation to be embarrassed.

"Hm," says Doctor S. "It's state law that we record your blood pressure every five minutes, but that's when you're on anesthesia, and you're *not* on anesthesia, so I don't think we need it at all!"

"*Thank* you *so* much!" I gush. I hate the auto cuff machine, which squeezes my fat arm too tightly, even when it behaves; I've gone home with bruises all around my upper arm like botched tattoos.

"Let's get started," Doctor S says. I breathe deeply, relieved because I'm running out of ways to keep myself mentally occupied before the Big Event.

"A small pinch." He injects lidocaine to numb the site a bit; then he'll put in the real needle. It aches nonetheless. He puts the lidocaine in four times, one for each side of the L5-S1 and the L4-L5 disks. Then it's really time; Doctor S puts the real needle into my back.

When I was prepping for the first injections six months ago, I visualized that the nerves next to my herniated disk were trapped in my flesh and only a needle could get in to rescue them, like a firefighter crawling through a collapsed building to extract a trapped victim. Instead of fight-

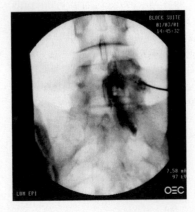

X-ray of the author

ing the needle, resenting it piercing it piercing my flesh, I had to welcome the needle, love how it could wiggle in between most of the cells, and push deep into where it could deliver desperately needed fluid help.

The imagery worked a little.

I'm watching the fluoroscope now, which is in front of the bed and slightly to the right. The fluoroscope takes real-time X-ray pictures of what's going on. I asked Doctor S if he isn't putting his hands in danger, exposing them over and over to the X-rays. He replies that yes, there is some hazard, but that's what he does for a living. I wanted to kiss him for being so noble as to do this icky task. Shoving needles into someone else's back can't be that great a job.

I watch the needle push in, black on the screen against the filmy white layers of my spine. Doctor S warns, "Putting in the contrast now." Once he thinks he has the needle in place, he injects some dye—"contrast"—so that he can see where the steroid fluid will flow. When the needle is not in the right place, the dye pools dully at the tip of the needle, but if he has the needle placed just right, the fluid blossoms into the

LIDOCAINE HYDROCHLORIDE

Lidocaine hydrochloride is an amide-type local anesthetic that prevents the generation and conduction of nerve impulses by interfering with the sodium-potassium exchange across the nerve cell membrane.

Common adverse reactions are skin reaction at the injection site, swelling, or potentially dangerous anaphylactic shock (an allergic reaction).

If blood pressure is high, use of lidocaine hydrochloride can lead to anxiety, blurred vision, ringing in the ears, shivering, seizures followed by drowsiness, unconsciousness, and potentially life-threatening respiratory or cardiac arrest.

Doctors are cautioned to keep resuscitative drugs and equipment available.

—Editor

cavity, like cream poured quickly into coffee in a glass mug.

I'm not totally happy with the cream-in-coffee analogy, so I ask: "Doctor S, how would you describe the flow, when you get the needle in the right place?"

Doctor S likes to chat during the procedure. "Well, when the contrast dye gets into the epidural space, that's how it flows, that's the shape of the space itself."

"Yeah, but I've been trying to figure out how to write it down. I can't think how to describe it, what it looks like, you know?"

Doctor S launches into an unhelpful description of myelial sheath and spinal cord nerves and dura, which I am wholly unable to hang on to because the anxiety of the procedure itself has kicked in. Doctor S's poetry is in the work itself. I will have to be satisfied with that.

"Okay, now the cortisone. This may burn for about five seconds and you may feel it in your leg. Let me know if it becomes unbearable and I'll stop."

It stings a little, but is only mildly irritating. The pain in this procedure comes when Doctor S hits a nerve, which results in a deep, dull ache unlike anything else I've ever felt. It's startling and aggravating, but I know it will disappear almost as quickly as it arrives. Nevertheless, my heart rate is up to ninety-seven beats per minute, I'm drenched

in sweat, and all my deep breathing exercises have gone by the wayside to be replaced by panicky panting.

After the first injection on the right side of the L5-S1 disk, I feel the medicine in my right foot. It's a nice tingly numb sensation, a mini-high for my foot. Doctor S goes for the next injection and it takes several tries to get the dye in the right place. It flows outside where we want it. Doctor S tells the tech to rotate the fluoroscope to show me the lateral view to illustrate what he was explaining about where it's supposed to flow, but I'm getting rapidly uninterested in taking mental notes and increasingly interested in not throwing up. Like the other times, we're halfway through and I'm ready to heave up the tiny amount of stomach acid in my dehydrated tummy.

I look away from the 'scope, hoping that will help. I stare fixedly at four boxes of latex gloves, size 6½, 7, 8, and 8½. "These gloves are made of natural rubber latex which may cause allergic reaction in some." This is not enough to distract me.

Doctor S is doing the third injection.

"Doctor S, I *very much* don't want you to stop, but I should tell you that I'm pretty queasy."

He heads toward my heplock with a needle. "I'll give you some anti-nausea medicine."

"Oh, no, please, I can pull it through!" There is sheer terror in my voice at this point; anti-nausea medicine is as frightening to me as anesthesia. It knocks me senseless, and that's the very last thing I want. (Control issues.)

I'm biting *hard* onto my left thumb in lieu of a bullet. He does the last injection with lightning speed. I worry that he'll botch it in his rush, but then he leans his arms on my bare ass for leverage. The touch of his warm skin against mine is yet another arousing reminder of a gentle touch in the midst of a harsh BDSM scene.

"OK. We're all done. Do you need a basin?" he asks calmly.

"Nope, I'm fine now." I'm fully into my beloved altered state and grinning insanely. This is fun as all fuck. I thank Doctor S over and over. Finally he escapes.

After a while the tech comes back and I roll onto a gurney. He pushes dizzy me into a slot in the recovery area. The nurses sit me up and give me the tiny cup of gloriously wet cranberry juice and a little package of Lorna Doones, which never taste good any time but now. I grin some more, relaxing into the afterglow. I shut my eyes and wiggle my feet to get the feeling back.

When I try to stand—with a chair, a walker, and a nurse at the ready—my right leg crumples. My butt is having a lidocaine party, getting all sorts of numbed-out thrills whenever it scrapes the bedside. I dress myself while sitting on the chair and am hustled over to a waiting area because there are so many other patients today. (I bet they won't have half as much fun as I did.) I spend a long time stomping my right leg and talking to it, to no avail. Finally I use the walker to get out to the car, which Jewel has pulled into the patient pickup area.

I babble all the way home. I'm high as a kite and loving it. Jewel gets me all settled in bed, takes my McDonald's order, and heads back out to retrieve sustenance. He's freaked but won't admit it. I call my folks in Florida, who are equally freaked and relieved to hear that I'm okay.

How did I manage to get more blasé about this than everyone else? I guess it's a survival technique. I know I'm going to be getting a bunch more of these injections before I'm all healed—hell, I might be getting them three times a year for the rest of my life—so I *have* to look at it as a somewhat routine event. But it's even better to be able to view it as a ritualistic, radical, body-modifying, kinky act of bravery.

I honestly enjoy having needles in my spine.

HERNIATED DISKS

by Dalton Graham

A hernia is defined as an organ or body part that protrudes through connective tissue or through a wall of the cavity in which it is normally enclosed. (Yum!) But how can a *disk* herniate? Disks are the shock absorbers for the vertebrae of the spine; they actually have a slightly soft core called the *nucleus pulposus*. This core starts out being jelly-like and useful when a human spine is young. As the years go by, the core slowly dries and becomes rubber-hard (which is why we shouldn't pogo to the Clash's "Should I Stay or Should I Go" when we get to the nursing home).

Unfortunately, it is possible to mess with the spine such that the inner core of a disk *pops* out from the outer disk membrane. When this happens, it may press against tender nerves nearby, which become understandably pissed. These nerves protest by causing pain that can be debilitating. If this pain radiates down one or both legs, the victim may be a candidate for disk aspiration (sucking the jelly core out of the herniation so that it doesn't press against nerves) or other surgical solutions. If the pain remains primarily in the back, a doctor may use injections for diagnostic purposes as well as treatment. The way the pain responds to various types of injections narrows down the source of the pain and points to treatment options.

Herniated disks can be difficult to diagnose, as they do not readily show up on X-rays. An MRI is often required to definitively identify the naughty little rupture. It is possible for herniated disks to heal, after a fashion: the hernia can "scar over" and the pain can lessen. Physical therapy, especially pool therapy, also helps by teaching the hapless spine owner new, safer ways to move to minimize the pain and prevent further injury.

It is much better never to herniate a disk in the first place, so use those legs when you lift!

Additional information: www.spinecare.com

Man-o-gram:
Guys Shouldn't Give Milk

by Maurice Broaddus

The plastic plate of the X-ray machine lowered with a whir as I stood against the cold metal beast, naked from the waist up. All I could do was stare at my breast while it was positioned to be compressed between the plates, wondering, *How the heck did I get here?*

Early in her pregnancy, my wife's doctor diagnosed her with a condition called placenta previa. While the doctor explained to both of us the nature of the condition, all I heard was, "You can't have sex with your wife." Seven long months later, my wife was still recovering from her C-section. As a first-time mother settling into a routine of nursing, any broach of her bosom area was met with the rebuke, "Those aren't for you," and getting my hands slapped. At that point, I didn't trust myself bumping into furniture. My Saturday nights were reduced to TV watching and cold showers.

Before the Divinyls' "I Touch Myself" gets cued, let me get on with my story. Once in the shower, I spied my wife's breast self-examination chart. Okay, it had been there the length of our marriage, but each time I stepped into the shower, all my mind registered were pictures of breasts. Every time, it took a minute for me to realize why they were there. Today was different. I looked around (because that's what you do when you are about to do something potentially embarrassing) and performed the self-exam.

I felt the lump.

Now would be the time to mention that I suffer from hypochondria. Unfortunately, it matched my great dislike for doctors, so I sat around a lot, obsessing about what I might have, while not actually going anywhere to confirm it.

I noticed a pain in my bosom (I'm trying to say bosom as often as possible, not necessarily to avoid offending anyone, but to

233

hide my soon-to-be-copious use of–read: obsession with–the word *breast*). The pain was so great, I decided to . . . call my sister. This wasn't as bad as it sounds. My sister was in nursing school. (Well, she was taking English and speech and other prerequisite stuff.) She told me that the lump might be an ingrown hair or an infected spider bite. So I was like, "Cool."

The next day, the pain in my bosom woke me up. I decided to squeeze my breast. White liquid came out from around my nipple. And it hurt. A lot. I spent the rest of the day lying around in pain. My wife went into full–but loving–harangue about how I ought to go to the doctor.

Two days after I first discovered the lump, I finally went to my doctor. It was a Friday. She (yes, my doctor is a woman. I know that there are various schools of thought on the subject, and while I am by no means a homophobe, if someone is going to touch me anywhere near my naughty parts, it is going to be a woman. Okay, maybe that came off more homophobic than I wanted.) poked, prodded, and squeezed my bosom.

"How long ago did you notice the lump?" she asked.

I responded with, "The best I can tell you is when I noticed the pain."

She sat across from me with her best grave "I have something serious to discuss with you" face. "There are three possibilities: It could just be an infected cyst. It could be breast cancer. It could be a benign brain tumor."

Things became rather hazy at that point, though I remember how she emphasized the word "benign" as if that would help when accompanied by the words "brain tumor."

My mind locked up with competing thoughts, trying to grasp the enormity of what I had just heard. Cancer didn't run in my family. However, I worked in an environmental toxicology lab and had sort of resigned myself to the possibility that any of the numerous chemicals I am exposed to might give me cancer. I mean, newspapers can report all they want about how coffee *might* cause cancer, but I worked with some chemicals labeled *mutagen*.

I managed to ask about the whole brain tumor thing. The doctor said that there was a type of tumor that caused the brain to screw up one's hormonal levels, which would explain–how did she put it?–"I'm not positive that you are simply discharging pus." Tiptoeing around it, trying her best to cushion the news–emphasizing that now was not the time to panic–only panicked me more. She finally said the magic words: "You may be lactating."

"Lactating?"

"Lactating."

Sometimes a circumstance is so absurd, all you can do is laugh. I'm all for extreme support in marriage; for example, when my wife had gestational diabetes, I gave up desserts. But I didn't think I had ever identified so much . . . I didn't think I had ever been so jealous . . . I didn't think that I was so sympathetic as to start lactating on her behalf. I mean, I got up in the middle of the night (okay, I was usually already up, but the thought was the same) to take care of the boy. But that was to change a diaper. When he was hungry, I was good with getting him a bottle. Being too lazy to walk downstairs I can see, but I can't see being jealous of her being able to deliver straight from the tap.

Anyway, my doc drew blood for some tests, telling me that I needed to schedule a mammogram. She'd put a rush on it and get it scheduled for Monday, sensitive to the fact that we'd want to know the results as soon as possible. She re-emphasized that, "Now is not the time to panic." Actually, I could think of no worse time to panic, especially after having been told to schedule a mammogram. I couldn't imagine the last time anyone prayed to have a pus-filled sac in his or her chest. (As an aside, I debated on the word *pus-filled.* I was going to go with *pus-y* or *pusy,* but I figured in a quick read, that was too close to something else and, boy, would that take this story in a new direction.)

I left her office in a daze, realizing that I had a whole weekend to dwell on the possibilities. My first call was to my wife. She asked, "When will you find out the results?" but the only response I had was, "Sorry, honey, but once I heard the words

"Asylum" by Kimberlee Traub

'breast cancer' and 'lactating,' I was pretty much done taking in new information."

My next call was to my friend whom, for the sake of this article, we'll call Laura. She was over the age of forty and every time she made her annual pilgrimage to get a mammogram on her birthday, she called me to tell me about it. Admittedly, it is an odd friendship, but it works for us. I knew she would be the one to give me real mammogram advice. She informed me that it helped to have big boobs—not that I had much say in this, although I follow a strict non-exercise regimen. Wearing deodorant was a mistake (apparently the X-ray machine picked up flecks of some deodorant as cancers trying to get started). Finally, she told me, "Don't schedule it around your period." As that point, I hung up on Laura.

This is a good time to discuss the sensitive reactions of my friends. Don't get me wrong: I love my friends. On the whole, these people would walk through fire for me, but we all dealt with trying times the same way: with (sadistic) humor.

Dan called while I was sitting on my couch brooding about my news. He wanted to inform me that he had been sent home from work because he had injured his back and was going to have to have an MRI done.

"I bet that I can trump your test," I said.

Dan—the same Dan who, when I had spinal surgery as a teen to insert a rod to correct my scoliosis, visited during my recovery to see if magnets would stick on my back—began laughing so hard I thought I was going to have to go over to his place and perform CPR.

In addition to being my pastor, Rich was one of my closest friends. I know that if anyone else had come to him, he would have been full of all sorts of pastoral wisdom. Since it was me, someone who shared his often twisted bent, I got, "This explains why you like shopping so much and dress so nice." (In his defense, he has since spun this as trying to "alleviate the weightiness" of the situation by making a joke. He went on to say that his response contrasted with that of our friend I'll call Rob who "delighted in your misfortune.")

Rob laughed so much that I had to let him go. When I called back, he was still laughing. In fact, he had called Rich to continue laughing. And despite Rich's protestations to the contrary, Rich's wife informed me that he was so giddy at the opportunity to be there for me, he nearly broke his finger trying to call me back to make a comment about the possibility of my having ovaries.

With a whole weekend to kill, I turned to the one place I knew would answer all my questions, that would comfort me in the cool embrace of useful information: the Internet. For the record, the Internet is a wonderful tool, especially for finding information. It is not a place where hypochondriacs should wander alone.

I didn't even know men could get breast cancer until I saw it on an episode of *Oz.* The American Cancer Society estimates that each year 1,500 new cases of breast cancer in men will be diagnosed in the United States. The symptoms included nipple discharge (usually bloody), nipple inversion, a lump, or, occasionally, local pain, itching, or a pulling sensation.

If I was indeed lactating, my condition was called galactorrhea: the secretion of breast milk in men, or in women who were not breast-feeding an infant. It could be caused by a pituitary gland tumor, other types of brain tumors, head injuries, or encephalitis (an infection of the brain). Men could possibly experience loss of sexual interest and impotence. Then I came across the single most disturbing article on the topic: "Milkmen: Fathers Who Breast-feed." It was about men who purposefully stimulated their nipples to produce milk. It had pictures.

Pictures.

• • •

Monday eventually arrived and, with it, the mammogram. I thought that I would feel odd, a guy waiting in the office that performed mammograms, until it occurred to me that I looked like a guy waiting on his wife. Even when they called my name, no one looked up over her magazine. But that's my own self-involvement speaking; they couldn't have possibly been concerned about their own impending mammograms.

The technician did her best to calm me, while handing me wipes to remove any deodorant I might be wearing and a gown to wear. I only wore the gown from the changing room for the four steps it took to get to the X-ray machine. She had me put one hand behind my back and the other on the machine, presumably to steady myself, though it might have been just to give my hands something to do to keep me from clawing at the machine.

There was a whole lot of tugging and pulling and clamping down of things. Most of my writing career has been as a horror writer, but let me tell you, no matter how dulcet the tone, the new scary phrase for me was, "Let me guide the tissue." That cued the pancaking—and there is a reason that the word *pancake* can be used as a verb—of flesh (and I don't have a lot to work with). Two plates pressed together to flatten the breast as much as possible. It was one of those, "You may feel an uncomfortable pressure"–not to be confused with pain–situations. All told, it took only a few moments to get the two views of my breast, one from above and one angled from the side.

Luckily, a doctor there read the results for me. She made me nervous at first, because she asked to have a couple of re-shots, saying that she wanted to see "my nipple in profile." I always imagined that a woman saying that to me would be grounds for divorce, but then she came back with the news that my condition looked like an abscess of some sort. Probably caused by an insect bite or ingrown hair. Antibiotics were prescribed to clear it up within a couple of weeks.

All in all, things turned out well. Granted, I can't remove my shirt when I play volleyball for fear of breaking some obscenity law by exposing my nipples. At the very least, the scare reminded me not to take my time, my family, or my friends for granted because I didn't know how long I would be with them. And my son appreciates how great my maternal instincts were.

✧

Beyond Death: Exploring Behind the Curtain

✧

Ephemera from the editor's collection

Finding Paul

by George V. Neville-Neil

Several years ago, I lived on the third floor of a three-flat Victorian in San Francisco. In the backyard was what's called an earthquake shack. These "shacks" had been built after the 1906 earthquake to house the workers who rebuilt the main houses in that area. The shacks are now considered quaint to live in. At that time, my landlord Paul lived in the earthquake shack, which was actually two shacks combined. It had a front room, bedroom, and a kitchen.

My lover Richard and I both commuted to work via a combination of bicycle and train. We kept the bicycles in the garage behind the earthquake shack. One morning in October, I was the last one to leave the house. I walked down the back staircase and out the small sidewalk to the garage, which we shared with Paul.

When I entered the garage, I noticed that Paul had left his car running. This seemed odd to me. The garage smelled of car exhaust, a bit worse than riding a bike in traffic. For some reason, I looked down while passing the back of Paul's car and noticed a vacuum cleaner hose coming out of the tailpipe.

I realized immediately what was happening and rushed to the front of the small station wagon. The hose was jammed into the window of the rear right passenger-side door. I opened the front passenger-side door, reached over, and turned off the ignition.

Paul was lying in the fetal position in the backseat of the wagon. I opened that door to see if I could do anything for him. His skin was all mottled red, like a bad sunburn with patches of white, which is the effect (I later learned) of carbon monoxide poisoning. I didn't find a pulse.

I don't think I ever took three flights of stairs faster before or since. I called 911. They identified my location as the front of the building, so I spent what seemed like an eternity explaining to them that the garage, where Paul was, was at the back of the building on another street entirely. After giving all the usual information, I went back down to see if there was any first aid that I could give Paul.

When I returned to the garage and surveyed the situation, it seemed to me that there was nothing I could do. Paul had no trace of pulse. I'd only shaken hands with him before and now I was making sure he was dead.

He was still warm and kind of clammy. His body, skin, and face had the aspect of a corpse. I knew how to recognize this because only a few months before a terminally ill friend had died while I was with him. I saw then the difference that death makes in a body.

Even under heavy sedation, the body retains a basic animation. The muscles pull at the skin. The skin itself has a basic glow that shows a person has life. A dead body is missing all these signs of life. The limbs hang literally lifeless. The skin somehow loses its glow. It's easiest to see death in the face, where the muscles, losing all their pull, do not animate the face but allow it to sag—so that the deceased, unless made up by a mortician, has the look of a mannequin. Paul had that dead look about him, no question about it.

I opened the garage door and paced around the garage to wait for the ambulance.

I heard the sirens but, of course, the dispatcher sent the fire department EMTs to the front of the building. They smashed in the door to the basement/backyard and raced to the garage. All I could think was, *You idiots, I said Douglas, not Ord!*

They confirmed my belief that Paul had been dead for hours and called the coroner. They said Paul had probably been in the car all night.

At this point, I needed to have someone around to talk to. I realized that a good friend of mine was perhaps not too busy at work. I paged him. He said he'd be right there.

My friend showed up before the coroner did and we talked about the whole situation. In fact, we joked about it. We'd both lost friends recently to AIDS. I'd lost other people before in my life. One thing you learn from having death around you is that humor is really a natural response. This seems true in professional death circles as well, because when the coroner showed up, he joined in on the jokes. He told us about the corpse he'd just pulled from the lake in Golden Gate Park. I don't remember the story, but I do remember laughing.

The cops came, but everybody left once it was clear that only the coroner was necessary. I gave the coroner a tour of the area and showed him to Paul's house in the backyard. There, on the kitchen counter, we found a good bottle of red wine that had been half drunk. Nothing else. I'd hoped we would find a note.

Paul had always seemed affable and pretty cheerful. He'd been my landlord for less than a year. During that time, he'd thrown a few BBQs for friends. He always seemed to have cool, interesting people around him. He also didn't seem ill in any way. I felt somehow that having found his body, I had a right to know why he had killed himself.

I signed some sort of certificate for the coroner, then he left.

A few days later, I was walking back from the garage after parking my bike and noticed that the door to Paul's house was open. I went to check what was up. A few members of Paul's family had come to pack up his things. When I told them who I was, they recognized my name from the coroner's paperwork. They apologized to me for having to find Paul. I asked if

he had left a note. I told them that the coroner and I had looked, but hadn't found one. I said I was surprised at Paul's suicide. They said they weren't, but didn't elaborate.

To this day, two things still puzzle me. The first is why Paul killed himself. The second is why Richard never even noticed the running car in the closed garage, with a vacuum cleaner hose clearly running from its tailpipe to the window.

I guess my final words about the experience are these: If you're going to off yourself, please arrange not to surprise anyone.

"The House Before the Cemetery" by Dorian Katz

CARBON MONOXIDE POISONING

The heart doesn't take nourishment from the blood passing through it. Instead, arteries wrapping the outside of the heart feed its muscles. Once the oxygen flow decreases, the muscle suffers. The heart beats faster and harder, trying to pick up more oxygen to feed itself.

A constant supply of blood is also necessary for the brain to function. Since the brain can't hold oxygen in reserve, it demands a constant supply from arterial blood. Within fifteen to thirty minutes after the onset of oxygen deprivation, the brain begins to starve, resulting in irreversible brain damage.

Due to a design flaw, the hemoglobin in blood prefers carbon monoxide to oxygen by a factor of two hundred. The victim of carbon monoxide poisoning dies because his heart and brain can't draw sufficient oxygen from the newly minted carboxyhemoglobin.

In addition, the carboxyhemoglobin makes the blood significantly brighter in color than normal, which gives the skin and mucous membranes of a carbon monoxide victim a "remarkable cherry-red tinge," according to *How We Die: Reflections on Life's Final Chapter*.

—Editor

RESCUE BREATHING

If you find someone who is not breathing, call 911.

To begin assisted breathing, first touch the person's shoulder, shake him gently, and ask, "Can you hear me? Are you okay?" If the victim does not respond, place one hand on his forehead and the other hand under his chin. Gently press the jaw upward as you tilt the head back.

Using your hand on the victim's forehead, pinch his nose closed. Take a deep breath. Place your mouth tightly over the victim's mouth and blow until you see the chest rise.

Remove your mouth and turn your head so that your ear is over his mouth. Listen for air leaving the lungs.

Repeat the procedure, giving one breath every five seconds.

After five breaths, check the person's neck for a pulse. If there is no pulse, you're trained in CPR, *and* help is on the way, begin cardiac compressions. However, if help is not coming shortly, face the inevitable. People's hearts do not suddenly start to beat like they do in the movies. CPR keeps blood and oxygen flowing to the brain, which may allow the victim to be resuscitated by EMS or hospital technicians, but the odds of rescuing him without drugs, shock paddles, and all the other paraphernalia, are pretty slim.

—Editor

CENTURY-OLD TEMPORARY HOUSING

Immediately following the big San Francisco earthquake on April 18, 1906, up to 300,000 people slept outside in city parks, either in fear of another tremor or because their homes had become uninhabitable. In June, the city erected large canvas tents to house the homeless. Three encampments stood in Golden Gate Park. Others sprung up in every relatively flat area in town. Running water, bathhouses, and sewers were provided in each park. Despite the crowding, public health was remarkably good.

By the autumn of 1906, the number of refugees had dropped to around 17,000. In anticipation of winter's rains, the tents were replaced with two- and three-room wooden structures called cottages. They became popularly known as "refugee shacks." The Lands and Building Department constructed six thousand little houses in more than a dozen locations. Each two-room cottage cost $100 to build, including plumbing. The three-room version cost only $150.

Most cottages were occupied by families or by widows with children. The relief committee demanded proof of need before refugees were allowed to rent a cottage for $2 a month. That money was held until the day that the family moved their cottage to their own lot. In fact, moving the cottages to lots owned by their occupants was part of the original plan.

Late in the summer of 1907, workmen jacked the cottages up, set them on horse-drawn carriages, and hauled them to new sites. These "shacks" were often the first homes ever owned by many of their occupants. Some continue to stand, including a pair on Funston Avenue near Lincoln.

—Editor

In Grandpa's House

by Trilby Plants

Summertime in Michigan's Upper Peninsula: ninety-five degrees, and it was early afternoon.

It wasn't just the heat that had put me out of sorts. I shouldn't have come. Even a small family reunion—my father's siblings and spouses—was trying. The pain of my brother's death was still too raw, my grief still unresolved.

My youngest brother, Eric, had been killed fourteen months before in a terrible car accident. On his way to school, he turned his car in front of a loaded logging truck and was killed instantly. He was sixteen.

The accident happened the morning my second child was born—a boy we named Todd. In a strange twist of fate, Todd was delivered at about the same time Eric died. A life for a life, if you believe in fate, or karma, or whatever. Reincarnation? Wasn't it Darwin who believed that if there was life after death, it was a wonderful reward, but if death was the end, then it would be a well-deserved sleep? He opted for the sleep theory. It made sense to me.

I sat in the family room of an uncle's house. The conversation of the older people buzzed around me: stories of the good old days. They were my father Roy's family: his sister, Lona, and brothers John, Raymond, and Duane. I hadn't seen some of these people since I was a youngster. They only managed to see one another once every ten years or so, so now they were catching up on all the minutiae of the last decade.

My mother sat quietly, mostly listening. I knew she must still be sad, too. I leaned toward her and said, "How're you doing, Mom?"

She smiled wanly at me. "Fine," she said softly. "But they haven't talked about the accident." I nodded. She sighed and said, "It's like he never existed."

I tried to give an encouraging smile. "Maybe they think it'll make you too sad." I touched her arm and she patted my hand. I saw pain in her eyes, in the new wrinkles around her mouth, and I knew she missed Eric, too.

I was caught up in the joys of raising a toddler, made bittersweet by the loss of my brother. Because Todd had been delivered by C-section, my doctor hadn't allowed me to attend Eric's funeral. Money, job, and circumstances didn't permit me to go afterward. I felt like I hadn't really grieved. I hadn't really said good-bye. Since I hadn't seen Eric for nearly three years, it was as if he had just gone away somewhere, that one day he would walk into the room and simply say, "Hi," and he'd be back.

A horn honked outside. A cousin excused himself to tend to the needs of a customer who had pulled his battered pickup into the junk-infested yard. The cousin had announced he was a businessman, a worm farmer, and he also kept a huge tank of minnows, which he sold as bait to fishermen. He asked me if I wanted to see his minnow and worm operation. I tactfully declined.

The good old days and raising minnows and worms for a living. I looked at the faces around me and realized I was sinking into a bottomless pool of ennui. Unless I escaped, I told myself, I would become fascinated by a worm farm and minnow business.

"Hey," I announced, "I'm going to sneak off and take a shower before dinner."

"Great," my aunt Val responded. "I want to clean up, too. But you go first." She was only a few years older than me.

A no-nonsense Yooper, a Finn by heritage, she smiled easily and seemed unflappable.

As I left the room, I heard my father begin his recounting of the time he cured himself of lockjaw when he was a youngster by eating a bowl of pickled beets.

Val followed me to the kitchen. "Thanks for rescuing me," she said.

I grinned at our duplicity and pointed upstairs. "Towels?"

"I'll get you some," she said and headed for a cupboard in a corner of the kitchen. "But don't use the shower. There's something wrong with the water pressure. It only trickles out of the shower head. Take a bath—that works fine—and if you want to wash your hair, use the kitchen sink."

"Sure," I said. "No problem."

She handed me two bath towels. "Take your time," she said. "I'm in no hurry. It's so hot, I thought we'd eat later when it's a little cooler."

"Can I help?" I offered.

"Oh, no," Val said with a smile. "Everything's under control. I went to town yesterday and bought take-out fried chicken. We can nuke it. We won't have to use the stove and add more heat to the kitchen." She fanned herself with one hand.

"Sounds great," I said. "On to the bath."

I made my way up the narrow

stairs, suddenly conscious of the house around me. My uncle Raymond had taken over the property several years before. He had remodeled an existing two-story structure that someone had built in the early seventies, remodeled it, and moved in with my aunt Val and his three sons. He had recently added a large family room. It was a comfortable house. I remembered another house on this property: my paternal grandfather's, Raymond's father.

The old man, a Scottish immigrant, had built a house on this same spot. The property extended into the forest, including a large meadow my father once told me had been planted

"Holy Woman" by Suzanne Dechnik

with potatoes during the Depression. Grandpa bartered potatoes to half the town. No one went hungry and his still was well supplied. My father remembered the still. I recalled, as if in a dream, gathering dandelions for my grandfather's dandelion wine.

My grandfather's house had had shiny wood floors. I always thought they were shiny because Grandma dusted and polished them. Once, when I had described my memories of the house to my mother, she told me the floors were shiny because they had been hand-cut and laid by my grandfather, then washed and waxed by him. Apparently my grandmother didn't do much around the house. The walls were clean and white, and the windows unspotted, because my grandfather took pride in what he had built and maintained it well.

The summer I was ten, 1955, Grandpa's big white house had burned to the ground just before we arrived in Upper Michigan for a visit. The fire had started in the cellar in the ceiling beams and was never explained. It was the third house Grandpa had built on the same spot. They had all burned. That house—the one I remembered—was Grandpa's last. That last fire took the energy out of him and he made no effort to rebuild. Grandpa's heart failed; he died a year later.

Now the house was full of relatives, my grandpa's five remaining children and their spouses. It was a boisterous group, all vying to tell about their lives.

I ran the water and sank into the tub. My mind sank into maudlin thoughts. I railed against fate, what-ifs, and my own inability to accept my brother's death. I felt tears gather and was afraid that, once they started, they wouldn't stop.

I hurriedly washed, got out of the tub, and dressed. I rinsed the tub and ran water for my aunt. I sat on the edge of the tub and tried not to think of anything sad. When the tub was full, I went downstairs to the kitchen.

"Your turn," I greeted Val.

After she went upstairs, I began washing my hair at the sink. Cooled by the bath and lulled by the indistinct buzz of voices from the family room, I rose from the sink and buried my head under a towel. The day was so hot, I decided to just towel dry. Lost in sorrowful thoughts, I gently massaged my head with the towel.

I heard footsteps descend the stairs, a heavy tread. The footsteps came up behind me and a warm arm went around my shoulders. I was pulled back against a warm body: a tall, masculine presence.

I started to pull the towel off my head.

"It'll be all right," a deep voice said softly in my ear. I felt the warmth of someone's breath on my neck. Again the soft voice. "It'll be all right."

The arm around me was warm, comforting. It made me feel less sad. My despair eased. A great sense of peace flooded me; I felt that a burden was somehow lightened. Maybe it was just knowing that someone else knew exactly how I felt. Someone shared my sorrow and that made it easier to bear.

I pulled the towel off my head, still safe in a warm embrace, and turned to see who had made me feel so peaceful.

There was no one there.

For an instant the warm arm stayed around my shoulder and then vanished.

There was no one there.

I screamed. Screeched, would be a more apt description of the incoherent sound I made. Everyone came running from the family room. Snippets of conversation revealed that some had thought I might have fallen down the stairs, scalded myself on the hot water, cut myself, or perhaps seen a mouse scurry across the kitchen floor. My mother immediately disabused everyone of that notion; I'd never been afraid of mice. She was worried I had encountered a spider.

She led me to a chair in the family room and eased me into it. Val arrived, breathless, wrapped in a terry bathrobe. When my near-hysterics were soothed, I recounted what had just happened to me. My aunt and uncle looked at each other. A long, searching look. Val nodded to him.

Uncle Raymond sheepishly hung his head and said, "We didn't want to alarm any of you, but we honestly didn't know if this would happen to other people." He had grown up in this little town in the Upper Peninsula. He was a practical man, not given to romantic notions.

Val said, "There's a . . ." she hesitated, "a presence in the house." She must have seen dismay on my face, because I saw it on everybody else's. My uncle John cleared his throat. Val hastily added, "Oh, don't worry, it's benign."

"Benign?" I said incredulously.

She nodded. "Didn't you notice I don't have anything breakable in the kitchen cabinets?"

"Well, yes," I said, not knowing what that had to do with anything. "I figured it was preference."

She chuckled. "Preference by necessity."

I saw the skeptical expressions on the faces around me.

Something clattered in the kitchen. I jumped.

My uncle held up a hand. "I'll get it, Val. You tell the story. It's just some plates."

The cupboards had sliding doors. I remember them being closed. I started, "But how—?"

"That's what we mean," Val said with a rueful smile. "It doesn't happen much during the day. The cupboard doors slide open and dishes tumble out. When we first moved, a lot of my breakable things got smashed. They aren't thrown. Just fall out. I replaced everything with plastic. Put away the good stuff." She nodded to a corner cabinet in the family room. "Doesn't happen in this room at all. Just the kitchen. The plastic stuff falls out, makes a terrific racket—wakes us up at night—but nothing breaks."

Val scanned the gathering. Some of the relatives looked uncomfortable. My mother had a strangely peaceful expression: acceptance?

Val chuckled. "You're all probably thinking we're nuts. But I don't think any of you should be frightened. It never feels cold, or angry, and it's never done anything really harmful. Just little mischiefs."

"Mischiefs," I said. "Like the dishes."

She nodded. "And the lights."

"The lights?" my Aunt Lona asked.

Val said, "Yes. But it's strange. Raymond rewired and replumbed the entire house. There's nothing left of the original stuff. Sometimes the lights just go on or off for no reason. The only time it's really annoying is at night when I'm going up or down the stairs and the light goes off, or when we're asleep at night and they come on. Every light–except the family room–including the television in our bedroom. The kitchen is over the spot where the living room of the old house was located. The family room isn't on an area where any part of the original house was."

Raymond entered the room and sat down in his recliner. "Just a few cups," he said with a shrug. "No harm done."

I looked at him and then Val. A shiver went up my spine. "Doesn't this scare you?"

Val shook her head.

Raymond said, "It's not malicious. Nothing harmful. Since we replaced the dishes."

I took a deep breath. "Have you ever felt a . . . a physical presence, heard voices?"

Val didn't move. I glared at my uncle. After a long pause, he nodded.

Val said, "Yes, often."

Raymond said, "But it's always pleasant. Kind of comforting. Especially when it's been a bad day for some reason."

"Calming," Val said. "Not at all distressing. And we haven't told a soul."

Raymond laughed. "We don't want to get a reputation as a haunted house."

I looked at him and shivered. "Is that what this is?"

Raymond's expression became thoughtful. "Probably."

Val put a hand on my arm. "But it's not bad. Whatever it is, it's not bad."

"Whatever–" I started. "You mean *whoever*."

Val smiled. "You're probably right. Whoever."

The gathering was silent. Finally I asked, "Who is it?"

Raymond said quickly, "Who did you think it was?"

One of my earliest memories of my grandfather is of sitting on his lap in a wooden rocker. The details in the room are vivid. I remember the creaking sound of the rockers on the wood floor.

I had skinned my knee. I don't remember the circumstances of the accident, but I distinctly remember the pain of the scrape. I'm sitting on Grandpa's lap, my head against his chest, listening to the slow *thump-thump* of his heart. There is an old-fashioned brass floor lamp near the rocker with a green shade and a pull chain. The house in my memory–the last one that burned–faced east. I remember the midday sunlight slanting through the windows.

My grandfather points a finger into the sunlight and says, "See the sunbeams? They're fairy ladders. And some of those little floating specks are fairies. If you believe, and you look close enough, you'll see which ones are fairies. They're the specks with wings."

My mother remembers the skinned knee incident. It was a nasty scrape and needed more than just basic first aid. She thought I might need stitches, but that was a big decision, as it was so far to a medical facility. She tells me I was no more than three years old.

But the most intense memory I have of the skinned knee incident is my grandfather's voice. Although he was tall and very slender, he had a surprisingly deep voice. Sitting on his lap, I heard his voice rumble in his chest: "It'll be all right."

I gazed at Val. "It was my grandfather," I whispered.

"My dad," Raymond said, and it was not a question.

Val nodded. "Yeah," she said, "that's what I think, too."

So maybe it is possible that people who die are not truly lost. Maybe they *do* simply walk into a room and say, "Hi." Perhaps they greet us in ways we don't want to recognize with our rational minds.

Perhaps I *can* believe.

Going into Tombs

by Hugues Leblanc

Not far from my home in Montreal, a cemetery occupies the southwestern side of Mount Royal. It is immense, some five hundred acres: hilly, forested, covered with tombstones. All kinds of trees have been planted; all species of birds fly by. There's even a family of foxes running around. It is a very beautiful place, right in the middle of a major city, itself in the center of an island. It's a pleasant place to experience the changing of the seasons, the turning of the leaves in fall, for example. In winter, it's just cold out there!

In most tombs, the inner chamber consists of two parts: a public area often adorned with an altar and possibly kneeling chairs and a sacred, more cryptic area where coffins are slid into niches. Once the coffin is in place, that opening is covered with a marble plate. Coffins are kept apart, individualized. To the contrary, in Montreal, whole families are kept close to one another in one space: eternal peace with the loved ones.

This cemetery is the only one I've visited so far where you can see coffins inside the tombs. The ornate metal doors—with little openings in the shape of crosses, spikes, rosettes, and so on—reveal the full content of the tombs, cut off from the world of the living. Coffins are piled up inside large vaults made of brick. The walls inside are whitewashed, but sometimes the paint flakes. A grid of pipes holds each coffin up, stacked one above another until there is no more room. Coffins line both sides of the interior. In some cases, even the central alley is filled.

Most of these monuments date from the last half of the nineteenth century. They are usually situated at a natural elevation of the terrain. Their façades are either like Greek temples or vaguely based on Catholic-looking churches with a central bell tower. Using a wide-angle lens through the openings of the doors makes for great photographs. But I wanted more.

The First Tomb

Going into the cemetery after dark was a risky business, but the moonless sky helped cover our tracks. My friend and I were on a mission. As we dodged tombstone after tombstone, a mild nervousness made us take even more care. A lot of our friends had been caught in such midnight strolls. We headed toward a row of monuments whose façades were being renovated. I had noticed a few days earlier that one of the doors behind a plastic fence held a chance of being opened. A simple bar was bolted to the ornate metal door. That lock could be removed by lifting the end that crossed the door frame. My initial idea was to somehow bend the door and create a stable opening by jamming something into the slit. For that, I carried a small log. Then I planned to slip through the narrow gap.

When we got there, I got the bar out of the way and attempted to bend the door. It just would not bend enough. As I worked the door—under a few tons of stone—I was constantly afraid of rock toppling down on me. It took a while before I figured out that my attempts to move things wouldn't disturb such a weight. Desperation set in. The door would open a little, which meant nothing was actually blocking it from the inside. I applied all my strength until the massive hinges broke free of their rusty hold. This unexpected turn of events scared the shit out of me. We moved away for a while.

As we drew close again, the dark world inside pulled on my curiosity, but in my mind was the heightened sense of going into the unknown. What if nightmares are real? My little flashlight gave me an idea of open space, devoid of anything. When I stepped inside to the lower ground, my feeling was that the earth would somehow swallow me. There is something about lowering yourself into the dark, even only a few inches. I went in.

The crypt was a bit of a disappointment at first because it was so empty. Inside the vault was a cement platform—a catafalque—on which lay one normal-looking wooden coffin on the left and two wooden boxes, one atop the other, on the right. I remember thinking: *How long has it been since this place was visited?*

My friend followed me in. Being in an enclosed space is overwhelming. Who would know if you were trapped there?

We both ended up entombed, where nothing else existed, face to face with our demons, in front of three coffins that held the grail of our quest. We were stunned into immobility.

The Little Lady

I lit the candles we brought. The place acquired a darkly romantic feel, haunted house-with-dungeon style. The coffin on the left had collapsed. Touching it might have led to further degradation, so I opted for the wooden boxes on the right. The one on top was made of particleboard. Its lid was littered with debris from the vault. The lower end of the cover seemed loose, so I pulled it up. Thanks to the humidity and the nature of particleboard, the cover—which was in two parts—lifted quite easily. Ordinary nails had rusted to the point of being nonexistent, so I put that part of the lid out of the way without moving any of the dust inside.

I had taken hold of the wrong end. What was revealed to us were the legs of the deceased. The little feet bones had collapsed.

My friend was eager to see more. I carefully went for the upper half of the lid.

In front of our eyes, lit by candlelight, lay the remains of a mature woman, age unknown, in her coffin, at rest, in eternal peace. It was a lovely sight. I was very impressed by the stillness. It slowly dawned on me how beautiful this scene was. The appearance of life, a person sleeping, undisturbed. Shreds of the fabric that lined her coffin had fallen onto her face, an appropriate reminder that all things fall apart. I brushed the fabric away. She held dried flowers in her hands, obscuring our view of her body. We realized later her prominent teeth were dentures. She was very skinny, dressed in clothes from another age. What had her life been like? What had she died from? Why was she buried in a particleboard box? Her body had definitely shrunk, leaving bones covered with only a remnant of flesh. The skull was well preserved, but the skin wasn't there anymore, only a layer of casing from necromantic insects. Every inch had been inhabited by a small being whose life had ended there. I placed three candles around the coffin and proceeded to shoot some photographs.

We looked at the coffin on the other side of the vault. The collapse had created quite a puzzle as to how to open it. Through the small gap at the bottom, only dust could be seen.

Time seemed to disappear. Maybe twenty minutes later, we exited the tomb. It was easy enough to close the door tight and set the metal bar in its place. One thing was certain: We felt a little lighter about what we were doing there. We had been where we wanted to go. We walked euphorically on the roads, but still avoided the regular exit, opting for the long way out of the cemetery.

Second Visit to the First Tomb

I returned to the same tomb two weeks later with *ma compagne*. She likes me because I am such a cemetery freak. I wanted to show her the crypt, but I also wanted to make a better picture of the inside of the vault. The previous pictures were insufficient, although the close-ups were very good. I brought a lot more candles, enough to light up the whole place.

For me, it was still an experience to re-open that door. The mass of the churchy façade weighed heavily upon my awareness as I signaled her to enter.

Being with a different person changes things. The thrill of the first time had somewhat dimmed, but there remained an incredible silence inside the crypt. *Ma compagne* got used to the inside much faster than I had the first time. She was very kind to help me place the candles around without creating further disturbance to the catafalque. All the candles held themselves upright without any incidents. Once the first few shots were taken, we posed in front of the camera, for posterity. We managed never to make a candle fall.

At last, I opened the wooden box for her. The Little Lady had not moved a bit.

I lightly touched the skull, then moved my hands down to the remains of her own and held them.

A corpse looks so fragile. To *ma compagne,* it looked less creepy than the photographs had. The illusion of life was intense in absolute stillness. I had acquired a lot of sympathy for my Little Lady.

Ma compagne went out to breathe a bit of fresh air and returned ready to investigate the conventional coffin on the left. The walls of it had collapsed. I tried to work the lid, which opened facing the wall. A body, especially the hands, could still be seen. Oddly, the skull was missing. The rest was all destroyed fabric, which had probably held the whole coffin together.

We replaced everything as it had been and took off into the night.

The Second Tomb

Ma compagne and I were walking through the cemetery late one Sunday afternoon when we came upon another row of monuments undergoing renovation. An orange fence blocked the way to the doors, but I was very surprised to see a loose wooden panel covering the front of one.

Several nights later, I went back alone. The windy night was a little cool, but the long walk kept me warm. The spookiest thing about walking into this cemetery is that a road runs alongside it. Headlights of cars that take this scenic route, lights from the lampposts along that road, and lights from faraway buildings all reflect off the tombstones. Long rows of square, glowing stones create an eerie atmosphere. As you move up the mountain, lights appear before and behind. You think that someone else is there. The sparse sections of bushes and trees rest your eyes. You try to make sense of the acoustic world. Birds or nocturnal animals rattle in the distance. This sound-and-light show follows you around. You've got to enjoy these moments, surrounded by darkness in a necropolis. I made it to the right church façade, removed the wooden panel with some difficulty, and went into the vault.

I knew that a light this high up in the mountain would attract attention, so I closed the metal door behind me before surveying the whole area with a candle. It was a mess inside. There were a lot of coffins, but sadly most of them were compressed on top of one another. The wood from one coffin had rotted and its aluminum inner sleeve had collapsed, leaving it in an upside-down position, tilted to one side. It was evident that no walking zombie would come out of the upside-down coffin. Its best feature was a glass window where the head had been.

A longish piece of aluminum had been trashed in the narrow corridor, so that had to be removed. Extinguishing the candle, I went back to the night, dragging the metal out of the tomb.

Once I closed the door again, I placed a number of candles around the area and took my pictures. Intuitively, I knew there wasn't enough light. I tried any-

"Interior of the Second Tomb" photographed by Hugues Leblanc

way, looking at things meticulously. This was a much more interesting crypt because it was so full and old and decayed.

I looked around some more. There was another body in the open, right on the floor behind the door. It seemed as if it had been tucked away under the carpet. I looked up. The overlying coffin was at mid-height, resting between two metal bars. Its bottom had given way and the body had fallen through, without its head. I placed candles around the remains, within the confined height, and took some pictures that turned out nicely, but of no great value. The missing head made it tasteless to view the rest. The body had been dressed; what was left was extremely dusty, looking more like a dummy filled with hay.

I was more successful with the other caskets. On top of the cadaverless coffin, one was broken enough to allow a view of the interior. Inside lay a skeleton, totally skinless. The bones of the spinal column were still holding onto one another. Ribs had fallen in the proper order. The skull had fallen onto its side, so I moved it back to fit with the toothless lower jaw. I took more photographs of it, but the light was insufficient. I had to put the whole camera into the hole, which eliminated all the light. I was in a bind using candlelight.

On the other side of the vault were coffins too well preserved to reveal their secrets, except for one, its side panel fallen, which held the partly decomposed body of a man dressed in what appeared to be a Sergeant Pepper coat. The coat's high collar obscured the lower jaw. Some leathery dried skin still covered the eyes, giving the skull the aspect of an Egyptian mummy. The face was certainly still apparent, the nose visible. Another hole in the coffin showed the hands: very sinewy, shrunken. I tried taking pictures again but could only predict a negative outcome, so I decided to return with a better setup.

Beyond the corpses, the floor was littered with coffin parts. Handles, carved nails, decorations lay in the dust. At the far end of the crypt, I found the chevron-shaped lid of a small coffin. It was hardly longer than my arm.

Outside, the wind howled. I called it a night.

Second Visit to the Second Tomb

Ma compagne wanted to see the second crypt, do a second expedition up the mountain, a second night among the dead. It was warmer by then, a solid breeze shaking the trees, dulling the sounds. High up there, facing a valley of tombstones, one is easily fooled by distractions reverberating in the dark. I guess cemeteries have to be creepy at night.

We were by then a very good team, used to the security issues involved. She sat on a big rock facing the tomb while I removed the wooden panel. I also removed the aluminum from the inside. We closed the door behind us. I had no flash, but *ma compagne* brought her Instamatic, so that I could use the photons of her camera to light up my negatives. I wanted a shot of the crypt undisturbed so we did the flash thing rather quickly and efficiently. Then I wanted to do the other ones, but the preparation took more time than I'd expected. *Ma compagne* was busy by herself, looking at all those little pieces on the floor, decorations from coffins that had fallen.

Looking at the floor reminded me to look at the ceiling. At the top of the shelves, two small boxes hinted at smaller corpses. I took a chance, knowing the bottom had already collapsed out of one coffin. I climbed up the metal pipes constituting the shelves and got myself in reach of one of the smaller boxes, broken and tilting to one side. In it was a lot of debris. The small coffin it had contained was disjointed. The top cover had broken into four or five parts. The

little coffin must have been so pretty, but there it lay, smashed, spilling part of its contents onto the coffins below. Only the central parts remained.

It occurred to me that the body must have collapsed in situ way before the wood rotted. I examined further and found small curved bones—flat, very thin, as from a broken eggshell. I found that two little ones were elements of a small skull, fitting together at the suture. At the moment of death, the bones had not yet totally joined. This had indeed been a small infant, sinful enough to have been alive, weak enough to have failed at an early age. Other parts of the skull were easily reassembled. Only the upper jaw pieces were missing. The baby was held once more in human hands before being left to wait further disintegration.

This was such a complex vault. Whole families had had their remains put in this place so that they could be close to one another. Little ones hinted at a difficult childhood; older ones at lives well spent. After a last look around, we went down the mountain again.

Later in the fall, high winds flipped the wooden panel away and the cemetery workers permanently secured it with new bolts. Another eternity awaited the inhabitants of this tomb, happy people from harder times.

Third Visit to the First Tomb

When I returned less than a year later, the light of the full moon flooded the whole landscape. It was so bright, one could almost pretend it was daylight. That only made me more wary. There were many more reflections on the tombstones than usual. I think going through that desolate black-and-white world made it a special experience. A different friend and I took a break to enjoy the surroundings and a lovely little cross that had fallen from its pedestal.

Upon our arrival at the tomb, he instinctively guarded the area, too close to the main entrance for our taste. I felt like a tour guide. The only element missing from my understanding of the tomb: what was in that big box under the Little Lady? I carefully moved away the accumulation of dead leaves from the front of the door and found the rest of the operation quite easy. I still needed to break rust from the door's hinges but, overall, I thought it had turned too much into an open house.

Right after coming in, my friend tried to close the door a bit behind him, an action that I thought wasn't so wise because rust works both ways. I lit a candle and handed him the small flashlight. Moving around, he immediately found a metal plate on the side of the collapsed coffin on the left. On it was the name of the deceased. I'd overlooked this in my previous visits because it was so near the wall. There were plates behind the particleboard coffins on the right, we later discovered. That meant that this place had once held more coffins than it presently contained.

By then, I had gotten hold of a camera flash. I took one picture of the nameplate. Satisfied, we moved to the right side of the vault and I got the upper half of the particleboard lid out of the way. There lay my Little Lady, impeccable. My friend illuminated her. She was his first full skeleton. She was still very beautiful, her dentures enlivening her facial features. Somehow, she showed much less volume. The illusion of a body was faded because of the flat look of her garment. In pictures with the candles, the skull was enough to give the impression of a personality, the rest an old garment covering decay.

My friend looked on, taking in the details that I pointed out: the empty eyes, the flowers, the hands, and so on. He was pretty relaxed about it, but I was, as usual, pressed by time.

I went to one end of the lower box, which held promise for the evening. By lifting the lid, I could see a bit of the inside. I couldn't lift the cover very high because of the particleboard coffin on top. I had leverage but very little angle to play with. My friend helped and we used a wooden block to hold up the cover. I took more photographs, encumbered now by the flash module that took a lot of space atop the camera. Taking a picture through an eight-inch hole while thinking of the angles you're covering is not an easy business; you hope for the best. The flash worked every time and the box was a real treasure house. There were two obvious skulls at our end and what appeared to be a body at the other. My camera couldn't get closer. That lid was too big a problem. It couldn't be lifted without compromising the integrity of the Little Lady's particleboard coffin above it. I feared damaging the Little Lady, so we left the lower coffin in place.

The Little Lady, unshaken by the disturbance, had not suffered. As I replaced the lid over her, I tried to imagine the history of this tomb. I saw the leftover elements, what remained of decades of funerals. There presumably had been more coffins in there at some time. Coffins had decayed and wooden planks had fallen apart. Skeletons had been displaced. Upon reopening the tomb every so often, cemetery workers would have removed the debris and deposited the various human remains in the big box. The Little Lady may have been the last survivor of her family. One had the sense that no one had been buried there after she was, that there were unlikely to be any other burials. It is ironic that from her high position atop her family ossuary, she would eventually fall through to the bottom with all the others.

Outside, I closed the door easily and reshuffled the leaves in front of it. Back in the moonlight, hiding behind giant shadows in the shape of trees, my friend and I headed back toward civilization.

I stopped in front of another row of tombs to look at the sky, at Orion, Hercules, and Cassiopeia. I couldn't dream of a nicer landscape in which to transform into that little fox, roaming around, hiding the night away within shadows.

Musings

There is more to cemeteries than monuments, grave markers, and pretty statues. In my wanderings, I've jumped into holes, I've touched half-decayed coffins, I've kicked around mounds of earth that revealed human bones. Being in cemeteries at night—sightseeing crypts and cadavers by candlelight—is adventurous and romantic. However, it is not something that I would do every day. My goal has been to explore the effects of decay on the body. Montreal happens to have century-plus-old tombs. Although one automatically thinks of spirits, souls, and immortality in the afterlife, it's been obvious in the photographic essay that came from these cemetery visits that the ultimate fate of our physical bodies is gradual disappearance, the loss of flesh until only bone remains. Decay is slowed but not stopped. As opposed to in-ground burial, where flesh is expected to last up to a year, keeping cadavers in open vaults increases their dignified chance of survival as maccabees, those walking skeletons of the *Danse Macabre* of the fifteenth century. The entombed people from the last century knew how to preserve themselves. Instead of having bodies disappear in flames, the emphasis was on quiet preservation. They built church-like tombs to approximate still older values.

Part of the better preservation in tombs here in Montreal probably lies with the climate. Sub-zero temperatures in the winter slow down the decomposition of the flesh considerably. Aboveground, away from worms and rainwater, the dehydration of tissue is facilitated by the flow of warm summer breezes within the tombs. Age, however, always gives way to chaos and entropy. Skeletons, wooden panels, and clothing all eventually deteriorate, decay, decompose, and finally turn into powder.

By taking photographs of the Little Lady and the others, I have a sense of prolonging even further the manifestation of their existence here on earth, of experiencing a bit of their personalities. This sounds grandiose, but then popular culture has not kept ancestor worship in its bag of tricks. In ancient times, would going to see one's ancestor in the middle of the night have been more understood? Cadavers would have been looked at, questions asked, and even the atmosphere would have provided answers.

Death walks beside us, until dust does us part.

Postscript

Since I took these photos, all these tombs have been renovated and their doors replaced. My photos were the last views of the interiors of these tombs.

Love Among the Tombs: Adventures in Forensic Archaeology

by Leilah Wendell

"The orgasm that creates life is nothing compared to the rapture of Death."

–Anonymous, 1897

Imagine the anticipation and sense of excitement Victor Loret must have felt when, in 1898, he unearthed one of the great royal caches of Egyptian mummies—sixteen in all! Imagine what was going through the minds of those whose "job" it was to unwrap the bandages. Of course, let us not forget that this was all done in the name of science. A far cry from Victor Ardisson, a Loret contemporary, whose reason for doing basically the same thing under, shall we say, less than scientific circumstances was, "Each of us has our passions. As for me, the cadaver is mine!" This reasoning would be echoed by another of their contemporaries, Henri Blot, whose infamous words at his own trial are still recounted in various texts: "How would you have it? Every man to his own tastes. Mine is for corpses."

In the end, all three examples boil down to mankind's unending *fascination* with the dead body, whether in the name of science or . . . romance. The dead, in their various stages, continue to intrigue the living.

Remember the scene from *Indiana Jones and the Last Crusade* when Indy discovered the secret entrance to the crypt beneath the library? He flung open the knight's coffin and straddled the corpse to take a rubbing from the shield in the dead knight's hand. No doubt, Blot and Ardisson would have found that scene highly erotic. I did! But then, we necromantic types have been misunderstood and vilified for ages. While it's okay for science to "fiddle with the dead," it's an act of grave (no pun intended) abhorrence for the rest of us to do the same. Go figure!

From Sergeant Bertrand to Ed Gein, the label of *necrophile* continues to have inherent shock value. Perhaps the most misunderstood area of human attractions, the mere concept of necrophilia inspires emotions equivalent in nature to mankind's ever-present fear and denial of death itself. Yet these are the same people who will rubberneck around a bloody car wreck.

The general consensus, even among serious psychological researchers, is that *all* necrophiles are inherently "sick and perverse" individuals. "It [necrophilia] is the true perversion," writes Dr. Erich Fromm, a prominent early-twentieth-century researcher into the field. "While being alive, not life but death is loved, not growth, but destruction." Necrophilia has been conjoined to the heading of *psychopath*. Because *true* necrophilia is so rare and misunderstood, it cannot possibly be documented fairly.

Most available research, a term I use loosely, on the subject paints a distorted and repulsive picture of the practice by folks who are either ignorantly or deliberately *sub*jective, rather than *ob*jective. For instance, according to psychiatric documentation, nearly all practitioners of necrophilia have been sexually abused or rejected (or both) in some way. Most, if not all, have some history of mental disorders and exhibit other forms of "sociopathic" behavior. *Necrophile* has become an unthinkable label simply because the great majority of those who claim its title are only doing so (with fresh corpses, might I add) for an "easy lay." The whole dominance and submission thing comes into play. No fear of rejection or complaint. No worries about performance. The corpse is viewed solely as an inanimate plaything, rather than a sacred catalyst. The *true* necrophile cares *nothing* about any of these concerns and desires only intimacy with Death. The crypt is what separates the necromantic from the (textbook) necrophile.

I don't know about most people, but a fresh cadaver does nothing for me. To me, such a state is still quite representative of life. A fresh corpse (or what I like to call a *gooey louie*) contains many living organisms and bacteria working at a frantic pace to achieve their goal: decomposition. Only when this is complete will the last aspect of Life itself die.

When the bathroom-tile green of the morgue dulls your senses and the formaldehyde sterility of the embalming room clouds your head, there is still a place where the feel, the aroma, and the aura of Death prevails: the crypt. At this level, you are not dealing with any shred of human individuality; you are dealing solely with Death itself. Therein lies the rub, the sticking point in any study of necrophilia. It is the all-important difference between necrophilia viewed as a "sexual deviation" or as an intimate encounter with Death.

While the distant and fanciful adventures of Loret and Jones are out of reach for those of you out there who truly want to get intimate with Death Itself, there remains one sanctioned possibility. It has no prestigious title. You won't make a lot of money, nor is it the stuff of movie adventures, and it's definitely *not* white-collar: It's simply referred to as forensic disinterment re-evaluation. What I like to call forensic archaeology. Those of us who have done it casually refer to it as "exhumation detail."

In most parts of the civilized world, this is usually a job performed by a branch (which we used to call the *ghoul squad*) of the medical examiner's office, i.e., the county morgue. Sometimes the actual disinterments are done by a subcontracted party, such as the local gravediggers' union, private cemetery maintenance crews, or even landscaping contractors. In more remote parts of the world, the job of disinterring the dead falls upon relatives of the deceased, with the help of local villagers.

A corpse is exhumed for various reasons, from the most ridiculous to the most newsworthy. For example, bodies are routinely exhumed from graveyards when family members relocate, to take their dead with them, so to speak, to be reburied in the new locale. Disinterment takes place more notably for the purposes of a coroner's inquest, when foul play or other suspicious or overlooked causes of death are in question, such as in the case of a homicide or suicide. Other disinterments occur on a more frequent basis in such so-called remote places like New Orleans, where bodies are casually discarded or whatever remains is push-broomed into a special lower crypt chamber to make room for a fresh burial. This is a practice, I must admit, I have never encountered in any other part of the country. I realize that land is at a premium here, but who draws the line between decency and practicality?

If you're fortunate enough to participate in an exhumation, you'll never run out of stories to tell your grandchildren on those dark and stormy nights! There are few things in this world more exciting than opening an interred coffin and viewing the remarkable. One of the more intriguing digs I've had the privilege of working on was up in the Northeast. It was well over fifteen years ago, but the memory is as fresh as yesterday.

After the power shovels removed the initial five feet of packed earth and clay, it was up to us modern day "sack 'em up men" to finish the job and retrieve the prize. In this particular case, we exhumed a very decayed cheap pine box that was completely enveloped in weeping willow roots. If you know anything about these trees, you'd know how tenacious and unique their root system can be. Resem-

bling thousands of long thin tentacles, they are extremely strong and completely invasive. They have been known to crush and infiltrate heavy iron water mains to quench their voracious thirst.

Under the shadow of gray storm clouds and armed with an odd arsenal of everything from bolt cutters to barber's scissors, my associate and I descended into the opened grave, carefully snipping around the coffin's cracked lid. After fifteen minutes of work, we finally got a prybar into the crevice and gently wrenched the lid free. It broke into splintered sections from the dryness of the unique northeastern soil. We felt like Burke and Hare as we shone the makeshift kerosene lantern into the opened casket. (We never used flashlights if we could help it. They're just so rude.) The whole corpse was literally enmeshed in a formfitting macramé of spidery tendrils. It looked like something straight out of *Invasion of the Body Snatchers*. The basic form of the corpse was beautifully mummified by a combination of its spiny green wrappings and the natural desiccant quality of the clay.

The next step was a delicate and time-consuming process. The decision was whether to remove the corpse from the grave still

Illustration by Erik Rose

LEILAH WENDELL

encased in the roots or to painstakingly snip away as much growth as possible and hope that the body would remain intact enough for transport. After debating over a few beers and watching the sky grow increasingly more ominous, we opted for the latter. I started at the head, while my associate began at the feet. The roots had literally penetrated the corpse and had been feeding upon its elements. In places, like around the head, the roots could be cut and peeled away in large chunks, much like peeling an orange. Beneath, the withered body had the preservative quality of a freshly unwrapped Egyptian mummy. (Natural mummification *always* results in the most exquisite find!) We could tell that the body had not been embalmed. A plus, as embalming is a sure way to wreak havoc on the natural decomposition of the human body. Sure, you may look "great" for three or four days in a viewing room, even keep your shape for several weeks underground. However, once embalming fluid and the progressive bacteria interact, it's nothing short of a grotesque experiment in the name of human vanity, denial, and greed. Nothing nice to look at all, let alone to get intimate with!

As the sun was going down,

we were nearly done. Carefully we loaded our prize into our customized truck and prepared for the four-hour trek home. We earned our $6 an hour (plus mileage) that day! My cohort cranked up some tunes on the eight-track in the cab, shot me a sly little smile as I finished securing our "friend" for the journey. Boy, was I beat. I sprawled out on the shag-carpeted floor as "Nights in White Satin" poured like molasses from the speakers. "A little romantic traveling music?" My associate grinned, a knowing glint in his eye. I nodded and he turned back to face the long expanse of highway ahead of us.

Away we rode into the sunset, like Indiana Jones. For the rest of this adventure? Just exercise your imagination, won't you!

This is but one of the many modern day adventures available for the aspiring forensic archaeologist with a real *passion* for his or her calling. All one needs are some old clothes, high-top boots, and a sense of adventure. Who knows, you too could bring home a real "find" to add to your collection. The moments to enjoy your find may be fleeting, but the experience will be a permanent installation in your personal museum of memories. I have quite a collection!

LOVING THE DEAD

Sex Crimes in History: Evolving Concepts of Sadism, Lust-Murder, and Necrophilia from Ancient to Modern Times says "the classical case of necrophiliac perversion" is that of Sergeant Bertrand in the middle of the nineteenth century. Described as handsome and "sensitive" in appearance, Bertrand had a lifelong habit of willfully breaking anything that came to his hands. He began his criminal career as a child by mutilating animal corpses he found at the roadside. This progressed to torturing and killing animals, one of the stepping-stones acknowledged by most sex criminals. While Bertrand fantasized about abusing and killing women, he took up with female corpses first. These he would "overwhelm" with passionate kisses and caresses. Always, the exhumations ended in mutilation. Bertrand said, "The urge to dismember the bodies was incomparably more violent in me than the urge to violate them." Twenty-five-year-old Bertrand was a French soldier at the time of his arrest.

Henri Blot, a "not unattractive" twenty-six-year-old, was caught asleep in a grave after he had ravished the female corpse within. Apparently, his necrophilia was linked with a sort of epilepsy, which dropped him into a trance state after the act was accomplished. The most romantic of his victims was an eighteen-year-old ballet dancer whom he disinterred in Saint-Ouen Cemetery (near Montmartre in Paris) in 1886. At his trial, he showed no remorse for his actions and won some immortality with his response: *Chacun a son goût.* Each to his own taste.

Victor Ardisson fulfilled the stereotype of the necrophiliac who couldn't get a date. He proposed to several living women—who laughed at him—so he took to following women and masturbating when they stopped to urinate in public restrooms. After he began exhuming corpses, Ardisson brought home a severed head, which he called his bride. His necrophilia was discovered after he brought home the decaying corpse of a three-year-old girl.

The morbid bible *Death to Dust: What Happens to Dead Bodies?* defines necrophilia as "a morbid fondness for dead bodies." Fewer than ten percent of necrophiles are also necrophages, meaning they cannibalize the dead. Only seventeen percent of necrophiles can be classified as psychotic, which suggests the others are well aware of what they are doing and how society would view it. Seventy-nine percent of necrophiles are heterosexual. The overwhelming majority are male.

—Editor

269

Grandmarama

by Allegra Lundyworf

Last year, a few days before Mother's Day, I sat in a small San Francisco café on Noriega Avenue near the ocean to write a card to my maternal grandmother, the lady I had grown up calling both Grandma Jean and Grandma Butterfly. I was worried about her. She and my grandpa liked living so near to their sons in Arkansas. She was in reasonably good health, but my grandpa's health had declined so far that my grandma couldn't take care of him at home. She had to move him into a rest home, where she visited him every day. Throughout this time, she talked to my mother every week; lately, she sounded very sad, Mom said. My Grandpa Tiger was suffering from dementia and becoming increasingly disoriented. The man who had been Grandma's strength—her rock—for most of her life was weak and lost.

I didn't write to her about that, though. I told Grandma Butterfly that I was thinking about her, that I loved her. I told her about the café where I wrote the note, with its mermaid-themed mosaics and funky maritime décor. I thought she would love it. She would have thought it was "very California."

All my life, my mother's parents lived far away. I only recall two visits to their homes: once, when I was very small and they lived in Arizona, and once when I was in junior high school and they lived in Arkansas. Instead, they visited us in Southern California. My Grandpa John wasn't much of a talker, but he had a low rumbling growl of a laugh—and what seemed like perpetual stubble—so my big sister called him Grandpa Tiger. It seemed only fitting that my Grandma Jean should have a nickname as well, so she became Grandma Butterfly, who loved flowers and gave us butterfly kisses, giggling as she brushed our cheeks with her eyelashes.

A few weeks after I sent that note to my grandma, Mom called to say that Grandma Butterfly was dead. The last time they had spoken, Grandma said that John had not recognized her when she visited him. She also said that she had received my card and it made her smile. Days later, she had taken her own life, neatly and quietly.

On the morning of the day she died, Grandma Butterfly phoned one of my uncles. She spoke briefly with my aunt. *No, she said, it's not urgent. I don't need to talk to him right away, but could you ask him to stop by this afternoon?* When her son arrived several hours later, he found his mother in the car, in the garage, motor running, window open, garage door shut. It was clear to her children that she had not wanted too much time to pass before her body was discovered. And she didn't want to be found by strangers. She had left the house newly cleaned and tidied—the clothes washed, pressed, and folded—no dirty dishes in the sink.

She didn't want any sort of memorial service. I'd wondered about that. I wanted to say my good-byes, but wasn't looking forward to visiting Arkansas again. Most of my memories of my Grandma Butterfly were linked to my childhood homes in SoCal, not halfway across the country. No, my mom said, she would fly back, but only to help deal with the aftermath, the sorting of belongings and signing of papers. And to see her father for the last time.

In the meantime, I needed a

way to say good-bye in San Francisco. I wrote to my friends about my grandmother, remembering the things she liked, the way she moved, the things she'd said. I told them grandma stories and the response I got was immediate. Some asked for more grandmother stories. Some told me grandma and grandpa stories of their own. I decided that even though a last-minute invitation would probably mean a low turnout, I needed to take this exchange of stories and turn it into the good-bye that I wouldn't otherwise have.

I sent a message out, inviting my friends to help me say good-bye to my grandmother with a bonfire at Ocean Beach:

If you and anyone you know would like to join me in saying good-bye to a grandma who's gone; tell stories about grandmas, good or bad, who are still going strong; talk around the fire about grannies, nanous, grandmamas, nanas, mammaws, babushkas, memaws, grandmothers, abuelas . . . *them* . . . come join me.

Bring firewood and stories. Wear warm clothes. (Your grandma wouldn't want you to catch cold!) If you have a recipe handed down from your grandmother for something we can eat on a windy beach, go ahead and bring it. I'll probably drink beer, myself. If you never had a grandma, or if you wish you hadn't, come and ask people about the ones they had. Maybe some of us wish we could trade. If you can't be there but you want your story heard, send it to me and I'll share it with whoever shows up.

About an hour after sunset that Saturday night, my husband and I picked up firewood and beer from the supermarket one block from the beach. We found a spot where we didn't think we'd get washed away by the tide, where we weren't too close to a loudly singing Christian youth group. As we tried to remember how to build a proper fire, friends arrived in twos and threes. When there were about eight of us and a decent fire, we got started.

I talked about how my Grandma Butterfly used to make matching outfits for me and for my dolls, about the way my Grandma Alice met Grandpa Lucky. I talked about Grandpa Tiger, gruff and scratchy and full of laughter. I talked about people I'd loved and who had loved

me, regardless of whether we'd understood one another, people who had raised my parents well. I listened to stories of cruelty and mishaps and gifts, of odd accents and culture clashes. There were immigration stories and stories of punishment, stories of family meals and family jokes. Rachel talked about the ranch she had loved as a child, the place that felt like home in a way nothing else connected to her family ever had. I told the story of Michel's grandfather, the convicted chicken thief. Karissa talked about fruit her grandmother had picked. Dave told us that grandparents like ours came along only once in a generation. This got a tentative laugh. Some stories were retold for latecomers. Someone went

Illustration by M. Parfitt

back to the store for more wood.

Finally I excused myself and went down to the tideline, which had been steadily advancing on us. I looked out at the waves, the moon, the clouds, the night sky: the closest thing to infinity I can imagine without leaving the atmosphere of this planet. It didn't matter that she'd last been east of me, not west. There was no direction to where my grandmother was now.

"Good-bye!" I yelled. "Good-bye, Grandma! I love you!"

And that was what I had needed. I came back to the fire. My friends hugged me and smiled. Before long, our fire burned down and it was time to get home. Even though she'd left instructions that she wanted no service, I didn't feel like I'd gone against Grandma Butterfly's wishes. What she didn't want was a room with her children and grandchildren sitting in it, along with the one or two friends who'd outlived her and would still remember her, shedding quiet tears over her passing. Instead, I wanted to make sure other people remembered her, people who had never known her in life. That there were people who, when they heard about Grandma Butterfly, would smile and think of sharing memories around a fire right next to the ocean.

• • •

Since my grandma's death, Mom and I have started talking every week on the phone, just like she used to do with her mother. Only a few weeks passed before my mother called to say her dad had died. The feeling in the family was unanimous: He'd finally realized that his wife was gone. That Jean was not coming back. So he went, too. In the weeks before, he'd told his children, "She's very busy." It was the way he explained her absence, the end of her daily visits. When at last he understood, he died of a stroke.

My grandfather, too, had requested that there be no memorial service held for him. I'd already said my good-bye to him there on the beach, knowing even if he had stayed around, I'd never get to talk to the grandpa I had known: He would never again see my face and know he was looking at his granddaughter.

I will host the Grandmarama again, this year and for as many years as it feels right. I'll plan a little further in advance, but I still won't mind if I don't get a big turnout. I'll invite my friends to come down to the beach, build a fire, and share stories. About grandmas, about grandpas, and about us: the ones who remember them.

The Keeper of the Shop

by Jill Tracy

For no apparent reason, I've been drawn to particular "found" objects throughout my life. I find a sense of divination—a feeling of function, purpose, and communication—through seemingly insignificant items.

Curled along the sidewalk, rubber bands denote a wish granted. "Stray" playing cards, revealed during treks through New York and San Francisco, have forged a path of cosmic poker, foretelling and reassuring me about poignant personal events.

Fans of my music now reward me with their own found-card collections, adorning the stage with them. (They know the nine of hearts is my most propitious; queen of spades, certainly a close second.) Puzzle pieces discovered at intersections have directed me through difficult decisions. The magic is always there; the trick is to allow myself to be observant enough to recognize it.

I became transfixed when stumbling upon the strange little shop in 1992. Having just moved from Manhattan, I was exploring San Francisco's Haight-Ashbury and was instantly lured into the magical storefront. Its textured walls were laden with curios: gargoyles, handcrafted religious icons, occult supplies, voodoo dolls, taxidermy, Chinese money for the dead. Bric-a-brac crowded every inch of space, displayed haphazardly from nails, pushpins, and fishing line. Towering toward the ceiling, this evoked a glorious sense of peril, especially in a city known for its earthquakes. Some of the shelves were so dusty, it looked as though the merchandise had been unearthed from past centuries. Basket upon basket held odd toys and talismans, licorice pipes, and dashboard saints.

The woman behind the counter possessed a cold, exotic air. Clad in an antique velvet dress, dark curls bundled loosely on top of her head, she appeared as a dark queen reigning over her unsuspecting subjects. When she noticed a particular book I was carrying, she struck up a conversation. Kerri turned out to be the store's manager.

She smiled subtly when I asked if they were hiring. In a hushed tone, she replied that yes, they did need someone, but hadn't really put the word out. I gave her my telephone number. I felt I'd found a kindred spirit.

As I walked further down the street, I encountered a shiny nine of hearts at the very edge of the curb. San Francisco was proving to be lucky for me.

My interview to meet the owner of the shop was scheduled the following week. Getting the job rested on whether Jeff liked me or not. When I spoke with Kerri initially, she informed me that Jeff could come across as a bit odd, but not to worry.

Nevertheless, I did. Following my second cup of coffee, three aspirins, and no breakfast, I entered the shop. Peggy Lee cooed on the stereo. Through black curtains concealing the back office emerged a small, older gentleman with slumped bookseller's shoulders. He beckoned me to the desk. He wore a dull tweed cap, thick-rimmed eyeglasses, and an unfashionably wide tie. His full gray beard gave him a cartoon walrus appearance. His eccentric character melded with the décor.

Hardly had we exchanged formalities when the conversation took an enjoyable shift into very non-work topics, from Eartha Kitt to mystery novels, fifties mambo music, and our shared travails in New York City.

Needless to say, I began the following Monday.

Monday was the slowest day of the week by far, so additional tasks included dusting, straightening up the displays, and conversing by the cash register for long hours while drinking coffee, exploring every imaginable subject.

At first, I found Mondays agonizing, being alone with the boss for the entire day. I longed for other coworkers. But as the weeks passed, I felt more and more affection for this curious shopkeeper. I began to look forward fondly to Mondays, when Jeff and I could share our stories.

Jeff was actually headed for Portland, Oregon. His "stopover" in San Francisco had lasted seventeen years. He resided in an old Victorian apartment building across the street from the store. His daily routine encompassed no more than three city blocks. This existence appeared hardly exceptional, but his life was a collection of extraordinary events and occupations. Jeff delighted in telling his tales; every muscle in his petite frame clenched with excitement. His hands gesticulated wildly, salt-and-pepper eyebrows wriggling like caterpillars. Every Monday revealed an adventure more compelling than the last.

Being a gay man in New York City during the early 1970s inspired him to become a photographer, capturing drag performers on and off stage. He went on to gain popularity instructing old-fashioned burlesque and striptease dancers to disrobe with extra panache. He confessed to publishing several X-rated pulp novels under a pen name he would never reveal.

Mastering the art of grooming standard poodles, Jeff spent some of his New York days clipping "show cuts" on the precious pets of Mafia members. He liked to go into great detail about the variety of classic pom-pom poodle styles, the "Metropolitan" a favorite among clients. He'd also sold antiquarian books, been a radio announcer, champion cribbage player, and an expert at hand-beading couture evening gowns.

Jeff's current routine included daily jaunts to the Haight Street Goodwill, where he never failed to score. Jeff excitedly bestowed upon me a plastic Infant of Prague floating inside a Jell-O-red lucite cube, followed by a drinking mug that stated "Dating is a Tug-of-War . . . just one big jerk after another."

Having now achieved a prominent and avuncular role in my life, Jeff was bewildered by my penchant for long-haired, tortured artist types. When boys of this sort swaggered into the store, Jeff waited until they exited, then burst into laughter. On some occasions, he hid in the stockroom to control his giggling fits when one of them paid me a visit. He would say in his grandiloquent tone, "Honey, you've got to get over it."

Nearly two years passed and my living situation in a nearby flat became unbearable. Following a scary ordeal, I had to evacuate my home in mere hours, while the San Francisco Police Department detained my male (long-haired) roommate overnight for questioning about a possible felony. Jeff invited me to move all of my earthly possessions into the store's cramped rear office, while I crashed on a friend's sofa.

The little shop literally became my home for three months. I made daily treks in and out to retrieve necessary items from my desk and bureau. Cardboard boxes of my clothes, books, and memorabilia shared shelf space with Tiki barware, tarot cards, and Elvis Presley toilet-seat covers. Jeff made what could have been a devastating situation reassuring. He constantly joked about selling my belongings by mistake.

One particular Monday, while I rung up Marquis de Sade

healing candles and glow-in-the-dark rubber squids, a customer paid for his purchases with a $2 bill. I exclaimed to Jeff that twos were a good luck token; I held onto them whenever they found me. But that's just it: for the magic to be genuine, I had to happen upon the bills, not purposely procure them.

I swapped the lucky charm for two singles from my wallet and carefully stashed the bill in the top drawer of my black steel desk, still housed in the back office. The auspicious two worked its magic. Soon I found an ideal apartment and roommate, mere blocks away.

Another summer inflicted itself upon Haight Street. Tourists shoved into the narrow storefront, both intrigued and outraged at our collection of curiosities. They destroyed our carefully arranged displays, as well as our patience.

Kerri and I were working on a Tuesday when Jeff failed to bring in our paychecks. In fact, neither one of us had seen him the entire morning. This was completely out of character for Jeff. According to his delicate and systematic methods, Tuesday was always, without fail, Pay Day.

We questioned other merchants in the neighborhood: the man at the corner store where Jeff purchased his cigarettes, the used bookstore clerks, the owner of the corner coffeehouse. Jeff's fixed routine was embedded into our brains. No one had caught sight of him all day. After several more hours passed, we had to investigate. This was very strange indeed.

I tended to customers while Kerri crossed the street and ascended the stairs to Jeff's apartment. Through his third-story front door, she could hear his cats scrambling across the hardwood floors, mewing plaintively. Where had Jeff gone? He wouldn't just take off and not inform us, nor leave his precious cats behind.

We made phone calls and left messages, the final one—by late afternoon—to Jeff's landlady. We all had that gut feeling that something terrible had happened. No one actually remembered seeing Jeff since closing time the previous Friday. Monday had been a holiday, so the store hadn't opened.

His landlady assured us that she would allow entry into his apartment; however, she would not return until seven P.M. The remainder of the afternoon was torturous. We trembled anytime the phone rang, hoping to hear Jeff's voice. The entire staff had been notified by Kerri; most of them rushed to the store, huddling around the cash register, waiting.

As we padlocked the metal gates across the doors at closing time, Jeff's landlady appeared, clutching a cumbersome ring of keys. Kerri and I followed her into the apartment building's dank, carpeted entranceway. Years of urine and mildew stains mingled inconspicuously with the ugly floral pattern. The other employees stayed in the stairwell as the three of us climbed to the third floor.

Kerri stopped abruptly in the dim hallway. I noticed her eyes were moist with tears. "Please, you go first," she sobbed.

Devoid of expression, the landlady turned the key in the lock. I took a slow breath and walked in.

I'd never been in Jeff's apartment before. The barren living room was pungent with kitty litter and stale cigarettes. Remnants of the day's sunlight cut blandly across the shadowy abandoned clutter. I felt like a trespasser, but couldn't help eyeing his vast collection of rare books and record albums and merchandise from the store. The cats had quieted down.

The glare of a lightbulb came from the left corner. The door to the bathroom was ajar.

As I approached, I noticed an obstruction in the light. There was Jeff, slumped on the floor, one hand clutching his stomach, the other languidly extended across the commode seat. Gentle and balding, naked save for a dingy white T-shirt, Jeff lay dead on the floor. For the first time, I witnessed him without his familiar tweed cap and glasses. Kerri's cries echoed through the hallway.

I thought how anticlimactic death was. There had been no dramatic buildup or stirring violins, no edge-of-your-seat crescendo, no digital special effects, no parting soliloquy. This was reality: a man alone, drawing his last breath, coiled in a fetal position on a cold bathroom floor.

What must have gone through his mind? I recalled Jeff's gleeful recitation of the tale of silent screen actress Lupe Velez: "She staged the most glamorous suicide ever imagined as a finale to her faded career." He had chuckled. "Selecting her finest evening gown and encrusting herself in jewels, she posed dramatically in her bed, awaiting the world to discover her elegant corpse. The pills sent her racing to the toilet several hours later."

That's how they found her, just like Jeff. Neither of them had planned it that way, but that's how their stories ended. I knew Jeff would get a fine laugh out of that. Then again, he wouldn't be around to share the story with me on Monday.

I peered down at his peaceful, ashen body and simply closed the door.

The autopsy report showed that Jeff died of a massive heart attack at age forty-nine. How ironic that a man who was so terrified of dying from AIDS, who proclaimed celibacy for the last fourteen years, had been defeated in the end by sustenance on McDonald's cheeseburgers, coffee, and cigarettes.

Jeff had no close relatives and no will, so the store was court-awarded to the next of kin, residing somewhere in the Midwest. They, of course, had no interest in the business, so it fell upon Kerri and the rest of the staff to liquidate the shop's inventory and go through his personal belongings. We all knew Jeff would have wanted it that way. To his relatives, he was a misunderstood outcast, but to us he was a comrade. While sorting through his apartment, we each saved—as a cherished memento—one of Jeff's ever-present ties,

selecting the most loud and hideous in the collection, recalling each one with amused admiration. Several months later, the store closed its doors.

Six years have passed. I can't help but think of Jeff often; my apartment is still adorned with ornate mirrors, statuary, and unusual treasures I obtained while working for him.

Recently, while reconfiguring some furniture in my apartment, I cleaned out the black steel desk, the desk held safely in the store's stockroom years ago.

Hidden in the top drawer, beneath scotch tape, scissors, and postage stamps, was a $2 bill. I remembered receiving the bill during my days at the little shop. I noticed writing on it. In black ink, it plainly read, "Jill, I love you, Jeff 7/12/94."

That was odd. I didn't recall Jeff writing on that $2 bill, or

From the author's collection

what happened in July of 1994. That seemed to be about the year the store closed.

Intrigued, I went to the hall closet and pulled out my 1994 datebook, wedged behind bulky coats and suitcases. I flipped through the gold-edged pages to July 12. Had Jeff given me another bill as a gift that day? Had there been a celebration of sorts at the store? I didn't have any other close friends named Jeff, then or now. It had to be from him.

I gasped in astonishment. The datebook revealed that July 12 was the very Tuesday I discovered Jeff dead in his apartment.

The coroner reported that Jeff had passed away during the weekend. On July 12, 1994, Jeff had been dead for three days.

The next time I saw Kerri, I asked if she had any samples of Jeff's handwriting. She pulled out a few old Christmas cards. We compared the signatures with the $2 bill. The writing was identical.

Naysayers might search for a logical explanation, but I believe that Jeff merely wanted to bid me farewell by means of the "profound" objects he knew I so adored. I'd like to think he finally made it to Portland after all.

LIVING ON IN DEATH

After dancing behind Fanny Brice in *Music Box Revue,* Mexican-born Lupe Velez got her break in 1928 as the wild mountain girl in *The Gaucho,* starring Douglas Fairbanks. She worked for D. W. Griffith in *Lady of the Pavements,* then went on to make *The Wolf Song* with Gary Cooper, *East Is West, The Squaw Man, The Cuban Love Song,* and more than forty other films. She was best known for the seven *Mexican Spitfire* movies she made. In the 1930s, she took a break on Broadway, where she starred in *Hot-Cha!* with Bert Lahr, then *Strike Me Pink* with Jimmy Durante. She returned to Hollywood to join MGM, where her husband Johnny Weissmuller was starring in the Tarzan movies. Their marriage didn't last.

Thanks to the notoriety brought by *Hollywood Babylon,* the suicide of Lupe Velez transcended fact to become tragicomic myth. The reality may have been more mundane.

The Hollywood Book of Death describes the December 13, 1944, passing of Maria Guadalupe Vélez de Villalobos. After the Hollywood premiere of her Mexican-made vehicle *Nana,* Velez returned to her Beverly Hills mansion alone. She put on her "favorite blue silk pajamas," climbed into her oversized bed, and swallowed an overdose of sleeping pills. The devout Catholic was four months pregnant by Austrian (sometimes labeled French) actor Harold Ramond, from whom she had become estranged. The *Time* magazine obituary later that month quoted her suicide note, which said that she couldn't stand the thought of bearing an illegitimate child.

Despite a dispute between the L.A. coroner and the Beverly Hills' district attorney, no autopsy was performed. The world may never know for certain if Lupe's death was from the bottle of pills, choking on her own vomit, cracking her skull on the commode, or drowning in the toilet bowl. *Hollywood Babylon* does provide a photo of Velez in her flower-bordered coffin, rosary looped over her manicured hands.

Glendale's Forest Lawn Cemetery hosted a nondenominational service for Velez at the Church of the Recessional, before her body was returned to Mexico City for burial at the Panteon Civil de Dolores Cemetery.

In 1945, the contents of Lupe's Rodeo Drive home were auctioned off. Her fabled eight-foot-square deathbed sold for a mere $45.

—Editor

Ephemera from the editor's collection

✦

Epitaph:
The Final Word
on Morbid Curiosity

✦

Ephemera from the editor's collection

The Mortician's Gift

by Loren Rhoads

Ten years ago, my husband Mason, my dear friend Paul, and I went to New Orleans for the thirtieth anniversary party of the Westgate Gallery, the world's only gallery devoted exclusively to "Necromantic Art and Literature." We had the pleasure of linking up with *Morbid Curiosity* artists Mike Hunter and Lizabeth West for a magnificent dinner in the French Quarter before cabbing out to the gallery. Leilah Wendell, Westgate's owner, greeted us once we arrived.

As the first band began to play, people packed the gallery. Many of them had been to the annual Anne Rice Vampire Ball the previous night. Reprising their costumes, they were dressed in farthingales, powdered wigs, the whole deal. It was almost Halloween in New Orleans. The night was probably ninety percent humidity. I melted just looking at the vampire folk, so I escaped to the slightly cooler air of the porch with Mason and Paul.

Before long, Leilah tracked me down. "There is someone I would like you to meet. He's a mortician." Grinning, I followed our hostess back into the sauna of the gallery.

He was an older gentleman, dressed all in black (*quelle surprise!*). About my height, he wore a wide-brimmed hat and a black Inverness coat. A monocle glinted in his right eye.

He swept my hand up to be kissed. "I arrange autopsies for writers. I've done them for Clive Barker and Poppy Brite, among others. If you're interested, it would be my pleasure to show you anything you want to see."

My adventures in a previous cadaver lab have appeared in *Morbid Curiosity* and in *Tail Spins*. "I am flattered by the offer," I said, "but I'm in no hurry to mess with cadavers again."

"Ah, but I can show you things you've never seen before," he promised.

Hm, I thought, opening newly dead people *would* be much different from exploring preserved teaching cadavers.

While I pondered his offer, he asked if I had a strong stomach.

"Well," I reminded him, "I do publish *Morbid Curiosity.*"

"There's something I'd like to show you." He glanced over his shoulder. "We need to go someplace private, where no one can see."

Into my head popped the *Bizarro* cartoon of the guy at the dance with two left feet in a paper bag. *Oh, Jesus,* I thought, *where's Mason?*

Of course, we were standing in the hallway at Westgate, a Victorian house packed canvas to casket with 150 people. There really wasn't anywhere too private.

The mortician led me into the front room, under Leilah's twelve-foot-tall statue of the angel of death. He turned away from me to open his Inverness. *Oh,* I thought, *here it comes.* For some reason, I expected he would peel back his coat to show me that he was horribly scarred, mangled, had a conjoined twin dangling below his ribs, some kind of hideous physical deformity . . .

Instead, he handed me a Polaroid. I got lightheaded from the shock of the mundane. Then my eyes locked onto the image in the photograph.

A dozen heads rested on a morgue table. They'd all been severed at the neck. They represented varying stages of decomposition: some green, others yellow. Their eyes rolled upward. Mouths gaped. It looked like a scene from Hell.

I'd never seen anything like this in my life. The black-and-white images of Weegee's corpses, Luc Sante's *Evidence,* even the gory *¡Alarma!* carnage is all removed from the viewer by virtue of being captured on glossy pages, trapped between the covers of a book. Those cadavers had already passed through the hands of a photographer, author, editor, printer, distributor, and shop owner before they reached me. Death was safely at bay. Now I was facing a man who'd removed a dozen heads.

"Death Carries Off Another Victim"
by Kimberlee Traub

My voice may have squeaked when I asked, "Did you take the photo?"

"Yes. I did some work for a university in Texas studying the deaths of indigents. When I had all their heads off, the moment was surreal enough that I thought I ought to document it."

Old blood ran in dark rivulets down the stainless steel tabletop. Some of the dead people seemed almost peaceful. I studied them, noting one's straw-like hair, the jaundiced yellow of another's eyes, a third's cyanotic lips.

I handed the photo back with my thanks. I was all giddy. I don't remember too much of the conversation past that point. Mason located me and, after a brief introduction, I excused us.

It was all I could do not to skip as we left the party. As soon as we collected Paul, I burst out with, "You'll never believe what I've just seen!"

There's nothing like a little horror to make you glad to be alive. That was my aim with *Morbid Curiosity* magazine and now this book: because an inoculation of the real every now and again makes you treasure good friends, beautiful art, a deep breath, a good cry, a morning awakening without pain. Make the most of what you've got, because it's all gonna end too damn soon. And that's beautiful, too.

Acknowledgments

A book, it turns out, is a very different animal from a magazine. This book could not have come to life without the aid of Anna deVries, my editor and psychopomp at Scribner, and Hannah Brown Gordon, my agent and advocate at Foundry Literary and Media. I cannot possibly thank the two of you enough for your encouragement and support. Thanks also to all the contributors herein, some of whom have been with me since the earliest punk rock days of my little zine. I am thrilled to see your stories in print once more. And, finally, thanks again to the crew at Borderlands Bookstore in San Francisco, *Morbid Curiosity*'s home away from home.

Contributors to
Morbid Curiosity Cures the Blues

Christopher R. Bales has been showing his art in central and northern California since 1986, shifting from 2-D art to assemblage sculpture in 1989. He's written about his misadventures as a sculptor, the art at Dachau that inspired him, and dressing up as the Grim Reaper on a graveyard tour for *Morbid Curiosity* magazine.

Maurice Broaddus works as an environmental toxicologist by day, a horror writer by night, and a lay leader at The Dwelling Place, a faith community in Indianapolis. His stories have appeared in dozens of markets from *Weird Tales* magazine to the *Dark Dreams* anthologies to *Horror Literature Quarterly*.

Frank Burch was a media professor at a university in the south. He died in 2000. "Blood Gags," published in *Morbid Curiosity* #1, was written under a pen name for obvious reasons.

Kalifer Deil was an engineer at Sun and Apple and is now involved with a third-generation dot-com startup. He dabbles in writing, sculpture, and home design. He has written two plays: *Interview with an Alien* and *Flight of the Soul.* He confessed to perpetuating a UFO hoax in *Morbid Curiosity* #5. "The Jumper and the Crabs," about working for the Coast Guard in the San Francisco Bay, appeared in issue #6.

John A. Domeier is a social worker who hates long walks on the beach because sand gets in his metal parts and seawater can make him rust. "The Fruit of All Evil," which appeared in *Morbid Curiosity* #9, was his first published piece. In 2006, he read it on *Insight,* the daily interview program on the NPR affiliate in the California capital.

Jessica Eisner graduated with honors from the University of California at San Diego School of Medicine. In 2004, Dr. Eisner wrote and directed *Muffin Man,* a morbid and uncomfortably hilarious mockumentary about the obesity epidemic and social dysfunction that led to the extinction of the human race. She has worked and traveled throughout much of Asia, Europe, and Latin America and is currently in Ecuador, researching Amazonian culture for a new book. She wrote about processed meat for *Morbid Curiosity* #2, but "Happy Trails in Southeast Asia" appeared in *Morbid Curiosity* #3.

Computer artist **Dean Estes** wrote about his night terrors in *Morbid Curiosity* #6 and about being gay in Texas on the Fourth of July in *Morbid Curiosity* #5. "Gilding the Afterlife" was his first story for the magazine (issue #2) and was the most requested reprint.

Seth Flagsberg has studied at San Francisco's Writing Salon since 2000. When not writing, he practices law at the Santa Clara County Public Defender Office–where he has defended more than twenty people accused of murder. "Brain Salad Surgery," about one of his first cases, was published in *Morbid Curiosity* #10.

"Hell on Heels" was **Dana Fredsti's** first essay for *Morbid Curiosity.* She went on to write for the magazine about her work volunteering with tigers, learning to surf, hunting ghosts, and starring in B-movies. She was coproducer/writer/director for a mystery-oriented theatrical troupe based in San Diego. These experiences inspired her novel *Murder for Hire: The Peruvian Pigeon* (James A. Rock, 2007). Dana was also cowriter/associate producer on *Urban Rescuers,* a documentary on feral cats and *Trap/Neuter/Return,* which won Best Documentary at the 2003 Valley Film Festival in Los Angeles.

Gravity Goldberg is one of the masterminds behind the literary magazine *Instant City.* For *Morbid Curiosity,* she's written about starring in porn movies and doing Tantra in the graveyard. "The Black Mass" appeared in the first issue.

Dalton Graham is a software tester who is going to Library and Information Science school. She wrote two pieces for *Morbid Curiosity.* Both involved breaking her skin.

T. M. Gray's novels *Mr. Crisper, The Ravenous,* and *Ghosts of Eden* are enjoyed by a widespread audience of horror fans. With the nonfiction *Ghosts of Maine,* the ghost hunter's guide to more than one hundred paranormal hotspots throughout the state, Gray proves her mastery of research and devotion to Maine's darker history, legends, and folklore.

Michael Hemmingson's first feature film, *The Watermelon,* will be released in October 2008 by LightSong Films. Two more of his films are being shot, one an indie and one a studio extravaganza with movie stars and an inflated budget. Some of his new books include a critical work on Gordon Lish (Routledge, 2009), an ethnography about Tijuana sex workers called *Zona Norte* (Rowman and Little-field, 2008), and a postmodern study called *The Anthropology of Pornography* (SUNY Press, 2010). In 2008, Borgo Press released twelve of Mike's books, one each month, from reprints to new works of literary criticism, literary smut, and sociological autobiography. In addition to fending off enormous Barbies, Michael wrote about encountering a time-traveling version of himself and surviving his crazy neighbors for *Morbid Curiosity.*

Katrina James had her first short story published in 1998 and has been creating a steadily growing body of tales ever since. She coproduced the cult public access show *kittypr0n* and has acted in and worked behind-the-scenes on San Francisco stage productions, including *Batman, Night of the Living Dead, Hitchhiker's Guide to the Galaxy, The Twilight Zone, Zippy the Pinhead,* and *Creepshow.* She currently spends her days disguised as a mild-mannered office manager. The truth came out in "Feed," which is taken from *Morbid Curiosity* #8.

Since murder—or, in this case, assisted suicide—has no statute of limitations, **JD** declines to identify himself. "Killing Max" initially appeared in *Morbid Curiosity* #2.

Dorian Katz is a visual artist. She has shown her work in San Francisco at Kearny Street Workshop, Glamarama, Jon Sims Center, and Live Worms. Dorian was an illustrator for *Morbid Curiosity* from the very beginning. She contributed "This Is a Very Old Scar" to the final issue.

Montreal photographer **Hugues Leblanc** has written about "Italy's Undead," his work as a hospice nurse, and "Going into Tombs" for *Morbid Curiosity*. He's written about cemeteries in Northern Italy, New England, New Orleans, and Mexico for *Monument Builders*. His photographs adorn *The Goth Bible* (St. Martin's, 2004).

Although she had early aspirations of becoming a detective, a ballerina, and a herpetologist, **Allegra Lundyworf** has settled into a comfortable day job as a receptionist. Nights and weekends, however, she juggles cats, lovers, cockroaches, kung fu, storytelling, and a husband. For *Morbid Curiosity,* she wrote about her nightmares on the nicotine patch and her grandmother's suicide.

Darren Mckeeman was the editor in chief of Gothic.Net. His writing career started as the first-prize winner of the Georgia Prison Writers Association Contest in 1991. He wrote role-playing game material for White Wolf Game Studio. He is the editor of *The Best of Gothic.Net: 1997 to 2001* (Gothic.Net, 2005) and author of *City of Apocrypha* (Gothic.Net, 2005).

After receiving a Ph.D. in experimental particle physics, **Dan McQuillan** worked with people with learning disabilities and as a mental health advocate. He created *Multikulti,* an award-winning multilingual website for asylum seekers and refugees. After he experienced human rights abuses in Genoa (reported in *Morbid Curiosity* #6), Dan joined Amnesty International as their global web manager.

A. M. Muffaz is a young Malaysian writer living in San Francisco. Her writing has appeared in *Fantasy* magazine, Gothic.Net, *Chiaroscuro,* and *Star*Line.*

George V. Neville-Neil is a quiet Irish boy trapped in the body of a Jewish anarchist. For *Morbid Curiosity* he wrote about cruising, getting tested for AIDS, finding his landlord dead, and visiting the Communards in Père Lachaise Cemetery in Paris.

Artist and writer **M. Parfitt** has exhibited her collages and assemblages in more than fifty shows since 1985. Her artwork—incorporating blood, hair, lint, text, buttons, beads, dog fur, and other unexpected materials—has been featured in galleries all over the

United States. Her nonfiction essays also feature the unexpected: a toy box filled with garbage, a theatrical performance in a cemetery, a dead dog that smelled like flowers. Her tales graced every issue of *Morbid Curiosity*.

Trilby Plants is a grandmother and retired teacher who designs digital scrapbooking materials. She is the author of the novel *Gatekeeper* and many published poems and short stories.

Kimberly Poeppey-Del Rio is an antiques dealer from Milwaukee. She has been a paranormal investigator for many years. Some of her sightings have been published in the books *Hunting the American Werewolf* by Linda Godfrey (Trails Media Group, 2006), *Weird Wisconsin* by Linda Godfrey and Richard Hendricks (Sterling, 2005), and in Loren Coleman's revised edition of *Mysterious America: The Ultimate Guide to the Nation's Weirdest Wonders, Strangest Spots, and Creepiest Creatures* (Paraview, 2007).

Wm. Rage can be found with the horror-noise band Blue Sabbath Black Cheer and running the Enterruption label, promoting and releasing music and visual arts by underground bands and artists from around the world.

Claudius Reich is an aging Bohemian who lives in San Francisco. Some of his stranger essays have been published in *Lend the Eye a Terrible Aspect* (Automatism Press, 1994), *Death's Garden: Relationships with Cemeteries* (Automatism Press, 1996), and the odd-numbered issues of *Morbid Curiosity*. He has written about why we OD, hitchhiking on America's back roads, the graveyard where he grew up, and volunteering at San Francisco's Needle Exchange.

Prior to editing the cult nonfiction magazine *Morbid Curiosity*, **Loren Rhoads** edited *Lend the Eye a Terrible Aspect* (1994) and *Death's Garden: Relationships with Cemeteries* (1995), both published by San Francisco's Automatism Press. Her essays appear in *Pills, Thrills, Chills, and Heartache: Adventures in the First Person,* two of the *Travelers' Tales* books (San Francisco and Paris), *Sex Toy Tales,* and in national magazines like *Trips, Tailspins,* and *A Reader's Guide to the Underground Press.* She was the cemetery travel columnist for Gothic.Net.

Ten years ago, Ohio native **William Selby** escaped writing for film, theater, and television (including the new *Twilight Zone*) in Hollywood. Transplanted to San Francisco, Bill currently plies his trade as a graphic designer. Six cockatiels, three budgies, and partner-in-crime Christine add zest, joy, and meaning to life as he completes his first novel. He wrote two pieces for *Morbid Curiosity*.

Lee Smith is the Program Director of Theatre at Bellarmine University in Louisville, Kentucky. His most recent project was the ultra-low-budget movie *Creature from the Hillbilly Lagoon,* which features enough interspecies sex to satisfy even the most unsavory viewer. Lee was primary researcher for three seasons of *The X-Files*. He wrote about that job and raining down an insecticidal Armageddon for issues 3 and 4 of *Morbid Curiosity*. "You Lock it Behind You," which appeared in *Morbid Curiosity* #6, is the story most often mentioned in reviews of the magazine.

Julia Solis organizes scavenger hunts and exhibitions in abandoned spaces. She is the main instigator of the urban exploration outfit Dark Passage. In 2002 she founded Ars Subterranea, an artists' group dedicated to the creative preservation of ruined spaces. She is the author of *New York Underground: The Anatomy of a City* (Routledge, 2005), *Scrub Station* (a short story collection published by Koja Press in 2002), and is a co-editor of the small publishing house Furnace Press.

Mary Ann Stein started writing on a serious basis four years ago. In addition to *Morbid Curiosity* #7, her work has appeared in the *Noe Valley Voice*. She's the Merchandise Manager at Borders on Union Square in San Francisco, the largest bookstore in the city.

Christine Sulewski had two stories in *Morbid Curiosity* #1. Her writing also featured in the books *Lend the Eye a Terrible Aspect* and *Death's Garden: Relationship with Cemeteries* (Automatism Press, 1994 and 1996). Christine lives, works, writes, meditates, and observes the apocalypse from her front-row seat in New York City. She does not condone non-consensual torture of any kind, at any time. You can read further overshares at http://soundofrain.net.

R. N. Taylor has written for such publications as *Apocalypse Culture,* and the magazines *Seconds, Outlaw Biker Tattoo Review, Exit, Esoterra,* and *Cyber-Psychos AOD*. Today he is perhaps best known for his lyrics and performances with the neo-folk band Changes. He wrote about a rotting goat's head for *Morbid Curiosity* #2 and contributed "A Night in the House of Dr. Moreau," about working in a vivisection lab, to #3.

Brian Thomas's writing appeared in almost every Automatism Press publication. In the pages of *Morbid Curiosity,* he buried a cat, visited the Black Virgin in Poland, worked with a human skeleton that he didn't know was real, slept in a casket, and bought a severed head in Venezuela. "Souvenir of Hell," in which he found himself locked into a cell in Auschwitz, has been a reader favorite since it was published in *Morbid Curiosity* #2.

San Francisco-based **Jill Tracy** has garnered multiple awards and a devoted following for her evocative cinematic music, sophisticated lyrics, old-world glamour, and curious passion for strange tales. Her tune "Evil Night Together" was featured on the CBS TV show *Navy NCIS* and on the BBC series *Jekyll.* Her film score work appears in *The Black Dahlia.* Her memoir of being stalked as a radio personality graced *Morbid Curiosity* #8.

Geoff Walker is a visual artist and musician living in the Pacific Northwest. He is perhaps best known for his work with the psychedelic noise rock outfit Gravitar, but has been involved in numerous other projects including Basketcase and Blue Sabbath Black Cheer. He wrote three pieces for *Morbid Curiosity* about his experiences in prison.

Leilah Wendell is America's best-known necrophile and the world's foremost researcher of personifications of and encounters with Death. Author of fourteen books, she was also proprietor of The Westgate Museum in New Orleans, the only gallery devoted exclusively to "Necromantic Art and Literature."

Mehitobel Wilson was nominated for a Bram Stoker Award for her work as Gothic.Net's nonfiction editor. She's the author of the fiction collection *Dangerous Red* (Bedlam Press, 2003) and co-author with Maria Alexander, Christa Faust, and Loren Rhoads of *Sins of the Sirens* (Dark Arts Books, 2007).

Simon Wood is a California transplant from England. In the last seven years, he's had more than 150 stories and articles published. A number of his stories have appeared in several "Best Of" anthologies. His nonfiction appears in *Writer's Digest*. He's the Anthony Award–winning author of *Working Stiffs* (Blue Cubicle, 2006), *Accidents Waiting to Happen,* and *Paying the Piper* (both Leisure, 2007). *We All Fall Down* came out from Leisure in 2008. Simon wrote about falling off a mountainside for *Morbid Curiosity* #8, getting lost in a small plane for #9, and his knee surgery in #10, but his story about running down a bicyclist was the hit of every reading for *Morbid Curiosity* #7.

After his experience in "Be Careful What You Ask For . . . ," **Vance Yount** moved as far away from California's Humboldt County as he could. He now works as a hair stylist in Charlotte, North Carolina.